MUSKOKA
MIRACLES

John F. Holliday
Richard D. Holliday

MUSKOKA MIRACLES

80TH Anniversary Edition
Muskoka Baptist Conference

John F. Holliday

Richard D. Holliday

Foreword by Rev. Robert Irvin

Huntsville, Ontario, Canada

iUniverse, Inc.
New York   Bloomington

MUSKOKA MIRACLES
80th Anniversary Edition

iUniverse books may be ordered through booksellers or by contacting:

iUniverse
1663 Liberty Drive
Bloomington, IN 47403
www.iuniverse.com
1-800-Authors (1-800-288-4677)

ISBN: 978-1-4502-5224-9 (sc)
ISBN: 978-1-4502-5225-6 (e)

Printed in the United States of America

iUniverse rev. date: 10/12/2010

Foreword
Rev. Robert W. Irvin

In the little white chapel at Muskoka Baptist Camp,
I made a personal commitment to serve the Lord. In
time, our daughter was a summer waitress and our
son a counselor. While serving at Moody Bible
Institute, we made summer trips with our camping
trailer, to benefit from MBC ministry. Later, a fruitful
summer was spent as volunteer Chaplain to the staff.

The spiritual impact has been widespread and
challenging. May this record of miracles and memories
bless you and yours, knowing that 'the best is yet to be'.

"To God be the Glory, great things He has done!"

Dedication

The Founders
and those who laboured with them
to the glory of God

Contents

M Each use of this symbol identifies a "Muskoka Miracle"...
~ a supernatural act of God

Preface

3rd EDITION ~ 80th ANNIVERSARY

"MUSKOKA MIRACLES", a book telling the heart-warming story of the commencement and growth of Muskoka Baptist Conference, was published in **1970** to commemorate its *40th anniversary.*

In the succeeding five years, **1971 to 1975,** the Conference experienced unprecedented blessing. Development included administrative reorganization, expansion of facilities and the assistance of qualified leaders from many professional, technical and other trained groups. The second edition of Muskoka Miracles, also by John F. Holliday, was published in **1975**, celebrating MBC's *45th anniversary*. The author incorporated the pen and the perspective of his associate in leadership, Sydney L. White. These two men were the principal leaders who told the story and kept the records, but took no honours. They believed that <u>God</u> would do the impossible if the principles of His Word were coupled with spiritual passion in families and churches.

This *80th anniversary* edition 2010 incorporates the basics of the <u>first</u> <u>two</u>, as authored and published by John F. Holliday in 1975. His son, Richard D. Holliday adds thirteen chapters by word and pictures to show the <u>present</u> realities of "what God has wrought". Through eighty years of preaching, heaven's music, hospitality and recreation, there is a lengthening chain of **MUSKOKA MIRACLES** which now stretches to not just two, but three, four and five generations of families and churches.

To quote our founders, "one thing should be emphasized; *the original purpose* of Muskoka Baptist Conference remains unchanged... the determination to exercise a soul-winning and bible teaching ministry to an increasing number of persons, young and older. This is still the compelling objective of our existence. The directors must always realize that this goal can only be achieved by seeking the guidance of the

Spirit of God in making decisions, and by implementing those decisions with an eye single to the glory of God".

This edition concludes with the testimony of one of our "five generation families", **Jim and Elaine Ross**. The father and grandfather were members of one of the founding churches. The family has had continuous involvement and leadership to the present day. We thank God for the spiritual concern, hard work and faithful stewardship of a dedicated household.

Introduction

"Jesus showed Himself again to the disciples at the sea . . . Jesus stood on the shore" . . . At the lakeside an exultant disciple, cried: "It is the Lord". How precious were the lakeside experiences recorded by the fisherman apostle! How dramatic was the breakfast on the beach, prepared by the Risen Christ! How compelling were the calls to follow the Master and fish for men, reported by John Mark! How weighty were the lakeside parables! How momentous the miracles! After nearly two thousand years, Bible readers are still learning invaluable lessons from the inspired record of those Galilean scenes and sermons.

No longer do we see the Risen Christ in His glorified body. Gone is the time when "He showed Himself alive after His passion by many infallible proofs, being seen of them forty days, and speaking things pertaining to the kingdom of God" (Acts 1:3). He has not ceased to draw near in spirit to hungry hearts, nor has He relinquished the power to support His claims by supernatural acts.

In the pages that follow, it is our responsibility and joy to record spiritual experiences which parallel those lakeside intimacies with the Lord in the long ago. On the shores of Mary Lake, Jesus showed Himself again and again, and displayed His undiminished supernatural resources. Thousands, of men and women, boys and girls, have been made conscious of His presence and power. This anniversary booklet is an attempt to recapture some of the memorable examples of divine ministry and miracle, which have marked the eighty year history of Muskoka Baptist Conference.

FOR PERSONAL CONTACT:
Rev. Dr. Richard D. Holliday
1339 Bryanston Court, Burlington, Ontario, L7P3N7
Telephone 905/331-0420
Email – rdmj.holliday@sympatico.ca

Chapter 1

1930 ~ THE BEGINNING OF MIRACLES

Muskoka Baptist Conference was born in the great depression when pocket-books and church treasuries were empty. Besides the economic factors, the founders of M.B.C. faced unfavourable conditions of a very different nature. Canadian Baptists were being despoiled and divided by the encroachments of theological liberalism. Doctrinal declension was accompanied by compromise in other areas, and added to these problems, were attempting to stem the tide of apostasy. In this sea of unrest it was a miracle that M.B.C. ever came into existence.

This is how it happened. In the fall of 1928 young people from Christie Street and Fairbank Baptist Churches in Toronto confided in their respective pastors. They had found an unwholesome moral atmosphere in the summer resorts where they had vacationed. This had convinced them that there was a real need for a camp where Baptists in the moderate income bracket could blend recreation with Christian fellowship and helpful Bible teaching. The report of these young folk was presented to the newly organized Fundamentalist Baptist Young People's Association. It was then recommended to the Union of Regular Baptist Churches.

In 1930, under F.B.Y.P.A. auspices, the first camp was held at Fisher's Glen, eight miles West of Port Dover on the shore of Lake Erie. It was attended by 134 campers from 32 churches. Accommodation was provided in tents and in a rented hotel. Rates for the ten-day period were ten dollars for those in tents and twelve dollars for residents in the hotel. From a 1930 invoice file, we learn that the price of butter was 31 cents per pound, sugar less than 5 cents per pound, and a large can of pork and beans cost 13 cents.

The directors of the Fisher's Glen Camp were Mr. S. L. White, Rev. S. Lawrence, Miss (now Dr.) Olive Clarke, Miss Twiss, and this writer, (the chairman, Rev. John F. Holliday). Miss L. Wyse (now Mrs. W. Gordon Brown) was editor of the first camp paper "The Fisher's Net".

The unexpected emergencies of that first experiment in Canadian Baptist Bible Conference history make an interesting chapter in the forty-year administrative record of the project. A year later the "venture" became Muskoka Baptist Camp. Before all the registered guests had registered and arrived, the members of the hotel staff resigned. The complaint was that the manager had not advised them of the coming of so many guests (134 instead of the usual 25). The manager promised a wage increase. The program organizers enlisted campers to assist in the dining-room kitchen and room-care. Mrs. S.L. White was appointed to supervise purchasing, catering and table service. This brought the "strike" to an end.

A sudden drop in temperature occasioned the second dire emergency. Unaccustomed to camping, most of those accommodated in tents, had ignored the registrar's instruction as to what to bring. They had been asked to bring blankets, but had brought only sheets and pillowslips. When the mercury fell, it required a midnight trip to Brantford Y.M.C.A. to provide a hundred freezing campers with blankets.

M   Financially, Fisher's Glen was a bold venture of faith. With nothing in the treasury, two of the directors signed an agreement to pay $800.00 for the use of the hotel and the services of the staff, and accepted the responsibility of tent rentals, food supplies, advertising etc. A faithful God supplied the need, and when all accounts were paid there was a credit balance in the treasury.

The spiritual objectives and Baptist emphasis of that forerunner of M.B.C. are indicated in the Fisher's Glen advertising. On the 1930 folder, there are **five significant Scripture texts**:

> "Being **justified by faith**, we have peace with God through
>   our Lord Jesus Christ" (Romans 5:1)
> "For I am not ashamed of the **Gospel of Christ**, for it
>   is the power of God unto salvation to everyone that
>   believeth" (Romans 1:16)
> "Now unto Him that is **able to keep** you from falling
>   and to present you faultless before the presence of

His glory with exceeding joy" (Jude 24)
"Thy Word is true from the beginning"
    (Psalm 119:160)
"Forever, O Lord, Thy Word is settled in Heaven"
    (Psalm 119:89.

M   The spiritual, numerical and financial success of that Biblically based beginning assured the continuation of the camping enterprise. A large number of the Fisher's Glen registrants met at Fairbank Baptist Church on February 3rd, 1931. It was the first Camp Reunion. There was enthusiasm and thanksgiving when the announcement was made that the F.B.Y.P.A. had taken steps to purchase a property near the junction of Mary Lake and the Muskoka River. The new site had an area of 117 acres and included 5 tourist cabins and three other buildings, which could be used for accommodation. God set his seal upon this second venture of faith by bringing to the Association an unexpected legacy. This paid for the property and provided an additional thousand dollars for legal fees, essential equipment and repairs.

The records show that groups from the following churches were active in helping to establish the Conference at Mary Lake: Barrie, Boston, Central Brantford; Christie Street, Fairbank, Faith, West Toronto and Pape Avenue in Toronto; Flamboro Centre, Freelton, Hartford, Scotland (ON), Memorial Stratford; Oxford St. Woodstock; Wortley Road, London; and Calvary, Ottawa.

That first camp in the Muskoka Hills was another miracle, and also, in many senses another "Beginning". It demanded every bit of pioneering spirit that directors, staff and guests could provide.

DeLoss Scott, the 1931 handyman and popshop manager came to camp in luxury (?) with the director and his family. Twenty-five years later, when he was pastor of The National Tabernacle, Washington, D.C., he sent "Silver Anniversary greetings" to M.B.C. in a letter, which vividly describes that pioneering season: *Could we ever forget that first year on the present property?*

(1) *The ride from Toronto in your Plymouth loaded to the roof with articles and materials too numerous to mention and with yours truly seated high and dry on top of it all in the back seat.*

(2) The road into camp – ugh! The present one is like the Pan American Highway in comparison.

(3) The condition of the property. Grass and weeds everywhere were to the height of about three feet. That smelly old Chicken House by the back door. The old, and first Pop Shop in back of Spinster's Alley with a roof that leaked like a sieve. My stock that was not spoiled by rain was stolen by the squirrels. No profit for that year. And the sleepless nights because of a million mosquitoes!!!!

(4) The old tumble-down barn with the late J. G. Connor and about ten boys sleeping (or pretending to) in the hay loft. What a barnyard rumpus!

(5) The equally dilapidated ice-house located back of the house near to the old oaken bucket well by the front door.

I felt like singing, 'How dear to my heart are the scenes of my childhood', for the Camp has surely come a long way since then. But, in spite of the above, we had some great times back in those days of pioneering. *It was there my sweetheart and I made all of the plans for our wedding and approached the late J. N. Millar re tying the knot. Then, together, Jennie and I will not forget all the hard work we put in as Camp Hostess and Camp Superintendent respectively. We would gladly do it all over again.*

Now, after a fruitful evangelistic and pastoral ministry in Canada and the U. S. A., Pastor and Mrs. Scott are with us once more in Ontario, and head-over-heels in assisting wherever possible at M.B.C.

Mr. and Mrs. Knight were there with the advance party to repair roofs, remodel buildings, clean rooms, wash floors and windows, etc., etc. Mr. Knight cooked for the advance party on a stove set up in the middle of a field. One member of the party, finding it difficult to saw wood without a wood-horse, horrified everyone by sawing off the back of one of the few chairs on the premises. The director's wife, drawn to Muskoka by the description of its restful beauty, worked from daylight until dark from the time she arrived until the hour she left, and enjoyed it all. On the day camp opened, the cook, Mrs. Lowry of Christie St. Church, attempted to split wood for the cook-stove. Her intention was good, her muscular power unimpaired, but her aim was poor. She missed the wood, nearly took off one of her toes, and ended the adventure in a doctor's office in Huntsville.

At that first camp, directors and staff occupied tents. Meals were prepared in the kitchen of the old farm house. They were served on the wide verandah or in the newly constructed dining area, produced by tearing out one of the partitions inside the house. Women and girls on the guest-list occupied five cabins on the riverbank. This area was labeled "Spinster's Row" or "No Man's Land". Families and middle-aged men were accommodated in tents. In the Grove, not far from the farm house were the family tents. There was the Loveday Tent, the White Tent, the Goheen Tent, and the Holliday Tent. The big Connor Tent, accommodated Mrs. Connor and approximately nine children. The pup tent belonged to Dr. J. W. Browett. Young men were quartered in the "Round House", a place that left indelible memories upon the minds of many Baptist youths. Teen boys, under the supervision of Rev. J. G. Connor, slept in the haymow of the barn. This stood on what is now the site of the dining-hall. At night, the barn fairly rocked with laughter. This was natural reaction to Father Connor's bedtime stories and his own hilarious humour.

It is impossible to pack into these few pages the record of all the labour and sacrifice that went into M.B.C.'s early years of development. Every spring, advance parties motored to Mary Lake at their own expense. They worked from dawn 'til dusk, preparing the grounds and buildings for the coming of the guests. Directors and staff-members not only served voluntarily, but they also often paid the full rate asked of the guests. When the camp opened, staff and director relinquished in-door accommodation and moved into tents. The new registrants occupied the in-door accommodations. In those days of depression, our little churches were hard-pressed financially. It took all the loyalty, enthusiasm, and sacrifice of the old and young to keep M.B.C. afloat.

Every improvement was a triumph, every addition to equipment was a victory. -a patch on the leaky roof, - new mosquito-netting, - little mirrors on the walls, - canvas cots replaced by spring bunks, - straw ticks exchanged for mattresses – coal-oil and Aladdin lamps supplanted by electric lights, - home-made quilts donated by interested churches. Even these little improvements were much appreciated.

Before long a large tent superseded the verandah of the farmhouse as the Conference place of assembly. In **1936, a rustic chapel** replaced the tent. By way of preparation, a **1935** circular, appealed for funds to build the new Chapel. The circular of request contained the following: *Do you remember sitting in the big tent trying to listen to the speaker, while ten thousand mosquitoes attacked your arms and ankles? Do you remember the Sunday when the wind nearly turned the tent into a balloon? Well we are going to end these experiences by presenting the Camp with a brand new chapel. With lumber (cedar) cut from our own bush, and with volunteer labour, we expect to finish the whole project on $250.00.*

The fund brought a generous response from the F.B.Y.P.A. constituency. Interested men from the Muskoka district gave their labour freely. Rev. James Millar, of Wortley Road Church, London had been a carpenter before he became a preacher. He supervised the area helpers so that the Chapel was erected in time for use at the 1936 Camp. **A unique rustic pulpit** was fashioned by Bert Olan, the original owner of the Camp property. He used scraps of cedar that were left over from the chapel construction. That pulpit has been used ever since.

There was great variety of programming in those early camps: hikes to Blueberry Mountain, paper-chases, treasure-hunts in the camp bush and tennis tournaments were played on rugged turf courts. The tennis winner was the racket-wielder who was most familiar with the bumpy places. There was keen competition in connection with tent-inspection, water-sports, and miniature golf. There were ball games, which engendered as much excitement as any big league final. The most violent form of recreation was broomball. Even veteran preachers were crippled in those fierce conflicts. The Camp Paper was always a masterpiece and sometimes an embarrassment. The schedule was varied by travel excursions: a weekly boat-trip, a drive to Algonquin Park, a ride on "The World's Shortest Railroad." As time went on, the weekly feature included a trip to Callander to see the world-famous Dionne Quintuplets.

A morning prayer meeting, made a good start for every day. Chapel services were known for their strong Bible teaching, preaching that emphasized fundamental doctrines, and sound Baptist convictions with clear-cut separation from the world. God used those Bible hours to produce conversions, baptisms, restorations and dedications.

There were open-air meetings in Huntsville on Saturday evenings and two great services in Camp on Sunday. Usually, Sunday afternoons a large group of campers went to some neighbouring home or school to hold an evangelistic meeting. These were happy, wholesome groups of vacationers. Old and young were playing and praying together with no generation gap. It was such a great time that many of them wept real tears when their camp period ended. In memory we can see them standing around a car-load that was ready to depart, commending the travellers to God and singing earnestly, sincerely:

> *We're sorry you're going away,*
> *We wish that you could stay.*
> *We're going to miss you,*
> *Our prayers will go with you* (by many, *"we wish we could kiss you!"*)
> *We're sorry you're going away.*

In those early years, there were three men who contributed much to the maintenance and improvement of the physical assets of M.B.C. They are worthy of a very special mention.

Deacon T.E. Harley He was officially or unofficially, maintenance superintendent. His home was the halfway stopping place for every work-party that drove northward to the Camp. His has many business connections and was able to enlist helpers from our Barrie Church. Proximity to M.B.C. made him invaluable. His concern for the enterprise knew no limits.

The Ralph Knights moved to Brunel and either lived at the Camp or near it through all of their years. His labour included countless practical details and the oversight of numerous major projects. If he had not supervised construction of the dining-hall and Fellowship Center, those undertakings would have been improbable, if not impossible.

Rev. James Millar was the London preacher-carpenter, after whom the new conference meal service building was named, **"Millar Hall"**. He literally "lived M.B.C." all year round. Our files contain letter after letter, three and four pages long, filled with detailed plans or long lists of projects carried out. These tell the story of years of service and sacrifice to make the Camp a worthy channel for the Lord to use. Pastor Millar's last act in this world was the London purchase of a second-hand pump which he loaded into his car. He planned to install it at the top of the River bank, near the cabins of the lady guests. His purpose was to spare the women and girls the necessity of carrying pails of river water up the hill. Both Pastor Millar and Deacon Harley have been promoted to glory.

Chapter 2

MIRACLES OF GROWTH

Everyone loved the after-chapel wharf hymn sings, accompanied by the strains of DeLoss Scott's guitar. It brought singers of all ages near to heaven's shore.

A favourite solo . . . "*There's going be a meeting in the air, In that sweet, sweet, bye and bye*".

The young people loved it. There was Jessie MacDowell from Ottawa. She still talks about it. - There was Arnold Gillott, - Gordon, Bertha and Vera Bigham from Woodstock - Vera married Rev. W. (Bill) Tyler, OMF executive secretary for Canada. -There were the Milne sisters, violinists from Oakwood Baptist, Toronto. The campers called them "The Fiddlers Three". They usually played when Dr. George Cole of Buffalo was speaker (Old King Cole). - There were "The Bells of St. Marys", -"The Wrecks of the Hespelers" which included Jim and Lillian Ross, as well as Mary Reid. (She became the wife of Rev. Tom Summers), -There was the Dawes Road Mission contingent which included four Russells . . . John, Bob, Nora and May. The Dawes Rd. group included Rev. George MacAlpine and Frances Wood (his bride to be).

From **Fairbank** came Len Aylett and Nessie Smith (another couple that is going down life's pathway together), the Hulse sisters, Joy Brockman, the Gonders (Mrs. Gonder was the first camp mother at Mary Lake) and the Mildons. Albert Mildon gave his life in World War II. There was Lillian Softley from **Christie Street**, Cora Parney from **Brantford**, the Van Loons from **Hartford,** the Javens trio, Hazel Treleaven and Mrs. Bell from **Owen Sound** and Ruby Barnes from **Barrie**. She married George Wilkinson, the one-time director of Mini-Yo-We camp. This scribe had the privilege of tying the knot in Bruges Belgium during the War. The Lewis sisters, the Barron sisters, Cora May Carson, Sid Smith and Thelma Hill represented **Faith Church, Toronto**. Thelma was one of the campers who annually wept buckets when camp ended, but Sid Smith married her and wiped away the tears. From Faith, too, came Eleanor Annan, the four Nelson brothers and two sisters. Claire married Frank Smith; Eleanor married Earl who went to be with Christ a few months ago. On one occasion Stanley Nelson cycled all the way from Toronto to M.B.C. But it was worth it to see Joan. He married her later on. There were Kenneth and Helen Miles from **Boston,** Wilma Adams from **Meaford**, Lois Bower and the Chadwick's from **Hamilton**, Blossom Moore, Marj Hockney and Fran Carpenter from **London**.

These are some of the names, gathered hurriedly from the letters, minutes, reports and registration forms of a few M.B.C. seasons. They represent a host of Baptist young people who look back with thanksgiving to experiences of fellowship, which are unforgettable.

There were older folk who also revelled in the fellowship of the Camp; men like **W. Tyrell** from Christie Street. He attended M.B.C. until he could scarcely walk. In recent years his granddaughter Betty was office secretary of the Fellowship of Evangelical Baptist Churches, and handled a great deal of the Camp office work. **Dr. J. W. Browett** was another veteran Christian who loved, attended, and supported M.B.C. **Mr. Hare Sr.** of Galt, father of Charles Hare whose contribution to the business and administration of camp was incalculable.

Mr. Mansell from Owen Sound, a painter by trade, came annually to M.B.C. to wield his brush on camp floors and walls. **Mr. Raeburn** of Orangeville, led to Christ by Rev. John Coyle, one of the Camps capable directors, came to Mary Lake in 1960. He was lifted to the highest heights by the spiritual blessings received, and for the past ten years has come to M.B.C. at every possible opportunity to use his skill as a carpenter to build, repair, and assist wherever he was needed.

The Conference attracted families. Christian parents saw the value of exposing their children to the wholesome moral and spiritual atmosphere of a Baptist vacation centre. The **Parsons** came from London, the **Bulls** from High Park, Toronto, the **Nullmeyers** have returned again and again. Rev. Ernie Nullmeyer and most of his eight sisters, have not only come themselves, but have brought others. There were **six Pickerings** there one summer. One of them was fourteen-year-old Frank, now Rev. Frank Pickering, Fellowship missionary in Japan.

It is interesting to note that in the last few years, three grandsons of early camp pioneers have served on the Camp Staff. The **third generation staff** are John Roberts, Don Loveday Jr. and Paul Holliday Jr. In each instance father and grandfather before him had a share in building M.B.C.

Many young people who attended Camp with their parents when they were children, counted it a real achievement to be given a position on the staff. A spur-of-the-moment attempt to list some of these second generation pioneers, reminds us of Mary White, Sandra Fitkin (Kernohan), Carol Guest, Ruby Barnes, three of four Whitelaw's, three Roblin's, four Loveday's, five Holliday's, Marg Millar, two Aylett's, two Roberts, two Knight's, and two Lawson's. A further investigation would probably double or treble the list.

The children have been enthusiastic M.B.C. promoters. They have enjoyed the beach, the swings, the seesaws, the dinosaur, the dining hall and the weekly D.V.B.S. Many of these boys and girls have talked M.B.C. all winter long. The spiritual welfare of the children has been the motive that has brought many a parent to the shores of Mary Lake.

To those who are aware of the financial limitations faced by Conference administrators, physical improvements have really been miraculous. In **1934** the chicken houses were replaced by the five-roomed **"Harmony Row"**. Two years later, **1936**, the **first chapel** was built. In **1938, the dining room.** At that time, the Ontario Hydro Commission ran a power line through the camp, putting an end to the era of coal-oil lamps.

From **1943 to 1945** Rev. DeLoss Scott and Rev. C. P. VanDuzen worked together and in succession as Camp managers. Under their leadership we saw the erection of **Falconer cottage,** the **Director's cottage**, a new snack bar called **"The Hub"** and **Holliday Lodge.** The latter was built and named while this writer was serving in the military chaplaincy. The old Hub was relocated and improved to accommodate guest speakers. It was labeled **"The Prophet's Chamber"**.

Fellowship Center was added in **1946**, under the supervision of Ralph Knight. It met a long-felt need for cool-weather activities. The lounge furniture was donated by one of the directors, and the fireplace (a memorial to Mrs. J.T. Holliday, the writer's mother). It became the focal point of scores of heart-moving testimony/dedication services in teens and youth camps. In response to invitations or a public confession of Christ or dedication of life, camper after camper indicated his or her definite decision by moving forward picking up a piece of wood while giving a testimony, quietly dropping the wood into the fire. In that same year, the lakeside property with cottages and boathouse, were deeded from Rev. Fred Dyson to the conference.

The next few years saw many important advances – more miracles. In **1947,** at a cost of about $6,000, a water system was installed, which included modern sanitary equipment. **1949** witnessed another milestone. M.B.C. acquired from Ralph and Minnie Knight, the whole corner of hill and meadow bounded by Mary Lake and the Muskoka River. It included thousands of feet of lake and river frontage. In **1951,** the riverside was subdivided into cottage lots for controlled sale to pastors and members of Baptist congregations. This increased the constituency of friends summering in the vicinity, while also providing funds for expansion. In that same year, on the hillside, four family cabins were constructed.

A major addition to the physical assets came in the *Silver Anniversary Year* **1955.** A twelve thousand dollar masonry motel with perimeter heating and individual washrooms was erected on the brow of the hill over- looking the lake. Ten thousand dollars came into the treasury before the work on the **Lakeview Motel** was started. Total cost $12,000.

Many of our readers will be familiar with the spectacular progress during the years that followed. Improvements included the construction of an attractive tearoom and bookstore, which was erected not far from the masonry motel and was later, enlarged to include storerooms and central lavatory accommodation.

At a cost of approximately $16,000 a beautiful new *Memorial Chapel* was built and furnished in honour of all the friends of M.B.C. who had been called to higher service. It was dedicated on August 6, **1961.** Among those who helped to put the finishing touches to the building was Bruce Davidson of Mount Pleasant Baptist Church. His long list of service on maintenance committees of Baptist churches stretched into the tiling of the chapel floor.

That M.B.C. Memorial building reminds us of many precious believers: Rev. A. J. Loveday, Rev. J. G. and Mrs. Connor, Albert Holland, Frank Andrews, Rev. J. N. Millar, Mr. Hare Sr., Mr. Tyrell Sr., Dr. Ralph Hopper, T. E. Harley, Mrs. Hemmings Sr., Mrs. J. H. Peer, Rev. J. J. Roberts, Mr. Peters Sr., Mr. Truman, Mr. Bigham Sr., Dr. O. S. Clappison, Rev. W. F. Roadhouse, Mrs. Nan Loveday, Rev. and Mrs. R. K. Gonder, and others, many others.

1969 there was the acquisition of boats and canoes and the erection of a much-needed maintenance shed. A building, capable of accommodating 26 staff members, was acquired, dismantled and re-erected near the site of the original camp administration building, which was demolished. The structure, purchased for $1600, was recently valued at $30 000.

Mr. Earl Thompson was a neighbor who owned one hundred acres of hard maple forest. With his good will and great benefit to the conference, it was purchased. In **1968** part of this area was laid out for 35 sites for tent and trailer camping. The remainder has been sub-divided to provide locations for 41 cottages to be built in accordance with long-lease rental agreements.

On the north bank of the Muskoka River, stood an old tourist resort. In **1968** it was purchased for use as a separate site for full- summer children and teens programming. This acquisition solved immense problems in relation to change over times from children or teens to adult conferences. At long last, it was possible to operate teens and junior camps concurrently with Senior and Youth Conferences.

Generous gifts and weeks of hard work by several members of the M.B.C. Commission added to the Conference assets a $3500 eighteen-hole miniature golf course. Constructed in the most modern style, with carpeted fairways, this "Tall Pines Miniature Golf Course" will be one of the special features of *M.B.C.'s 40th birthday*, (1970).

As we have roamed through the files of forty years and examined hundreds of lists of tasks assigned to various committees, sub-committees and individuals, we have been staggered by the enormous mass of detail that has entered into the development of Muskoka Baptist Conference. Had we known or dreamed of the complexity, the diversity, and how far we would be led, we would have stopped e'er we began.

How was the objective accomplished? What is the secret of the achievement that is M.B.C? The answer is ***Miracles*: - *supernatural providences that gave to the Conference divinely prepared human instruments for every phase of its growth.***

The Lord supplied our spiritual leaders. **like Rev. A. J. Loveday and his son Dr. Donald Loveday, Rev. Tom Sommers, Rev. John Russell, Rev. DeLoss Scott, Rev. Cliff P. VanDuzen, Rev. Norman Pipe, Rev. Harold Buchner, Rev. T. Hunt, Dr. Ralph Hooper, Rev. Norman Forge, Rev. Leander Roblin, Rev. E. Sydney Kerr, Dr. Morley. R. Hall, and other men of God. Some of these will be mentioned elsewhere in Muskoka Miracles.**

Some of these leaders served through all or almost all of the Camp history, others were raised up to meet specific needs in particular periods. Among the outstanding leaders who carried heavy responsibilities were **Sydney L. White, Charlie Hare, Arthur Fitkin, T. Etric Harley, Ewart Page, Frank Andrews, George Simpson, Ralph Knight, D. Miller Alloway, Cyril Hemmings and Len Aylett.**

There were ladies too, who laboured, and we mean "laboured", in the development of M.B.C.: **Helen White, Luella Holliday, Minnie Knight, Margaret Hare, Jennie Scott, Margaret Simpson, Elsie Andrews, Ellen Becker, and Betty Tyrell, Grace Harmer.**

The limits of this book make it impossible to catalogue a host of other men, women, and young people, who prayed and worked for the spiritual and material success of M.B.C. We have in mind brethren: **J. H. Peer, Glen Wardell, Don Dinnick, Roy F. Lawson, Jas. Fraser, Robert Gordon, Jim Boyd, Ernie Nullmeyer, and other pastors who gave strong support.** There is another long list of notables, including Directors, assistant directors, song-leaders, nurses, hostesses, cooks and helpers in other areas, in greater number than we can mention.

We are mindful of the children and grandchildren, who have grown up, accepting the responsibilities for the operating and expanding Muskoka Baptist Conference. There are scores like them who are indefatigable workers: **Rev. John Bonham, Earl Heron, Frank Bowman**, and a great many more. The God of miracles has not ceased to furnish the people needed in His work.

In May **1950,** the F.B.Y.P.A. decided by vote of its annual convention to transfer Muskoka Baptist Camp property to its parent body, the Fellowship of Independent Baptist Churches. In March **1951,** the Fellowship accepted the camp from the Young People's Association, and assumed responsibility for its operation under a new name, ***Muskoka Baptist Conference***. With the merger of the Fellowship of Independent Baptist Churches with the Union of Regular Baptist Churches in Canada in **1953**, M.B.C. became the opportunity and responsibility of the new group of churches. It was in reality, the most important physical asset acquired by the merged Baptist body. It has continued to be one of the most effective missionary arms of the group.

Biblically oriented ministries, such as Muskoka Baptist Conference have always faced the opposition of our great enemy. No work for God will be achieved without "blood, sweat, and tears". It is interesting that the first conference at Mary Lake was arranged amid a tempest of criticism. In the early years the camp sessions were harassed by hoodlums and by members of heretical religious cults in the district. Roadway arrows pointing to the camp were torn from the trees. A big sign at the camp gate was riddled with bullets. Late one Saturday night, one or more of these foes entered the Camp chapel and deliberately broke those hammers in the piano, which controlled the notes most frequently used in normal church accompaniment. The Lord protected!

<u>**Emergencies**</u> in Camp life can call for quick thinking and swift action. There was the occasion when the propane gas system failed while <u>the cook</u> was preparing Sunday dinner for a congregation that filled the chapel. In less than an hour those hungry guests would be on their way to the dining hall. The cook (now Rev. Don Holliday) hurriedly transferred all his preparations to the old staff-house kitchen. A roaring fire was built in the ancient stove. When the stove-pipe and the floor around it caught fire, <u>Len Aylett</u> took up a position in the room above, pouring water on pipe and floor. The cook below kept the fire burning with undiminished fury. When the guests sat down in the dining hall,

the hot meal was ready to be served. Only the cook and staff knew of the near panic behind the scenes.

There was that other emergency when another cook, <u>Una Edwards</u>, barely escaped with her life when the kitchen propane stove exploded.

There was a summer day when the rains descended and <u>the floods came</u>. Some dams burst on the upper lakes, and the rivulets became roaring torrents. The director watched the rising river level as the water raced past the cottages. As Mrs. Aylett was returning from Huntsville with several staff members, she stopped at the edge of a ravine to join other motorists who were watching a stream in full flood. The camp hostess saw a tiny crack appear in the road. Calling upon her staff to join her, she leaped to the wheel of the car and drove it to the Camp side of the valley just before a vast section of road was swept away. In seconds the Conference was isolated from the eastern approaches to Huntsville. Within hours, the road to the South also became impassible. M.B.C. handymen had to take a long, long detour to make contact with the outside world. This was the night of *Hurricane Hazel.*

There were some humourous emergencies. There was the time when Pappy Knight was carrying out instructions to clear part of the riverfront of debris. There was one <u>obstinate large stump</u>. Pappy put an extra-generous charge of dynamite under the offending obstacle and blew the biggest part of that stump right across the river. It landed in the neighbour's boat, with disastrous results both to the boat and to the neighbour's neighbourliness. (We did pay for the damage.)

There were other forces that challenged the loyalty of the Camp administrators. Biblical principles and policies were important for our Christian testimony. The spiritual success of the Camp depended on these values. From time to time there were those who objected to the Biblical standards of Sunday-observance, modesty in clothing, separation from worldliness and responsible behaviour. It was not always easy to *draw the line* but the leadership of M.B.C. consistently sought to carry out a policy that put *the glory of God first.* That policy met with widespread support and certainly produced effective results. As a result, literally scores of Baptist leaders and church members brought gifts and funds to M.B.C. committee members.

It was an encouraging day on which there had been an appeal for friends to invest in a conference expansion project. A business man, not directly associated with us, came to the director: *I would like to have the privilege of lending a thousand dollars to Muskoka Baptist Camp. My reason for doing so is that I am interested in helping a conference that makes no apology for upholding Christian standards.*

On this *40th anniversary*, Muskoka Baptist Conference has no reason to be sorry for loyalty to Scripture principles.

Chapter 3

MIRACLES OF SAVING GRACE

The **1931** birth of a Baptist Camp on the banks of the Muskoka River was not the beginning of soul-saving ministry in that area. Port Sydney, at the other end of Mary Lake, was an early field of Christian service for young **Jonathan Goforth**. At the turn of the century, he became one of the world's foremost Gospel-preaching missionaries.

Just south in the Bracebridge district, a Godly Baptist teacher held meetings. His name, **Prof. P. S. Campbell**, attracted so many and were so charged with spiritual power, that the aisles were blocked by the large crowd. The professor had to climb over the backs of the benches, so he could explain the way of salvation to sinners who were in an agony about their lost condition.

In Huntsville, **J. H. Peer**, shepherded the Baptist Church during a season of unprecedented blessing. By the time the Baptist Camp was established in nearby Brunel Township, some of the effects of that revival had been dissipated. There were, however, many Christians in the vicinity, who pointed back to the "Huntsville Awakening" as the time of his or her conversion. It is not surprising that Pastor Peer became a strong supporter of MBC, and that he was the first person to order a copy of *Muskoka Miracles*.

MBC's **first known profession** of faith in the Lord Jesus was **Reg Knight**. He was the son of Ralph and Minnie Knight. Soon after, he was baptized in Mary Lake. In WWII he served in the Royal Canadian Airforce. He survived an incredible experience. Shot down by a German plane, he spent 2 days and a night alone in the ocean . . . just off the coast of France. Late in the second day, it was a **miracle rescue**. Reg married Naomi Trueman, who served on the Camp staff. She enriched many a chapel session with her heart-moving solos. Reg is now a schoolteacher in Barrie. He and Naomi are members and musicians of Emmanuel Baptist Church. They have a cottage beside the Muskoka River.

Dr. Paul Roberts is a well-known Toronto physician. He served for years as a missionary doctor with H.C.J.B., Voice of the Andes in Ecuador. He made a profession of faith when he was a boy in England, but knew little of the reality of Christian experience. As a youth of 17, under the preaching of Rev. A. J. Loveday at M.B.C., he came under deep conviction. This led to a definite commitment of himself to Christ. His decision was sealed by the assurance of salvation. The next year he returned to M.B.C. and was greatly blessed by the ministry of Colonel F. J. Miles of London, England. At that time he was baptized in Mary Lake by Rev. DeLoss Scott. Recently, in his office at Sunnybrook Hospital, Toronto, he witnessed to the writer . . . *Muskoka Baptist Camp had a profound influence on my life.*

Ewart and Nellie Page were enthusiastic supporters of M.B.C. from the very beginning. Ewart was Sunday School Superintendent and a Deacon of Fairbank Church in Toronto. His abilities as a draughtsman were enlisted many times by M.B.C.'s planners. Son, Robert and daughter Doris felt this was their summer home. Bob's son **Kenneth** was baptized in the waters of Mary Lake upon profession of his faith in Christ. It was this writer who baptized him. We stood together on the shores of Mary Lake, Kenneth, Bob, and the grandparents. Not long afterwards Ewart was promoted to glory. Bob has been a dedicated business man and a M.B.C. committee member for many years. His son, Ken is now a skillful carpenter serving many of M.B.C.'s area residents.

The M.B.C. files include many thrilling stories like the following letter from a missionary: *During the Friday night service I could not help but think of how much the camp has meant to our family. A younger sister had just responded to the invitation. A few years before my brother found Christ at Camp. Another sister, now on the mission field in South America, walked the same Camp aisle to dedicate her life to Christ. In that same Camp chapel I too had said Yes to the Lord as He called me to full-time service.*

In a two-week period of the Camp session, which produced that letter, there were 38 decisions for conversion or dedication. It is not possible or necessary to give a statistical report of the results of all forty Conference seasons. Statistics can be cold and sometimes do not convey accurately the true measure of a spiritual achievement. It is certainly significant that all forty files of M.B.C. history contain records of spiritual results.

Excerpts from minutes and specific files give year-by-year reporting of spiritual victories in individual hearts from 1930 to 1967.

M   Among the miracles of saving grace at Muskoka Baptist Conference there are some that stand out in memory, among them the <u>Y.M.C.A. secretary</u> registered for two weeks at Camp. He appeared to be very discontented. He was obviously unconverted, unsympathetic with the standards, and he did not attempt to conceal his hostility. Every effort was made to make him feel at ease, without apparent success. Weeks later, after having returned to his duties, he phoned to arrange an interview with the M.B.C. director. In his Y.M.C.A. office, he confessed that he was unable to cope with the power of sin in his own life, was woefully incapable of helping the young men under his care with their moral and spiritual problems. He wanted a clear explanation of the secret of Christian living, which he had seen exemplified during his weeks at Mary Lake. When the explanation was given, he humbly and sincerely called upon God for saving mercy.

M   There is a story which began with a Christian family from Sarnia. **Mr. and Mrs. Peters Sr.** rented a cottage in Cottrill's Bay, a short distance by water from the M.B.C. The Peters had a six-year-old boy named **Harry**, who loved the Camp. Year after year, he returned to Muskoka with his parents, becoming increasingly interested in M.B.C. activities, particularly the Bible studies. In the course of time, he opened his heart to the Saviour. God gave him a burden for the salvation of others.

There came a summer when the **Meyers family** from Buffalo "summered" in a cottage near the Peters. Not one member of that household knew Christ as Saviour. Their young son named **Frank**, became a friend to the Peters. Before long Harry began to bring him to the chapel services. Evening after evening they rowed across the bay. One night, Harry led Frank to a personal knowledge of Jesus Christ. Frank's conversion was real. Old things passed away and were replaced by the new things of the Spirit. His introduction to the Master was a spiritual breakthrough for the Meyers' household. Other members of the family were converted. **Carol Meyers** became a waitress on the M.B.C. staff. Frank trained for the ministry and is now a Gospel preacher in the U.S.A. Harry Peters continues to witness for Christ. For a time he served as director of an institution for underprivileged children. A few weeks before the publication of *Muskoka Miracles*, we addressed the Bible School of West Park Baptist Church, in London, Ontario. We were introduced by the Sunday School superintendent, Harry Peters. After the service which followed, he told us he was planning to be at camp for M.B.C.'s 40th birthday, and he ordered two copies of *Muskoka Miracles*. Mrs. Peters Sr. was at the West Park Service. She had come from Sarnia to London to renew the fellowship begun long years ago at Mary Lake.

M   Another Muskoka Miracle that we will never forget was the case of **Mr. Kemper**. His house adjoined the camp property, separated only by a picturesque waterfall and sparkling stream. There was a bridge across the stream, which was a frequent source of controversy between Mr. Kemper and some of his neighbours. He was a retired German stationary engineer, who had a Lutheran background, but had long since ceased to attend church. In the early years of M.B.C. he was often hostile to the Conference, particularly when he had been drinking heavily, which was not infrequent. There were occasional incidents in which his antipathy to the Camp created embarrassing situations.

There was the Chapel service when Mr. Kemper appeared at the door and demanded that his boy *be removed from that Baptist meeting*. There were the late-night bonfires on the Kemper property, when the wild drinking celebrations of Mr. Kemper's guests kept the Campers awake until the wee hours of the morning. There was the occasion when the Ontario Provincial Police interrupted a Conference service to investigate the report that there was a man with a shotgun fighting someone at the Camp gate. The problem turned out to be another argument about the bridge between Mr. Kemper and a neighbour. Mr. Kemper was there alright, with the shotgun. Up to that point there seemed to be very little chance of reaching Mr. Kemper with the message of salvation.

Then something happened which changed his attitude completely. At one of those midnight parties, when the fire was burning low, Mr.

Kemper used a can of kerosene to revive it. The can exploded in his face, burning him terribly. He spent weeks in Huntsville hospital, and during that hospitalization we visited him and asked the patient gently if we might be permitted to pray for his recovery. He assented and thanked us sincerely for the brief, simple prayer. Later he confided in one of the Camp staff, that the only person who showed that he cared whether he lived or died was the director of Muskoka Baptist Camp.

From that time on Mr. Kemper was a real friend of the Camp. He was a capable plumber and steamfitter. When he had recovered from his burns, he delighted to help Ralph Knight with the problems, which developed in the water system. The camp was expanding to keep pace with the erection of new buildings. He became a warm friend of the Knights and of many of the camp administrators. Because his house beyond the creek was his year round residence he kept his eye on the Camp in winter as well as in summer. Indeed, when the Conference was closed each fall, he constituted himself the unofficial guardian of the property. If any suspicious-looking stranger appeared, he shouted: *Get off this place you blankety, blank so and so. I'm the custodian of the Baptist Camp*. Though reports of his language on such occasions was a bit embarrassing to the Conference, his concern for M.B.C. was very real.

Old Mr. Kemper was good to us, very good, and yet he was still unsaved. This writer talked to him about the way of salvation. Almost every member of the Holliday family witnessed to him. Our three preacher sons tried over and over to tell Him what Christ could mean to him. The Knights and the Ayletts added their testimonies, but we all received the same answer, *I'm too old to change now*. He became ill and the illness lengthened, finally issuing in hospitalization. His M.B.C. friends visited him, continued tactfully and earnestly to endeavour to lead him to Christ, but still without success. Then one day, the M.B.C. office received a call from the hospital, requesting that one of the Hollidays visit Mr. Kemper as soon as possible. Pastor Don Holliday, who was on duty as director drove to the hospital immediately and found Mr. Kemper ready and waiting to open his heart to Christ. There was no need of argument, pleading, or pressure. God had prepared him and he wanted to be saved. In a few minutes the transaction was over and the sinner who had so long delayed decision had passed from death to life. Don immediately called Toronto, and when we heard the news, we jumped into our car and drove the 150 miles to the Huntsville hospital. As we entered the sickroom and took the worn hand, we said, *Oh, Mr. Kemper, what wonderful news! How can I tell you how glad I am that you have accepted Christ as your Saviour.* He answered, *Mr. Holliday, if you are so glad because I am saved, think how glad I must be.*

Mr. Kemper lived for months. He witnessed to former friends and neighbours. He often expressed the hope that he might recover sufficiently to just attend one service at the camp chapel that he had so long ignored. The Lord did not see fit to grant that desire. At his request, Mr. and Mrs. Knight came to his bedside as often as possible, and Mrs. Knight sang for him the old songs of salvation. He died in Christ. A great host came to the funeral service, which it was our privilege to conduct. Mrs. Knight and Pastor Don Holliday participated. There were few dry eyes as we told the story of the miracle conversion of Mr. Kemper. If Muskoka Baptist Camp had accomplished nothing else but the salvation of that precious soul, with the testimony that it meant to Brunel Township, and the glory that it brought to our Sovereign Saviour, it was worth all the effort that went into the establishment of a Christian witness on the shore of Mary Lake.

Chapter 4

MIRACLES OF JOY, PEACE, AND POWER

Every guest who comes to Muskoka Baptist Conference has a particular need. Some are bursting with vitality, some come to escape tensions, some are weary and want to relax. There are those who anticipate reunion with friends. The lonely are looking for companionship. There are the new converts needing the joy of Christian fellowship. They come from a variety of backgrounds. There are congregations which have lost their emphasis on the Gospel. Many sense the need of teaching. Some come with searching hearts, hoping that the counsel of mature Christians may lead them out of the mist. Some are physically weak, sad or deeply troubled in soul. It may be that there is the loss of the joy of their salvation or that they may never have come to Christ for salvation.

Muskoka Baptist Conference is a Christian vacation center, recognizing the authority and power of the Lord Jesus Christ. There is a need to apply the Scriptures to contemporary conditions. We must seek, by the help of the Holy Spirit, to encourage individual believers and to strengthen local Bible-preaching churches. Because of its Christ-centered and Biblically oriented program, M.B.C. has been used for forty years to meet the varied needs of all of divergent backgrounds. A visit to Mary Lake can be like a banquet, an oasis, and an armoury. It can be a source of joy, peace, and power. In the paragraphs of this chapter we will attempt to introduce you to some who have come to these hills and by the miracle-working power of the Holy Spirit have found richer joy, deeper peace, and greater strength.

MIRACLES OF JOY

Christians can have a lot of fun. One of M.B.C.'s earliest campers, Dr. J. W. Browett, used to say: *The Gospel doesn't make coffee-pot faces.* Some of our other pioneers described the Camp as a place of fun, food, and fellowship. In another place it was said,: *Jesus isn't a joy-killer. He is a joy-bringer.* How true! The Bible says: *Thou wilt show me the path of life: In Thy presence there is fullness of joy; at Thy right hand there are pleasures for evermore . . . Psalm 16:11.* Real joy is heaven-born. Christian pleasure is a variety of merriment, which does not leave behind a legacy of regrets. What happy times we have had at M.B.C. When we were penning these pages, Mrs. Holliday frequently challenges me: *Tell them what a good time we had at Mary Lake.*

The one-roomed Round House was equipped with about eight bunk-beds. It was the accommodation for young bachelors. In the memory of hundreds of boys, it was a synonym for fun. About 1950, Roy Lawson Jr., Art Fitkin Jr., Dick Holliday, and several other extraordinarily exuberant youths were billeted in that round house. A shy newcomer was allocated a place in the midst of that hectic conglomeration of dynamic teenagers. One wonders that he ever survived, but he did. He returned to camp several times. As the years passed he came to Rev. R.D. Holliday, M.B.C. Planning Committee Chairman, and said: *I was with you and Lawson and Fitkin in the Round House 21 years ago. They were the best years of my life. I am married and have four children, I want the members of my family to spend their summer vacations at Mary Lake, and so I would like to apply for one of the lots in the M.B.C. Acres subdivision.*

We had our bonfires, skit nights, hat contests, water sports, field days, boat trips, ball games, tennis tournaments, volleyball. These activities sometimes became a Free-for-all, but there was always genuine harmony around the dining room tables, at the old "Hub" and the new "Tea-room". What wholesome hilarity in connection with a thousand unscheduled happenings!

Do you remember the time when <u>Nelson Beckner</u> crept up behind the cook, Jack Adams, slipped a raw egg into each of Jack's back trouser pockets, and then gave Jack two resounding spanks?

Do you recall the occasion when two pastor-directors, preparing to return to their respective pulpits for Sunday ministry, accidentally consulted a long out-of-date time-table. They found no train at the station. Further delayed by a flat tire, they finally were thankful for transportation in a dusty, construction gravel lorry?

Did you ever hear of the incident when the director's trousers were hijacked? It had to do with the disappearance of the pants of a slender pastor and their replacement by the nether garments of a preacher weighing at least 240 pounds. One of the major problems in that emergency was to find a belt of sufficient dimensions to support the replacement. The difficulty was solved when someone produced a trunk-strap four yards long.

Then there was the camper who rushed into the kitchen, as she was about to leave for home, and demanded the parcel with her Sunday dinner roast, which she had stored in the Camp refrigerator. Everything came to a standstill in the kitchen while a nervous member of the staff went into the walk-in-refrigerator. They found what appeared to be the package with the choice cut of meat. This turned out to be a bag of giblets which the M.B.C. cook had set aside for soup. The members of the staff always wondered what happened when the camper opened the package in her hometown.

From long experience, we have learned that a sense of humour is a very important qualification for the Christian worker. We cannot help but feel that the time spent at M.B.C. probably contributed greatly to the development of that quality in the case of many staff-members and guests who were called to full-time ministry.

There were deeper experiences of happiness born at M.B.C. Some friendships blossomed into lasting love and the establishment of happy Christian homes. We have already referred to some of these Camp romances:

Rev. DeLoss and Jennie Scott

Rev. George and Frances McAlpine

Mr. Stan and Joan Nelson

Mr. Sid and Thelma Smith

Dave Taylor and his wife Ruth were both saved at MBC. They met at MBC and were married in the Chapel.

Rev. R. D. [Dick] Holliday and Marilyn [Aylett], Bruce Aylett and Fay (Garner) formed a lasting friendship while on the staff.

Bob Cripps of Guelph and Carol (Ratcliff) of Second Markham met at M.B.C. in 1967 and were later married.

Nelson Beckner and Isobel celebrate their 25th anniversary of their marriage this year, a marriage, which is the fruit of a camp romance. We will let Nelson tell you the story in his own words. . .

Dear Pastor Holliday:

I have been putting this letter off for some time but thinking a great deal about it in reference to the book you are going to write, Muskoka Miracles.

You know as well as I do, or nearly so, the blessing M.B.C. has meant to my Christian life. Before the 1939-45 war, I received encouragement from the fellowship of the Christian at MBC. That was a real help to me in the Navy, to "stand and therefore stand". The grounding of the Word I received at Benton Street, along with this fellowship, enabled me to take my stand, with the help of the Holy Spirit.

You also know, I first met my wife at Mary Lake. When our first child was born in February of 1947, we spent time, that summer, at Mary Lake for her first holiday. With few exceptions we have been at Mary Lake every summer since. This fall we will be married 25 happy years, so there is no doubt it was an excellent find.

Be assured, Pastor Holliday, of our prayers as you endeavour to put into print some of the blessings that have been yours and others down through the years. This summer it was thirty years since I first broke the silence of the Muskoka Hills and if the Lord tarry, I hope to be up there 30 years hence.

Yours in Christ, Nelson Beckner   I John 1:7

At Arnstein, in the North, <u>Pastor Walter Nichols</u> shared with us this personal testimony: *In May, 1942, while serving with the Canadian army at headquarters of Number One Military District, I was saved under the ministry of <u>Rev. G.F. Logsdon</u> of Central Baptist Church, London. A few months later I spent a "leave" at Muskoka Baptist Camp. To me it was the most wonderful place I had ever been. I had never experienced anything like it. I returned to the Conference in 1943 and 1944. After training in London Bible Institute and missionary service in Japan, my wife and I and family come back again* and again. In addition to service with the China Boat Mission, Walter Nichols pastored the Otterville

Baptist Church for ten years, and has for the last four years been the under-shepherd of the Arnstein Evangelical Baptist Church.

MIRACLES OF PEACE AND POWER

Volumes could be written about the refreshment that has come to a great host of toilers in the Lord's harvest field who have *come apart to rest a while* in the Muskoka Hills beside Mary Lake.

The following is a typical letter from a Christian mother, written after she returned home from a week at Muskoka Baptist Conference: *I wouldn't be happy if I didn't write and say a hearty, thank you, for the wonderful time you gave us. We truly enjoyed wonderful fellowship which we will never forget.*

In our M.B.C. files there are literally hundreds of letters from directors, committee members, staff workers, friends who have laboured voluntarily and sacrificially. These have been blessed in their association with the Conference and do not hesitate to say so. From this mass of material we have culled a few expressions of appreciation from those who knew what they were talking about. Most of them are selected from the files of the 1930/1940 years. It is not because there is less appreciation today, but because the workers and campers of yesterday had so much less for which to be thankful. Their gratitude is all the more impressive.

Splendid Christian fellowship and Bible teaching
Cecil R. Roberts, Field Secretary of Gideon's International.

Our Muskoka Paradise
Rev. James Fraser, Montreal pastor and energetic worker on many camp projects

I don't know of any place that I would rather go than to that beautiful lake.
Dr. H. H. Savage, First Baptist Church, Pontiac, Michigan

I am certainly looking forward to my visit at the camp. So many of my acquaintances spoke of the splendid time of fellowship enjoyed there. From a Woodstock girl, sending in the registration to M.B.C.

I enjoyed it so much last year. I just can't miss it this year. From Miss Bertha Belch, who served for years as a missionary in the Congo, and more recently in Colombia, South America.

I am looking forward to the time of fellowship and spiritual uplift-ing which one gets at the Muskoka Baptist Camp. <u>Nurse Alice Patrick</u> (now Mrs. Henderson)

Muskoka Baptist Conference holds many memories for me, because as a younger person I spent a couple of weeks each year at Mary Lake. It was at Mary Lake that I dedicated my life wholly to the Lord. A Kitchener Christian nurse

A 1937 Leamington camper writes this note in 1970:

"One of the highlights of my youthful days was the two weeks spent as a guest in the Dyson cottage. While there I attended the meetings on the Campgrounds. I still have a small memo pad which I purchased from the Tuck Shop. I wrote the choruses we learned:

- *Trust in the Lord and don't despair*
- *Chiefest of Ten Thousand*
- *He Lifted Me Up*
- *Lead me to some soul today*

I get blessings when I sing those choruses yet . . . At the time I was not a member of a Baptist church . . . When I sit and gaze at the present M.B.C. beach, I think of the Sunday, Aug. 2, 1937, when near this very spot I was baptized. We always enjoy, to the full, our stay each year at M.B.C."

From the influences of a missionary home and a Bible-believing Baptist church, Don Whitelaw not only brought something to M.B.C., but he also carried something away. Many who came to those Muskoka Hills went away stronger than when they arrived. Muskoka Baptist Conference proved to be more than a banquet, more than an oasis; it turned out to be an armoury. Their convictions were deepened, their faith was fortified. They obtained a clearer understanding of the issues separating truth from error, right from wrong. There was a more settled confidence in the triumphant power of the Lord Jesus Christ.

Chapter 5

MIRACLES OF BAPTIST INFLUENCE

You cannot fight a big war on one small front. Military strategists must consider every area where the enemy may be attacked or may be expected to attack. They must take into account economic, psychological and other factors. It was this principle, applied to spiritual warfare, which gave strength and determination to those who pioneered Muskoka Baptist Conference.

During the years in which the camp was established, foes of Christianity were making powerful thrusts into the ranks of Bible-believing Christians.

The threat, which loomed largest on the horizon was the massive assault of liberal theology upon the bulwarks of Baptist Faith. M.B.C. was started by the Fundamentalist Baptist Young People's Association. It was, as the parent organization name implies, designed to be a bulwark of *The Faith once delivered to the saints*. That was its position and purpose from the very beginning.

A second area of enemy penetration was in the realm of summer vacationing. The holiday resort business was mushrooming. In most cases, vacation centers were characterized by a moral and spiritual atmosphere which threatened the soul-health of Christian guests. Many places involved had questionable amusements, immodest fashions and a breakdown in Sunday observance. The M.B.C. pioneers, backed by their constituency, determined to make the new camp a witness against all three trends.

There was another aspect of that spiritual struggle, in which Muskoka Baptist Camp would play a vital part. Two tension-filled Baptist divisions had followed each other in quick succession. Many congregations were driven toward ultra-independence. The ties holding the Independent Baptist Group together were few and slight. The Camp became a rallying point and a strong connecting fellowship link.

The unifying influence of M.B.C. was felt among evangelical Baptist ministries for a long time.

There was also a concern about an over-emphasis upon inter-denominationalism. It was perceived that this could lead to a softening of Baptist convictions and the abandonment of Baptist distinctives. M.B.C. was grounded in fundamental doctrines, Scriptural standards of separation and an appreciation of the importance and value of true Christian fellowship.

A BLESSING TO BAPTIST PASTORS

The Conference has had an incalculable impact upon Canadian Baptist history. *This Dominion, His Dominion,* was the Centennial feature publication of *The Fellowship of Evangelical Baptist Churches in Canada*. The author, Rev. L.K. Tarr, wrote: *An observer today would concede that the Muskoka Baptist Conference, as it is now known, has exercised a far-reaching influence on evangelical Baptist life. The Mary Lake camp and conference grounds have been the setting for life-changing decisions. Conversions, dedications and commitments to full-time service have enriched the churches, and in God's hand, enlarged the kingdom.*

Perhaps the most important tributary to this stream of influence has been the Holy Spirit's work upon the lives of pastors and prospective pastors through MBC. In **1952**, we penned an article in *The Fellowship Evangel*. This was the publication of the Fellowship of Independent Baptist Churches of Canada: *"Every year scores of young people found Christ through MBC's services. Every year young people confessed Christ by baptism in the waters of Mary Lake. Every season scores of believers heard the call of God to surrender for service. This happened in the chapel or by the fireside. Many of today's pastors, missionaries, and students in training were powerfully influenced toward their life work while sharing in the services at Muskoka Baptist Conference."*

The writer's heart is strangely warmed as he thinks of the army of pastors who have played and prayed, worked and worshipped in these Muskoka Hills. They have driven out through the Camp gate to the world beyond, to experience the fulfillment of the promise on its cross-beams, **"My presence shall go with thee"**. The Master is bidding these men of God who have felt His touch . . . *"Come ye after Me, and I will make you fishers of men".*

A list of just names would certainly include many more than just the following:

Rev. DeLoss Scott and **Rev. Kenneth Miles** - the first two camp handymen - honoured servants of Christ in both Canada and the U.S.A. DeLoss, as a pastor and evangelist, Ken in pastorates and educational realms.

Dr. Donald Loveday - camper, handyman, registrar, camp director, commission chairman and pastored three churches . . . 25 years in Central Brantford, frequently preaching at M.B.C., President, of The Fellowship of Evangelical Baptist Churches and Central Baptist Seminary.

Rev. Ernie Nullmeyer - a baby on our church cradle-roll at the time the Camp was born: enthusiastic supporter, worker and MBC committee member, a capable pastor of three congregations and preacher to youth.

Rev. John Roberts - came as a lad, a tower of strength to the Camp, Teens committee leadership, home missionary and pastor.

Rev. Roy F. Lawson - father of Roy and Ed Lawson. He pastored Ontario and Quebec churches. When the Muskoka property was first visited by three board members, Rev. Lawson Sr. was pastor of Huntsville Baptist Church. He joined the three for the initial site inspection. He and his wife became ardent encouragers.

Rev. Roy Lawson, Jr. - teenager, teen's leader, program director, M.B.C. promoter (and dare I add, "Organizer of the Lion Hunt"). He made an immense contribution in Youth and Fellowship leadership, pastor of several churches, including Central Baptist in London.

Rev. Ed. Lawson - handyman, pianist extraordinary, now on faculty at Tennessee Temple U., Chattanooga, Tennessee.

Rev. George and Margaret Simpson - She came to camp from the beginning, and every year thereafter. Both have a long record of faithful service to M.B.C. George, a pastor, when in Ajax, he was used of God to lead some of the Heron family to the Saviour. Murray and

Lorne Heron have been leading pioneers of churches and evangelism in Quebec. Earl Heron is one of our chief helpers in planning and construction.

Rev. Norman Rowan – early MBC speaker, riverside cottager, strong pastor of rural congregations. Father-in-law of <u>Rev. David Clarke</u> who pastored the nearby Locks Church.

Rev. John Coyle – attended, promoted and later directed the conference. Faithful pastor and continued helper at MBC.

Rev. Claire Hoffstetter - came to M.B.C. at a spiritual crossroad in his life. One Sunday morning, in the first Chapel, this writer was warning young guests about serious moral and spiritual perils. Claire became deeply conscious of the seriousness of life. That moment became a turning point in his experience. He is now a dedicated, well-trained, capable Baptist pastor in Kingston, Ontario. **Sisters, Helen and Joy**, were among the top-ranking workers in the Camp Office and Tea Room

<u>This author</u> feels compelled to share his testimony. I came to the task of pioneering M.B.C. when I was a young pastor. The associations with the Conference have been a major factor in shaping our experience and the life of every member of our family. Ross is the business executive, Don, the evangelist, Paul and Dick the pastors, and Dorothy the missionary. They have all been profoundly influenced by association with the Conference. During the war years, Don was in the merchant navy. He was away from home and away from God. There was one place, which he longed to see again . . . the camp beside Mary Lake. As a family we are deeply indebted to M.B.C.

We would not want to leave the impression that all, who came to the Conference, were without faults. There were some who caused heartaches and problems. There were many times when a director needed much prayer and patience. As years passed, the skill of the divine Potter became evident. Some who had seemed to be the most "unpromising" became outstanding in their character and service. Looking back across the years we can see that a battle was being waged in their hearts. Satan saw their possibilities and sought to frustrate God's plan. Christ was sufficient and has made them *more than conquerors.*

Before we leave this part of our survey of Muskoka Miracles, it is important to note that the Divine supernaturalism was not confined to the calling and commissioning of pastors. A great host of Baptist deacons, Sunday-school superintendents, and prospective leaders in other departments of the local churches came to Mary Lake. Many were profoundly influenced by the teaching and fellowship of the camp.

In the early leadership of FBYPA and in the establishing of MBC, I was greatly blessed by the teamwork of godly friends: Sydney L. White, Ewart Page, Ralph Knight, Charlie Hare, Etric Harley, Art Fitkin, Gordon Bigham and others. The young lads of the M.B.C's yesterday, are dedicated leaders of Baptist Churches today: Reg. Knight, Bob Page, Duncan Findlay, Harry Peters, Miller Alloway, Vivian Gonder, Frank Bowman, E. Heron, and others.

What an impact on entire families who come to Mary Lake year after year !

- summer daily teaching ministry from the chapel pulpit, reaching as many as 400

- the seed of the Word sown in children's hearts through the summer D.V.B.S.

- special conferences for Pastors, Laymen, Ladies

- 2 or 3 weeks for children and youth became a separate summer camp ministry

- registrations have often outgrown available camp and cottage accommodation

- an influence beyond expectations is reaching outside our constituency

We meet the alumni family of Muskoka Baptist Conference everywhere we go. During the war, we met them in Britain, Belgium, Holland, and Germany . . . service men who had met the Master on the shores of Mary Lake and were now serving Him in army camps and barracks.

A few months ago we preached in Glendale Baptist Church in Hamilton. We were greeted by a father who said: *This little boy of mine made me come over to this service. He was saved under your ministry at M.B.C., and he wanted to see you again.* He was the bundle of suppressed dynamite, who, to the consternation of his parents, sat on the front seat of the chapel for five successive nights. Surprisingly, he was as good as gold. On Friday night, when an invitation was given to come to Christ, his was the first hand to go up.

In recent weeks of ministry, I was greeted at Churchill Heights by a song leader who was a camper at MBC. At West Park Baptist Church, in London, it was the Sunday-school superintendent, who was a veteran M.B.C. camper.

How wonderful that the Camp of *Depression Days,* that began with so little and so few, has enriched hundreds of churches and thousands of lives. In actual fact, the influence of Muskoka Baptist Conference has been woven into the fabric of the Fellowship of Evangelical Baptist Churches.

THE UNIFYING INFLUENCE OF M.B.C.

When the Fellowship of <u>Independent</u> Baptist Churches and the Union of Regular Baptist Churches were moving toward amalgamation, the Camp played an important part in preparing for the merger. Union pastors became speakers at Camp sessions. Members of churches, that had been divided from sister churches for years, met one another at M.B.C. There was joy in a common commitment to the Word. They could worship, play, and study the Word together. M.B.C. Pastors' conferences, involving both groups, drew them together in a close bond of fellowship.

Attempts to unite Eastern and Western evangelical Baptist groups appeared doomed to failure. It was at a Mary Lake Pastors' Conference, which included Western representatives that new impetus was given to plans for a Trans-Canada Fellowship. After several years, at a minimum of expense, this ultimately became *The Fellowship of Evangelical Baptist Churches in Canada.*

DEVELOPMENT OF A BAPTIST SUMMER COMMUNITY

Before the leaders of F.B.Y.P.A. thought of establishing a summer camp in Muskoka, the plan for a Baptist summer community in Brunel

Township was on the heavenly draughting-board. The project was actually under way. Three preachers and a like-minded family had purchased land. They erected cottages at the corner of Mary Lake adjacent to the farm that was later to become the camp property. The nucleus of a Baptist summer community consisted of Rev. Fred Dyson, Rev. C. J. Loney, Rev. P. B. Loney, and Mr. Mrs. Harry and Penelope Taylor.

As the camp developed, other believers, including some Conference administrators, purchased land and built cottages, bringing to about twelve the number of summer dwellings on the hillside, overlooking Mary Lake and the Muskoka River.

In **1951**, the Fellowship of Independent Baptist Churches received the camp from the F.B.Y.P.A. A section of the riverfront was surveyed and subdivided into lots. This provided eighteen cottage locations, and before long, there was a cottage on every parcel.

By **1969**, a large section of the newly acquired hundred-acre *Thompson sugar bush* was laid out in a plan of 41 leased cottage sites. In the first weeks six applications were made for the long-lease agreements.

This brings to 36 the number of Baptist families with cottages on or near Conference property. When allocation of the other 35 *M.B.C. Acres* lots has been completed and cottages built, the Summer Christian Community in Brunel will number 71. This is a very real source of influence for God in the Mary Lake area. In addition to this "miracle village" in the Muskoka Hills, there is a parallel story of the <u>Muskoka Mission</u> and the work of Muskoka missionaries during the past 39 years.

Chapter 6

MISSIONARY MIRACLES

This chapter is the best in the book. . . not because it is produced by a better writer ! It is the same scribe with the same ballpoint pen. Not because it was written at a more auspicious time than the other parts of this chronicle! Why then is it the best chapter? It is best, because it is the tremendous story of the <u>missionary</u> outreach from Muskoka Baptist Conference. It is the testimony to Brunel Township (our Jerusalem). It is the description of the enlargement of M.B.C.'s witness, a testimony now stretching across Canada (our Samaria). It extends in outreach to Africa, India, China, Japan, and South America (the uttermost parts).

THE MUSKOKA BAPTIST MISSION

The believers who attended the first Camp lost no time in initiating a witness to the area. Before the conference closed, the campers themselves held services in the neighbourhood. By October of 1931, a missionary had begun work in the Mary Lake district. One of the objectives was to reach as many areas as possible. The interprovincial F.B.Y.P.A. was appealing for 30 Bible Schools and Young People's Associations to give fifty cents a week each toward financing the project.

In the years that followed, community after community felt the influence of the <u>Muskoka Mission</u>. Regular preaching services were held in schools, public halls, or homes on the South Mary Lake Road, the Britannia Road, at The Locks, Grassmere, Newholme, South River, Novar, Elmsdale and Bardsville. Ultimately churches were also organized at Huntsville and Bracebridge.

Dedicated young pastors manned those missions and churches. These servants of the Lord included Rev. Fred Bell, Rev. George Wilkinson, Rev. Jack Adams, Rev. Gordon Rendle, Rev. Clayton Wilhelm, and Rev. David Clarke. Their flocks were in small, scattered communities. Their incomes were meager. The roads that they travelled were rough and sometimes impassable. The cars, which they drove, were of *ancient vintage.* The presentation, of a new car to Pastor and Mrs. Rendle, at an F.B.Y.P.A. convention, was a big event in their Muskoka career.

The limitations of a brief history confine us to one sample of the sacrificial service of the Muskoka workers.

As young people, **Fred Bell** and his fiancée **Maisie** attended the first Baptist Camp at Mary Lake. During those ten days their love for one another, and for their Lord, was deepened. What they saw and heard at M.B.C. gave them a strong desire to spend their lives in the service of Christ and produced a deep concern for the evangelization of the Mary Lake district. They were married two years later, but in the meantime Fred had become the F.B.Y.P.A. missionary to Muskoka. Together Pastor and Mrs. Bell gave themselves without reservation to meeting the spiritual and material needs of their flock. Mr. Bell went far afield, preaching in homes, schools and halls. He taught courses in religious education in five Brunel Township public schools and others as far away as Hillside and Dwight. His mandate included Bible teaching and the Gospel. He held regular services in Logging Camps and Road Camps. In a government depression-time project, he regularly addressed a hundred men.

Pastor Bell organized a church in the Britannia Road area, the first of a series of congregations that were to grow out of the witness of the Muskoka Mission. At one period of time he used a United Church building for meetings on every second Sunday evening . On alternate Sunday evenings the United Congregation held meetings there. The Baptists increased in numbers so rapidly, that before long the United Church cancelled the arrangement.

The Muskoka missionary, Fred Bell, was known for faithful visitation. When winter roads were impassable to buggy, cutter, or car, he used snowshoes or skis to reach his scattered members. On a bitterly cold day, while skiing down the frozen surface of the Muskoka River to prepare for the Camp's summer refrigeration needs, the ice beneath him gave way. He was all but submerged in the stream and nearly perished before he succeeded in pulling himself to safety. Later he recalled that shortly before the ice cracked it occurred to him that if such a thing should happen his ski harness would make it almost impossible to extricate himself from a hole in the ice. At that point, he loosened the harness on one of the skis, and when the accident took place a few moments later, he was able to kick off the one ski, disengage himself from the other, and get back on the ice. With his clothes freezing to his body, he made his way painfully to one of the Camp buildings, but was unable to find a match to light a fire. He struggled on to a neighbouring home about a quarter of a mile distant. There he was given hot tea, food, and dry clothing.

On another occasion, **Camp Director DeLoss Scott** had a similar narrow escape. He was with Pastor Bell on the frozen surface of the river when the ice cracked with a sound like a cannon. He fell backward, the lower half of his body submerged in the icy river. He lay perfectly still until Pastor Bell circled to a point on the bank behind him. Laying face down on the ice, he pushed his way out until he could get hold of Pastor Scott's hands, and slowly, inch by inch, pulled him to safety.

On a bitterly cold day, when the temperature fell to forty below zero, and a 40 mile per hour wind brought the chill-factor to 80° below, Missionary Bell's car stalled a mile and a half from his home. Facing the biting gale, he made the journey on foot. In sight of his house, almost spent, he literally hurled his body against the wind, using all of his failing strength to reach the threshold. Mrs. Bell, watching anxiously for him, threw the door wide open, and as he staggered through the opening, he collapsed in utter exhaustion.

In the "Depression" years, Baptist Churches and local F.B.Y.P.A.'s shipped tons of clothing and bedding to Pastors Bell and Wilkinson for distribution to destitute families. In **1939**, the secretary of the interprovincial F.B.Y.P.A. received from Brunel Township Council an official expression of appreciation for the *untiring efforts* of the missionaries to assist the needy in the region.

Many former guests of M.B.C. can recall with a thrill those great days when the Muskoka Missionary would bring the converts of the winter ministry to the summer conference lakeside. Amid the rejoicing by M.B.C. guests, and Muskoka congregations, young believers were baptized, by the missionary, in the waters of Mary Lake. During the winters, scores of Baptist churches were stimulated and strengthened by the testimonies of the Muskoka missionaries.

After twenty years of operation by the F.B.Y.P.A., (1931-1950) the "Muskoka Mission" was merged with the Home Mission work of the Fellowship of Independent Baptist Churches. With the improvement of roads and the consolidation of public school districts, the missionary strategy was altered to meet new conditions. The number of smaller causes was reduced and their congregations absorbed by the stronger missions and churches. The Britannia church is an example. After the organization of The Locks Baptist church, most of the people from Britannia, Newholme, and Fairyport came to The Locks. An attractive frame building was erected, combining both chapel and parsonage. A group from The Locks later seceded to form Faith Baptist Church in Huntsville, a company shepherded in recent years by Rev. T. L. White. He has been a long-standing supporter of M.B.C. Under the pastoral leadership of Dr. Clarence Hayden, The Locks Church has relocated to Riverside Drive, near Huntsville. This climaxed the Muskoka Baptist Mission witness with the erection of a beautiful modern edifice, dedicated this year (August 1970).

INFLUENCE IN CANADA

Many are the men and women of God who heard the footfall of the Master beside Mary Lake, and were powerfully influenced by their association with Muskoka Baptist Conference. Rev. Lorne Heron came in 1944 as a teenager. He was thinking seriously about the possibility of giving his life to the Lord for fulltime service. There was still a measure of indecision. Under the influence of Pastor Stover, Lorne made the decision to surrender. With his brother Murray and Bill Phillips, these drew *Muskoka encouragement* for their life-time ministries in Quebec Province.

Rev. Don Whitelaw's missionary parents were friends of M.B.C. from the beginning. It was there that Don met Marion Hurst, his future bride. With others of the Whitelaw family they have given their lives in pioneer ministry and academic witness. Rev. Don Dinnick, a builder of churches. He learned his greatest personal lesson years ago while at Muskoka Baptist Camp. More than 90 Baptist churches have been enriched by the pastoral ministry of men of God who responded to the Master's voice at Mary Lake.

TO THE UTTERMOST PARTS

Appointment to MBC's staff has often been a foretaste of Christian service.

Lorna Whitelaw and family operate a Bible depot and mission home in Mexico, S.A.

Sheila (Findlay) McNaughton is with the Evangelical Alliance Mission in Venezuela.

Vern Goheen (1931 camper) and wife Vivian . . . Wycliffe Bible Translators in Guatemala.

Bertha Belch, (camp nurse)served in Africa, Columbia, S.A.; Women's Missionary Society

Ivor and Ruth Greenslade frequent MBC helpers . . . served with ABWE, Peru

Rev and Mrs. Geo. McAlpine early campers. Served years in Africa & Field Director, SUM

Rev. John Russell, MBC cottager, pastor, administrator –SUM, EAM, Slavic Missionary Soc. Dr. *Bob & Belva Foster,* MBC director 1940, honoured missionary doctor, AEF

Herbert Foster early camper. Gave his life in missionary service in Africa, AEF

Keith Donald, once assistant-director at M.B.C. is with A.E.F. in the Copper Belt in Zambia. *Ross Alloway* also serving with the AEF

Len and Ness Aylett volunteer missionaries at the Mukinge Hospital station in Zambia. What a record they have in relation to the development of M.B.C.! As a young man Len Aylett attended the 1930 camp at Fishers Glen. He asked if he could come and do anything he could to help. Nessie came to her first camp at Mary Lake in 1931. The Ayletts have made an incalculable contribution.

John Whitelaw & sister Claire Jantz missionaries Western Congo, in crisis years

Dorothy Holliday CBFMS missionary in Eastern Congo during chaotic period.

Miss Hazel Fulcher, camp nurse in 1934, served in China.

1937 shows 6 *Pickerings* at MBC; Frank Jr. 14; He & Marion pioneer missionaries, Japan

Paul and Mary Kerr, MBC Assist. Director/Nurse: FEBC Missions including India

Tilly Goba is with International Christian Fellowship in North India.

Dr. and Mrs. Howard Searle Teens' counsellors 1959, Marilyn, Camp nurse, FEBC, India

Shirley Funnell (MBC staff) Wycliffe Bible Translators, Philippines.

Marg (Alloway) Gentry and her husband ABWE, Philippines, now FEBC Pastor, Edmonton

Enid Skuce missionary service in France.

Florence Young 25 years Esperanza Hospital, B.C. working with Shantymen Assoc.

Chapter 7

MIRACULOUS PROVISION

A RECORD OF GOD'S FAITHFULNESS BY SYDNEY L. WHITE

"I being in the way, the Lord led me"

Imagine trying to stage a Bible Conference in the middle of the black depression of the early thirties. The present generation cannot appreciate the conditions, which prevailed at that time. Those who are older remember that even tradesmen who were willing to work for two dollars per day could not find employment.

The small group of Baptist Churches that had come into existence only three or four years before, had been further splintered by controversy, and the dominant feeling was depression, disillusionment, and despair. God seemed to be saying, *"Forward"* as the need and challenge were impressed upon a small group who were themselves without financial resources or backing. Unknown to us, God had already made provision for our encouragement by leading one Christian lady to place a legacy in her will. Her bequest, made some time previously, became available just when it was needed most.

Let us go back to the launching of M.B.C., because our story really started in 1928, when the executive of the F.B.Y.P.A. asked the executive of the Union of Regular Baptist Churches to establish a Bible Conference. The members of the executive reacted favourably to the idea, but, no doubt because of other urgent matters engaging their attention, did not take any action. It is interesting to note that the motion requesting the F.B.Y.P.A. to undertake this work was made by Dr. T.T. Shields at the Union Convention in Brantford in the fall of 1929.

A Bible Conference or Camp for young people for the year 1930. No money! No location! No experience! What should we do?

It was found possible to rent a property at Fisher's Glen on Lake Erie, for ten days. The rental price, including a staff of three, was set at

$800.00. Although we did not know where we would find eight hundred dollars, or even eight hundred cents, the agreement was signed on April 5th, 1930, in Brantford, by the owner, and by John F. Holliday and Sydney L. White acting for the F.B.Y.P.A. The dates were set, July 25th to August 4th, and the call for registrations went out.

How anxiously we watched the mails! Would our young people respond? Would we make it a financial success, or would we go into the red? While we waited, programs were arranged and food and other supplies were purchased.   Our outlay came to more than $1,700. Registrations came in and the guests arrived. God honoured His Word. Some professed acceptance of our Lord Jesus Christ. The registration fees and other small items covered all our expenses and left a balance of $141.93. This was just the amount needed to cover the cost of camp cots which had to be purchased. Thus *we thanked God and took courage*.

The next question was . . . *where now*? A property in Muskoka was brought to our notice. The price was $4000., the down-payment $250. and there were other scheduled payments later. Dare we step out in faith again? Yes, because God was leading us on. A call went out to our young people for the $250. needed by December 31, 1930. "*Such a small amount*", you will say, and we reply, "*not in 1930*". Sacrifices were made. On the due date, the exact amount of $265. was available to us. Full payment was made. It was early in **1931** that we heard of a legacy of $5,000. This bequest was the biggest gift received during the forty-year history of M.B.C. It was sufficient to cover the price of the property, legal fees and to provide for some essential alterations and much-needed equipment. During the ensuing years, additional property was purchased. The land and buildings in Muskoka may now be realistically valued at a figure between $200,000. and $300,000., in accordance with current market prices.

God's faithfulness, however, is not measured by a year or two. The record goes on. We needed a Director's cottage . . . and a good friend supplied the funds to build it. Benton Street Baptist Church in Kitchener contributed the cost of another cottage to increase accommodation for guests. "**Benton**", the name given to the building, is still serving us well. One by one the old structures were demolished and new buildings took their places. To celebrate the Camp's Silver Anniversary, plans were made for the construction of a $12, 000. **masonry motel**. $10,000. in cash or pledges was set as an objective to be attained before work on the building was to begin. Hundreds of former guests and staff-members responded and the ten thousand dollars were received in time to build the motel and have it ready for M.B.C's 25th birthday (**1955**).

M   In **1952**, the provision of a large **walk-in refrigerator** was a special miracle that will long be remembered. In the early years of the camp, the refrigerator was a tall cabinet, with limited space for food. Above the food compartment, there was a container for big blocks of ice. These had to be cut from the lake in the winter and stored in saw-dust. To place those huge blocks in the top of the refrigerator during camp was a feat that endangered the life of more than one handyman. With the expansion of the camp, refrigeration became a pressing need, and though the treasury did not warrant an immediate purchase, a committee of two was appointed to explore the cost of better equipment.

Our good friend, <u>Rev. Norman Pipe</u> of Simcoe suggested that a relative of his, who manufactured such equipment, might help us. It was the writer's privilege to accompany him on the exploratory mission. We were graciously received, were advised that it was the practice of the firm to give an annual contribution to a religious or charitable institution, and since M.B.C. was the first organization to solicit help during the calendar year, we might select from the firm's catalogue a refrigeration unit costing up to a thousand dollars. There was an assurance that it would be **donated, delivered, and set up in the kitchen . . without charge**.

That room-size walk-in refrigerator has not only served as a storage room for perishables, but has made possible the purchase of large quantities of meat and vegetables in advance. This has enabled cooks to prepare such dishes as salads, jellies, etc. for large numbers of guests, and have them fresh and ready to serve. The story does not end there. Shortly after the refrigerator was delivered to M.B.C., the firm that donated it changed hands. The new management discontinued the annual gift to religious and charitable institutions. M.B.C. was the last organization to profit from that generosity.

The manner in which the two camp chapels were acquired was very different, but both were divinely provided. In the case of the first, both the lumber and labour were supplied by divine providence. Logs were taken from the camp bush, cut into lumber and built into a rustic chapel (**1936**). Interested men of Brunel Township provided all the labour under the supervision of Rev. James Millar. It served as a chapel for approximately twenty-five years and was a rendezvous with God for hundreds of Campers. By 1960, it was too small and inadequate for the growing conference. At that time the Lord moved on the heart of one of the Conference commission members to offer $3000.00 toward the cost of a new meeting place It was understood that M.B.C. would undertake to raise the balance needed. This was done, the Chapel built, and each summer it accommodates a congregation frequently numbering as many as four hundred. Our *"Memorial Chapel"* (**1961**) has served us well and many decisions for the glory of God have been made within its walls.

This account would not be complete without mention of the many persons whom God led to help in many sacrificial ways. *What more shall I say, for time would fail me to tell* of members of the M.B.C. organization first (committee), then (commission) who have sacrificed weekends and weeks of vacation periods to labour on the grounds. Often they have gone beyond their physical strength in their service. Others, in addition to physical involvement, have purchased and contributed urgently needed items of equipment. Many friends have come for weeks at a time to contribute skilled work as carpenters, electricians, etc. All of these are remembered with deep appreciation, as we *esteem them very highly in love for their work's sake.*

In our stewardship of these God-given provisions, the M.B.C. organization has taken meticulous care to administer the funds economically and efficiently.

From the inception of the Camp, a very conservative and realistic accounting program has been followed. As an example, throughout the forty-year history of M.B.C. we have depreciated property and buildings at a commercial rate. A procedure not often followed in normal church accounting. At the end of 1969, the accumulated depreciation reserve amounted to $51,127. Included in this policy, great care has been taken <u>not</u> to capitalize small items, but to charge them to current expense during the year in which they were acquired.

Throughout the years, M.B.C. has sought to provide accommodation for our Baptist people at approximate cost. In accordance with this policy, we have kept the rates down so that as many as possible could enjoy the facilities. With the steadily increasing costs (an increase in taxes of approximately one thousand percent) this has not been easy to achieve. It follows, therefore, that when large capital expenditures are made, the conference must look to other than operating revenues to procure these.

Various measures were taken from time to time to secure the additional capital needed for vital improvements. This included the subdividing and sale of river-front lots to Baptist families. This was a Silver Anniversary appeal in which $10,000. was contributed for the erection of a motel. From time to time, M.B.C. issued <u>loan certificates</u>. Some of these were retired by cash payment, and some by conversion to Fellowship bonds. It is significant that the success of the First Fellowship Bond issue was in no small measure due to the fact that part of the investment project was to be used for the development of M.B.C.

It is to be noted that M.B.C. funds derived from loan certificates, or Fellowship bonds, have been used for capital expenditures only.

M.B.C. committees and commissions have consistently followed certain revenue-producing strategies. In spite of pressures for extra features that appealed to one group or another, the organization concentrated upon **essential accommodation** and **improvement of accommodation**. This would maintain and increase revenue. Recent examples are:

(1) The setting up of 35 camping sites to take advantage of the contemporary enthusiasm for tent or trailer vacations

(2) The development of M.B.C. Acres, a sub-division containing 41 lots for cottage building on long-lease agreements. After the basic costs of survey, roads, water, and electric services, this latter project will provide funds, which may be used for the reduction of capital loans.

Among the revenue-producing strategies carried out by the commission, is the development of the timber potential of the property. Four years ago, representatives of the Ontario Department of Lands and Forests checked the standing timber. Trees were marked for cutting or preservation. At the same time ten thousand new trees were planted in an open area of the newly acquired *Thompson property.* The future value of the results of this project must be obvious to all.

In **1954**, by guidelines from the executive of the newly formed Fellowship of Evangelical Baptist Churches in Canada, there was official recognition that M.B.C. Teens Camp was a vital investment in youth that would continue to require a subsidy. The M.B.C. commission was to plan to maintain and develop this aspect of its operation with expectation of a reasonable subsidy from Fellowship funds.

In reviewing the financial history of M.B.C., it is to be noted that, apart from the above-mentioned subsidy toward the operation of teens' camps, the annual revenue of Muskoka Baptist Conference has covered all current operating expenses. In addition it has accumulated substantial surpluses. In recent years, M.B.C. has also contributed substantially to the general overhead expenses of the Fellowship.

God has supplied the money and the workers. As the Word has been ministered, the Spirit of God has added *the blessing of the Lord.* He has established and maintained M.B.C. for His glory. We give Him our praise in thankfulness for all the way He has led us . . . a way that has been marked by Miraculous Provision.

Chapter 8

THE MIRACLES AT M.B.C. YOUTH CAMPS

By Rev. Roy Lawson, Program Director

Young people pioneered Muskoka Baptist Conference. On a motion by Dr. T. T. Shields, the Union of Regular Baptist Churches was committed to the newly-formed Fundamentalist Baptist Young People's Association. Their task was to provide a summer-time ministry for youth. The success of the first camp at Fisher's Glen in 1930 was followed by the purchase in 1931 of 117 acres in Muskoka. Thus began the establishment of a permanent Baptist summer conference. The project was under the direction of the F.B.Y.P.A. It was strongly supported by young people, including many young married couples. It was operated as a general camp for young and old without age limitation. The youth emphasis has characterized its whole history. It was evident in the early years in efforts to reach the young people's constituency.

Arrangements were made for special train and bus rates for youth groups and organization of youth car-pools from London, Stratford, Woodstock, St. Mary's, Brantford, Hamilton, Toronto, and Ottawa. Much of the early history of the F.B.Y.P.A., is tied up with camp-related projects. These included missionary operations in various Muskoka areas and church planting by F.B.Y.P.A. missionaries in Brunel and adjacent townships. A "Depression" welfare program developed under the aegis of the Interprovincial F.B.Y.P.A. In co-operation with F.B.Y.P.A. missionaries, it distributed tons of clothing and bedding to destitute families.

The impact of F.B.Y.P.A. participation was reflected in the enthusiasm with which the young people's conventions received the reports of camps and missionaries. The three Baptist churches which were established still maintain a strong evangelistic testimony in the Muskoka region. The names of Alfred Bell, D. Wilkinson, J. Adams, G. Rendle, pioneers in the early days of F.B.Y.P.A. Muskoka Mission work, will long be remembered.

51

THE FIRST CAMPS FOR GIRLS AND BOYS

The story of the first camps for "Teens" is packed full of human-interest items. They were called "Camps for Intermediates" because at that time, the Fundamentalist Baptist Young People's Association was promoting local church programs and operating rallies for young folk from twelve to sixteen years of age. This was identified as the "Intermediate" outreach of the F.B.Y.P.A.

In **July 1937** the first Intermediate Camps were held. The "Girls" led the way, which made it necessary for the Girls' Staff to prepare the Camp facilities for both eight-day programs. Two days before the opening, Elsie Barrow (now Mrs. Frank Andrews) obtained her first licence to drive. The following day she borrowed her father's car and drove the whole staff (cooks, directors, and counselors – six in all) to Mary Lake. The trip took seven hours. The road from Huntsville to Camp contained small quantities of gravel and large amounts of mud, furrowed by deep ruts. The car stalled on the big hill near the spring. With plenty of pushing, they surmounted the ridge. When they reached camp, they found no water (except that which they could carry from the camp spring), no hydro (the light was supplied by coal oil lamps), no wood cut for the stove, and not a soul in sight. The girls cleaned the kitchen of the old farm house, washed the dishes in preparation for the girl campers who were due to arrive on the morrow. They looked out into the inky blackness of a starless night, and barricaded themselves in the farmhouse. Weary and a bit scared, they retired, but sleep did not come easily.

Suddenly, at midnight, there was a thunderous knock on the back door. All six ladies grabbed the available weapons, a poker, a shovel, a broom, etc., and prepared to do battle with the midnight intruder. Elsie Barrow, in the stern tone which the situation demanded, shouted, "*Who's there?*" From a gentle male voice the answer came: "*It's Paul Morris. I'm the handyman. I hitchhiked from Toronto and walked in from Huntsville.*" The relief of the six heroines was indescribable. The barricades were removed and the hero of the hour was admitted. He was permitted to find a corner of the building in which to retire. Six re-assured young ladies went back to bed with confidence that there was a man to protect them in the dark hours, and someone to carry water and chop wood when the sun came up.

Before the guests arrived, the heroines of the previous night had to clean the cabins. There were mice everywhere. The members of the staff stood on chairs and beat the mattresses with brooms while the mice made their exit.

At that first Girls' Camp, the distribution of staff duties was very simple. Two looked after the cooking, the other four served as program directors, disciplinarians, lighters of lamps, blowers-out of lamps, and general supervisors.

The following paragraphs are culled from a letter written by Mrs. Shelson, one of the members of that pioneer staff. The letter was dated July 12, 1937: *We are very happy that God has blessed our first attempt with the girls, for His watchful care, and also for lovely weather. We are grateful for the opportunity of operating a girls' camp. We are praying that God will richly bless and guard the boys this week. Above all, that His name shall be lifted up and souls saved.*

The first Intermediate Boys' Camp, also in July 1937, was just as successful as the girls', spiritually, and in all other ways. The boys claimed they had the better time. Notes were discovered for a Teens' Rally address promoting the 1938 camps. The following information about the previous year indicated the extraordinary program variety for the boy's. It was: *Wake up, breakfast, kitchen-fatigue, chapel, golf, swim, climbing Blueberry Mountain, sing-song, Bible message, picnic lunch, by car to Westjo (a neighbouring camp operated by a Baptist pastor), ball game, supper served to our boys at # 5 Schoolhouse by neighbouring people.* One boy bragged that he had nine pieces of pie, but insisted that the director must have had thirty-five pieces. Two other items in the program were "Watermelon" and "Tossed in a Blanket".

Along with the fun, there was spiritual ministry that had a profound influence upon many of the girls and boys who attended the first and succeeding Intermediate Camps. The first leader of this camping project was Mr. Herb Gooderham. In 1938, Mr. Frank Andrews succeeded him as chairman of the Intermediate Camp Committee. The

Toronto F.B.Y.P.A sponsored all the Camps of 1938 to 1941. In 1941 there was a considerable increase in registration and revenue.

The 1938 Girls' Camp reported a humorous story that is worth recalling. It was the case of a damsel in distress. The young lady was Miss Irene Kenyon, speaker of the week. About 3 a.m., terrified screams pierced the air. Miss Barrow and Mrs. Shelson threw on their bathrobes and raced to the speaker's cabin. They found Miss Kenyon sitting on the bed, her legs crossed tailor-fashion, and all the bedclothes wrapped around her. Beneath the floor, a porcupine was gnawing vigorously at something. The speaker would not believe that the animal was not right in the room under the bed, about to emerge at any moment.

As a result of war conditions transportation was a major problem. This led to cancellation of the 1942 Intermediate Camps. They were not reinstated until 1948.

PIONEERING PERSONNEL

The pioneers of M.B.C. youth work had a deep love for young people. We cannot exaggerate their devotion to the Saviour. This enabled them to cope with the limitations and frustrations which they met as they sowed the seed in young hearts.

Mrs. Frank Andrews (née Elsie Barrow) served the longest term in M.B.C. youth ministries. It stretched from 1937 to 1960. From that time to the present, she has continued to contribute to the progress of every department of M.B.C. She has also still been working in the Evangelical Fellowship office. Retiring recently from that post, she has become a fulltime staff member at the conference center to which she has given so much of her time and strength. Frank Andrews, to whom Elsie was married in 1956, was greatly loved by teens, young people, everyone associated with M.B.C. His campfire stories, poems, and his consistent Christian life made a lasting impact upon a host of young people.

- o   Many others made a notable contribution to the Conference youth work.
- ☐   **Rev. DeLoss Scott**, handyman in the early days, director of the conference for years, speaker to Teens in 1948

- ☐   **Dr. Jack Scott**, Youth camp director in 1948, and a real helper in bringing about a resumption of Teens ministry after the war years

☒ (*The following service record has been inserted by the author, J.F. Holliday. Since R. Lawson is the writer of this chapter we felt that a word about his contribution should be included.*)

☐ **"Rev. Roy Lawson**, serving for fifteen years with the Teens work, in various capacities – counselor, committee-member, director, etc. – giving the best of his energy and talents to it as representative of F.B.Y.P.A."

☐ **Rev. John Roberts**, invaluable assistant as a camp director.

☐ **Rev. Robert Irvin**, now dean of students at Moody Bible Institute was Teens' Camp director for approximately five years.

☒ Al Williams, Rev. A. Bell, Rev. T. White, Don, Paul and Richard Holliday . . . These, and others, have helped to shape the lives of many hundreds of young people who came to the Mary Lake youth camps

HIGHLIGHTS

1948 was a banner year in Conference outreach to teens. M.B.C. resumed operation of their camps. From the fall of 1947 there had been many requests for a resumption of this ministry. There had been a hiatus because of the war years. In May 1948, an enthusiastic Teens' Rally prepared the way for a new beginning. A committee, consisting of Rev. Jack Scott, Joyce Grundy, Frank Andrews, Joan Chapman, Elsie Barrow, Mrs. Shelson, Art Hodgins, and Rev. J.F. Holliday, made the plans. Rev. Jack Scott served as director and Rev. DeLoss Scott was the speaker. Registration and spiritual blessing showed that M.B.C. Teens were on the march again. The fine camp of 1948 was followed by good Teens' Weeks in 1949 and 1950. These were directed by Rev. D. Adamson and Rev. B. Hunt respectively.

1951 was another highlight. So many tents were required to accommodate the crowd of registrants, that the 1951 camp earned the title, "The Tent Village of Baghdad". For two solid weeks there were 175 teenagers and teen counselors on the grounds. On one weekend the number of campers, counselors, and guests reached an all-time high of 195. The Friday night testimony/dedication services were never to be forgotten events. Sixty, seventy, and eighty boys and girls rose to tell of new-found faith in Christ, restoration, or dedication to their Lord. Those two weeks cost $800.00 more than the children paid in rates, but it was an investment that returned immense dividends to our entire Evangelical constituency.

THE PURCHASE OF WIDJIITIWIN

From **1960 –** Youth and General Conference leaders began to sense the need of a dedicated property to house a separate youth camp. This would provide adequate time and separate facilities to develop Junior, Intermediate and Senior age camps. **In 1961**, a Youth Camp Investigation Committee was organized. Consideration was given to properties in other regions as well as to the possibility of developing a youth camp-site on an unused part of the M.B.C. acreage. The search ended in **1968** with the purchase of a summer hotel. It had adjacent cabins frontage on the bank of the Muskoka River, opposite the parent conference. The property had been used for years as a secular tourist resort. After much hard work by committee members and friends of M.B.C. youth leaders, it became a useful and popular centre for all summer camps for boys and girls.   The youth camp committee labeled the new site, "Widjitii-win", an Indian word meaning "togetherness"/ "Fellowship".

The 1974 Widjitiiwin report will give some idea of the value of this ministry to Youth: *The eight weeks of Junior Camp (8 to 14 years) operated at capacity, averaging 79 campers each week. The two senior weeks (14 to 18 years) were somewhat less. There were 714 campers for the year.* The report also records that *many young campers placed their faith in the saving power of the Lord Jesus Christ, while others dedicated their lives to His service. There are many thrilling testimonies . . . .* Director Abe Dueck is giving excellent leadership at this time.

A concern developed in the hearts of Teens' Leaders about the adequacy of this 2.5 acre site. The committee focused on plans for use of an available property located on the conference side of the Muskoka River.

Lack of space makes it impossible for us to do more than mention many other phases of M.B.C.'s outreach to children and young people.

- ☒ There was that time when members of a motorcycle gang turned up at Teens' Camp and were converted through faith in the Lord Jesus Christ and His work of redemption.

- ☒ There were those weeks when Benton Street Baptist Church sent 20 to 30 wards of the Children's Aid to camp. This resulted in many of the children coming to Christ.

- ☒ There were those exhilarating ball games between M.B.C. and the children from Camp Mini-Yo-We. There were those nights of inspiration when the whole Widjitiiwin Camp group crossed the river on The Muskoka Queen, and put on a program of gospel music to a chapel packed with three hundred Conference guests.

- ☒ There was that week of steady rain, when the roads were blocked, the hydro was cut off, the access to the outside world was blocked, the food ran short, AND the dinner feature was "porridge".

To tell the whole story of M.B.C.'s outreach to the younger generation, we would have a lengthy record: thousands of summer-morning "Craft and Bible Story Hours", the Sunday morning "Junior Church" services in Fellowship Centre, the thrilling F.B.Y.P.A. weeks and weekends that often climaxed a summer of mercy-drops, with showers of blessing. We would have to report the coming of hundreds of young people to the Winter Retreats of these two years, 1973-74. We have had a harvest of precious souls in these gatherings, as recorded elsewhere in this book.

LASTING RESULTS

We marvel as we look back over the history of Muskoka Baptist Conference. We marvel at its origin. We marvel at the leadership that God has provided through the years. We marvel at the provisions that have maintained and enlarged M.B.C. while similar institutions have dwindled and dissolved. We marvel at the providential care that has watched over the thousands and thousands of children during these forty-five years. We have had thousands of campers, but no serious injuries. We humbly thank God for His goodness.

We marvel most of all at the lasting results of the outreach to youth in the Muskoka Hills. We marvel at the number of missionaries who have been influenced by their contacts with M.B.C. At the moment, a few of these come to mind: *Len and Nessie Aylett* in Africa, *Craig Cook* with H.C.J.B., *Verne and Vivian Goheen* with Wycliffe Translators in South America, *Dave Taylor* in Quebec. Some of these are mentioned in a different connection in an earlier chapter of this book. We mention them here in the context of our presentation of the impact of the Conference upon youth. That impact has not been diminished by the passage of the years. It has lasted. We marvel at the influence upon pastors. The outreach of M.B.C. has experienced the blessing of God. It has produced a great host of Bible-believing, God-fearing, Christ-honouring men, women, and children, the backbone of many local churches. We marvel at the grace of our Lord Jesus Christ in revealing Himself to young and old at Mary Lake, as *He showed Himself to the disciples, centuries ago, on the Galilean shore.*

Chapter 9

MEET THE FOUNDERS

Dr. John F. Holliday and Mr. Sydney L. White

In the years **1928** and **1929**, Rev. John F. Holliday and Mr. Sydney L. White were active servants of the Lord in their respective local churches. Frank Holliday was the Pastor of Fairbank Baptist Church in Toronto, and Sydney White was a Deacon and the Treasurer of Central Baptist Church in Brantford. At the same time, Mr. Holliday served as a professor of Toronto Baptist Seminary and Mr. White was the President of A.G. Spalding Brothers of Canada. The two men shared a common interest in ministry to young people.

In the late 1920's The Great Depression created a climate of adversity. During the same period, there was a serious conflict concerning the entry of Liberal Theology into some ministry training institutions, and into many churches. **The Fundamentalist Baptist Young Peoples Association** was born. John F. Holliday was its first President and Sydney L. White its first Treasurer. At this time, some young people from Fairbank and Christie Street Baptist Churches, respectively, approached their pastors about the low standards of vacation resorts, and the need of a summer place for our Baptist young people and families. As the leaders of the FBYPA, Frank Holliday and Syd White shared that concern. They became God's instruments in the development of **"a Baptist camp for youth and families"**. In that period, the FBYPA was the youth arm of the Fellowship of Independent Baptist Churches, which in 1953 became the Fellowship of Evangelical Baptist Churches. In 1930 at Fisher's Glen and then from 1931 in Muskoka, it has been a meeting place where Christians could "come apart and rest awhile".

Dr. John F. Holliday ~ An article in the April 1990 issue of <u>The Fellowship Baptist</u> :

An Eloquent Man and Mighty in the Scriptures

Dr. J.F. Holliday, one of the founding pioneers of the Fellowship, went home to be with the Lord on Friday, March 2. He was 88.

Dr. Holliday served as a President of the Fellowship of Evangelical Baptist Churches in Canada, one of the founders of Muskoka Baptist conference, and founding editor of what is now *The Evangelical Baptist.* He also served as President of Central Baptist Seminary, and pastored the following Fellowship Baptist churches: Fairbank, Faith, Eglinton, Waverley Road, and Mount Pleasant Road Baptist Church (all in the Toronto area); as well as Tiverton, Kincardine, Charlton Avenue (Hamilton), and Second Markham Baptist Church (Stouffville).

He was born Jan. 29, 1902, in Quebec City, to John and Amy Holliday. His father died when he was only four. At 16, he moved to Toronto, to live with his aunt and uncle, the Tims family. There, he attended Boon Avenue Baptist church where, on his third Sunday, he responded to the invitation of the gospel given by Pastor F.W. Roadhouse.

One of Dr. Holliday's first jobs was as personal office boy to Sir John Eaton, to whom he gave his first testimony of salvation. Conscious of the call of God to prepare for service, he resigned and enrolled at Toronto Bible College. To his surprise, he was allowed to continue working part-time at Eaton's, and "Sir John" personally gift-funded his tuition.

Dr. Holliday married fellow T.B.C. student Luella Trombley. His work in mission preaching, student pastorates, and diligence in studies were complemented by "one Holliday after another" (children Ross, Dorothy, Don, Paul and Dick). The family knew a Dad who was fun to be with, loving, tender, and spiritually motivated.

Scholarship was evident in Dr. Holliday's classrooms. He earned a prize in Classical Greek at McMaster University, and later the Alumnus of the Year Award from Ontario Bible College.

At T.B.S. and Central Baptist Seminary, he taught Hebrew, Systematic Theology, and Pastoral Theology. He was editor of the Fellowship Baptist and published three books and scores of sermons.

World War II chaplaincy was a high-light of Dr. Holliday's witness. He served for the Pacific Command, in England and in continental Europe. Leading a sing-song while sitting on a cannon, playing his autoharp, defused tensions and warmed hearts. He preached on the field of battle, on parade squares, in barracks, jails and hospitals . . . always armed with the truth of God's Word. He logged more than 14,000 office counseling sessions. A year after the war ended, his voice was still broadcasting over the B.B.C. "Armed Forces Radio Network". During his absence in the military, M.B.C. still listed him as "Honourary President" of the Camp Committee.

- Later in his career, Dr. Holliday showed spiritual leadership in the following areas:

- He laboured with pastors in the founding of more than 40 churches

- He was principal leader in founding the Fundamentalist Baptist Young People's Association (F.B.Y.P.A.)

- He organized the "Home Missions Committee" of the Fellowship Baptist Churches, which in one year started more than 52 new churches.

- He was a founder of Muskoka Baptist Conference, along with Sydney White.

- He was the founder of Sky Force of Canada, a local church ministry to children and teens. www.skyforce.org . Teaching materials in English and French.

- He was one of Canada's first radio pastors; Hamilton's CKOC, Toronto's CHUM radio

Being a preacher of the Word was the highest profile of Dr. Holliday. Though he was organized, efficient in business and a consummate administrator, Dr. Holliday lived to preach the Word of God. He thrilled to the promises of the Bible. Faithfulness in doctrine, and consistent New Testament local church practices were the characteristics and bounds of his conscience. He contended for the faith, without being contentious, and he truly loved his enemies.

Dr. Holliday was a man of God, full of faith and vision. His personal piety was natural and unaffected. His prayer was real, and answers were evident. To his closing days, his only longing was to serve his Lord and to preach the Word. He never considered retirement. Like Elijah of old, *a one-man army has been called home to glory.*

Mr. Sydney L. White ~ by Mary (White) Donald

"A man of God . . .thoroughly equipped for every good work" II
Timothy 3:17

The history of Muskoka Baptist Conference has been well recorded
in Muskoka Miracles. What a milestone, to now celebrate eighty years
of ministry. God has truly been faithful. These brief words about Sydney and Helen White can only begin to express some of the precious
memories which I have. It is the perspective of their daughter, Grace
Mary Donald . . . nee White.

My Dad was born in England. With his mother and siblings, he
came to Canada as a very young man. During World War I, he served
in the Royal Canadian Navy for two full years, 1916 to 1918. His
assignment as a Wireless Operator kept him on the very lonely Sable
Islands.

Upon discharge, he worked hard in the business world. Under the
employ of the "A.G. Spalding and Bros. of Canada", he served from
1921 to 1962. He soon rose to be its President and General Manager.
For some years he was President of the Brantford Board of Trade.

Sydney White came to know Christ as his Saviour when in his
youth. I knew him to be a family man . . . godly father, husband and
grandpa. The local church was consistently a priority ministry. He
was one of the founders of the Central Baptist Church of Brantford
in Ontario. He was a life-long deacon for 56 years, many of them as
the Chairman of Deacons. One of his concerns and objectives was to
strengthen Bible-believing Baptists in their stand against modernism
in doctrine. He wanted to encourage dedication and effective service
for the Master.

As an extension of his local church, he was <u>the first treasurer</u> of the
Fundamentalist Baptist Young People's Association. This office he carried for several years. His friend, Frank Holliday was <u>the first President</u>
of the FBYPA. The two men gave leadership in arrangements for the
first camp which was held at Fisher's Glen in 1930, and in 1931 by
establishing the new Muskoka Baptist Camp. My father served on the
official board of MBC <u>every year</u> from its founding, until 1977. He

also served as the first lay President of the Fellowship of Evangelical Baptist Churches in Canada.

My brother Paul and I knew our father to be a great family man. This certainly included his love of quiet times, of reading, or a game of Rook. He also enjoyed golf, tennis, volleyball and ping pong.

My mother was born in London, Ontario. She came to Brantford as a young child, after her mother was widowed. Diligence led to her vocation as a school teacher. She was a <u>good</u> one ! She appreciated fine music and played the violin. Everyone knew her to be a great cook and a gracious hostess . . . with beautiful cups and saucers !!

Helen White loved her husband, her children. . . and as years passed, her grandchildren. Our fond memories include the enjoyment of canoe rides with her, as well as, boisterous games of Rook.

There are four words which come to mind as I reflect on the lives of my parents:

- Dedicated
- Courageous
- Faithful
- Unwavering

<u>Dedicated</u> to Christ and His Word, the Bible

<u>Courageous</u> – unafraid of taking a stand for what was right. With other couples, they stepped out by faith during the depression, to purchase the land for MBC, even though they had very little money.

<u>Faithful</u> to Christ and to each other. They were faithful to their family, to their local church, to their business commitments and to Muskoka Baptist Camp (later . . . "Conference").

<u>Unwavering</u> – Always they stood firm in their convictions and in a steadfast love of their family.

My Dad's favourite hymn? That is not a surprise!
How Firm A Foundation,   ye saints of the Lord,
Is laid for your faith in His excellent Word.

They say that "behind every good man, is a fine woman". That was my Mom. While Dad attended myriads of meetings in the interest of business, the local church and MBC, mother faithfully kept the home fires burning. As children, my brother and I were taken to Sunday School and Church regularly. Going to Muskoka did not change the pattern. Sunday afternoons in the north found us at the old Chapel, under the teaching of Mrs. Penelope Taylor. Every year we heard the story of Creation.

Driving to "the Camp" was always an adventure. There were no four-lane throughways! No air conditioners! Usually the car was packed to the ceiling. PLUS our Saint Bernard dog. We all knew that it was a big problem if we had to wait for a long, slow train at the Orillia crossing. That would add another hour to the journey.

Dad always had a boat. He taught me a great lesson about giving. It was his practice, no matter how busy, to take the Camp speakers and their wives . . . and many other guests for a ride. He enjoyed such opportunities to show off his beloved Mary Lake and to recount the history of the Lake and the Conference. This would be followed by cruising up the river to "the Locks". Back at the cottage, Mom would serve light refreshments.

As a member of the staff of A.G. Spalding, Dad was able to purchase sports equipment so that MBC always had the very latest. The Conference was a refuge and a relief for my father. It was a change from the pressures of business and church involvement. It was a place for spiritual refreshment, making and meeting friends, and enjoying good times.

I am grateful for the many wonderful people who touched our lives as a family, through friendships with my mother and father. Some of those people were my heroes of the faith:

Frank and Luella Holliday	Pappy and Mammy Knight
Cliff and Audrey Van Duzen	Pastor Don and Nan Loveday
Charlie and Margaret Hare	Len and Ness Aylett
Art and Nancy Fitkin	George and Margaret Simpson

DeLoss and Jennie Scott   Jack and Cora Adams

Yes, there were many more than these who encouraged me by their faith and example.

As I reflect upon past years, I am conscious of the heritage passed on to me through my Mom and Dad and through their friends. This treasure has enriched my children and now grandchildren. These now have active interest and involvement in Christian camping ministry. We can never adequately express our gratitude to God for Muskoka Baptist Conference.

As my Dad so often said, "GOD IS SO GOOD"!

Grace Mary (White) Donald
Beloved wife of Ken Donald

Captain J.F. Holliday, Chaplain WWII

Rev. Dr. J.F. Holliday, Pastor, Seminary Professor, Author, Editor

Mrs. Luella Holliday, granddaughter Kimberly Holliday

Mr. S.L. White, Royal Canadian Navy WWI

*President/General Manager of A.G. Spalding and Bros. Canada
Founder/life Deacon Central Baptist Brantford*

Mrs. Helen White, granddaughter Mary Lou Donald

Chapter 10

1930 to 1946 ~ FOUNDATION YEARS

THE IDEAL LOCATION

1930 - The Fisher's Glen Hotel, near Port Dover, was the place enjoyed by 134 campers from 32 churches. The rooms were filled to capacity and some occupied specially purchased tents. According to the 1930 printed brochure the following were listed as "Camp Directors": J.F. Holliday, S.L. White, S. Lawrance, Olive Clark, Catherine Twiss. The editor of the first edition of "The Fisher's Net" was Miss Louise Wyse (later known as Mrs. W. Gordon Brown). The spiritual level was the highest, however, crowded circumstances and colder weather made them feel that "this is not our permanent home".

PROPERTY DISCOVERY ! In the Fall season, Syd White drove to Toronto and climbed into Frank Holliday's old Ford. They drove to Barrie where they met Etric Harley, a deacon of Collier St. Baptist Church. The three drove on to Huntsville where they met their fourth friend, Rev. Roy F. Lawson Sr., pastor of First Baptist Church. Their mission was to investigate a property totaling 117 acres on the Muskoka River near Mary Lake. It was being sold for back taxes. The property had been a small resort owned by Mr. Bert Olan, however, it had fallen into disuse because of the depression. It had a big farmhouse, a 25 foot circular building (later named "The Round House") 5 riverside cottages, a building with 4 small rooms, a drive-shed, and a few small utility buildings. There was no running water, no hydro and no fireplace. It took an eye of faith to see the potential. They were entranced by the beauty of the trees , open fields and the river flowing into Mary Lake. The arrangements were simple:

-The land cost ~ $4000.

-Other charges levied would include transfer fees, registration of the property, back taxes.

-THE TOTAL would eventually come close to $5000.

-The first required   payment was due by December 31, 1930   ~ $250.

M After prayer and a thorough viewing, the four men left for home. There was enthusiastic agreement that this was the property of choice. In Toronto, Frank Holliday and Syd White agreed to commit themselves by making the payment on December 31, 1930. If they could not raise the funds, they agreed to use their homes as collateral. Just before December 31st, their efforts had produced **$265.**

1931 In early January, Frank Holliday received a telephone call from the Registrar General. He asked for Mr. Holliday's ministerial credentials, (Pastor of Fairbank Baptist, President of FBYPA, Professor, T.B.S.). This was followed by a question: *Do you know where there is a Baptist Camp for young people and families?* Mr. Holliday explained that in all his experience he knew of no such place in Canada. He added the information that the Fundamentalist Baptist Young People's Association had been authorized to proceed with the development of a Baptist Camp for young people and families. The phone call led to attendance at the Toronto office for the Registrar General. Confirming documents, including the information regarding sale and registration of the property, were verified to full satisfaction. The Registrar then explained that a lady in British Columbia had died and left a legacy of **$5000.** to be used by *a Baptist Camp for youth and families.* The cheque was prepared and handed to Frank Holliday. The deposit was made the next day by Syd White. God supplied the entire need with enough left over to pay for some equipment and repairs. The name of the lady is still unknown to us !

On February 3, 1931 a large number of Fisher's Glen registrants met at Fairbank Church for the first camp Reunion. It was an excited and enthusiastic group that heard the announcement that steps had been taken to purchase the property in Muskoka. The first FBYPA folder indicated *Summer Camp to be held at Muskoka River.* When Camp began, "Mary Lake" quickly became the identifying term.

Summer was about to begin. Ralph Knight, a member of Fairbank Baptist Church, was unemployed due to the Depression. He was an experienced carpentry foreman and concrete contractor. He had been involved in major construction projects in several parts of Ontario. With a month's salary from his Pastor, he was assigned the task of preparing the grounds at the new Muskoka site. The buildings had to be repaired and prepared for occupancy and use. Minnie Knight, assisted by others, came at the end of June to do the cleaning and outfitting of the kitchen to serve the campers. Their son, Reg Knight was the first person to make a profession of faith in Jesus Christ.

1934 ~ Harmony Row was the first accommodation building to be erected. It was built by Ralph Knight and volunteers. A very basic structure of 5 rooms facing a front porch. Those who lived there experienced the world's greatest sound system. An exuberant word at one end could be heard by the residents at the other. According to the Camp Paper of 1934 there were daily room inspections. *No sir-r-r-r. I made my bed before and now look at it ! The inspectors are coming ! Hurrah, Hurrah !*

THE FIRST CHAPEL AND THE PULPIT

The first place of meeting was the verandah of the farmhouse. They met in the grassy field nearby. Next, a tent replaced the farmhouse porch. In the Fall of **1935**, the depression-afflicted men from the Muskoka District, gave their time and skills to cutting cedar trees on the property. They used the nearby sawmill to cut the logs into boards. An appeal went to churches for a Chapel donation. The cost was to be no more than $250. Supervision of the construction project was by Rev. J. N. Millar. The new "pole barn" Chapel was completed for summer use in **1936**. Mr. Bert Olan, the former owner of the property assisted in the local team effort. As chapel construction was nearing completion, he collected the unused cedar tree tops. While working on this project he was heard to say, *I'm going to make a pulpit that these Bible-thumping Baptists can't shake apart*. Through every year it has continued as THE central symbol of Muskoka Baptist Conference.

Forever, O Lord, Thy Word is settled in Heaven (Psalm 119:89).

Sydney L. White wrote about the Pulpit as follows . . . July 31, 1979

"This pulpit was made by Mr. "Bert" Olan, who was the owner of the land bought by MBC in 1931. He constructed it from trees cut on this property.

On presenting it, "Bert" intimated that he had noticed the propensity of <u>*Baptist Preachers*</u> *to* <u>*pound the pulpit*</u> *and its massive proportions were designed accordingly. This was the year 1936. May it ever be* <u>*used*</u> *to the Glory of God."*

1938 ~ <u>Ontario Hydro</u> ran electricity lines through the properties of Brunel Township. This not only ended the era of the coal-oil lamps, but made possible much more extensive use of all buildings in the evenings.

Because food service was now beyond the capacity of the farmhouse, Ralph Knight and Rev. J.N. Millar laid the plans for a new dining hall/kitchen. With the help of local workers and volunteers, the building was constructed. What a help to connect the new facility to the hydro electric supply. The cost of this building was $1500. During the construction, Pastor Millar commuted between the conference project and his church in London. Skill as a carpenter prompted the church to grant his time for MBC involvement. Having loaded a water pump into the trunk of his car, bound for use at Mary Lake, he was suddenly called home to Heaven. The new building was named *Millar Hall* in his honour.

1939 to 1946 ~ Ministry continued during the war years. Sydney White assumed the leadership of the Camp Committee. He regularly corresponded with Frank Holliday, about M.B.C. blessings and the ongoing programming in spite of war time limitations. During the war years when Frank Holliday was serving in the Canadian Army Chaplaincy, he continued to be recognized as "Honourary Chairman" of MBC. It was really Sydney White who co-ordinated the work during that time. Transportation being a problem, it was necessary to suspend the intermediate camps from 1942 through 1947.

1945 ~ Property improvements continued under the building expertise of Ralph Knight. **Holliday Lodge** became our best accommodation, with 8 guest rooms. It was built on the hill, beside Harmony Row. Non-flush wash room buildings, located at strategic places, were the only kind available.

1946 ~ Fellowship Centre was constructed at the edge of the property, farthest from Mary Lake. Behind it was the beautiful stream and waterfall. In later time, the road to Camp Widjiitiwin's property would pass by. This building was needed to accommodate informal activities. It had the first "truss style" roof, providing a large indoor area for recreation and ministry to children and youth. It was outfitted with comfortable rattan cushioned furnishings. A big stone fireplace was a welcome feature for prayer meetings on cool mornings, and for testimony evenings. The furnishings and fireplace were a memorial gift in the memory of Amy Holliday, mother of J. Frank Holliday.

Leadership ~ 1928 to 1946   (Speakers and Committee Men)

Rev. F. Bell, Rev. S.L. Boehmer, Dr. J.W. Browett, Mr. G. Bigham, Dr. O.S. Clappison, Rev. J.G. Connor, Rev. R.K. Gonder, Mr. C. Hare Mr. T.E. Harley, Rev. John F. Holliday, Rev. A. Jones, Rev. S. Lawrance, Rev. A.J. Loveday, Mr. A.H. Mildon, Rev. J.N. Millar, Rev. J.H. Peer, Rev. J. Russell, Rev. DeLoss Scott, Rev. T.E. Summers, Rev. C.P. VanDuzen, Rev. G. Wardell, Mr. S.L. White

Other Speakers: Rev. G.W. Allan, Rev. H.W. Bower, Rev. Cole, Rev. R. Day, Rev. A.S. Evans, Rev. A. Glass, Rev. Clarence Keen, Rev. D.A. Hackett, Dr. C. Heaton, Rev. W. Hotchkiss, Dr. A Hughes, Mr. S.F. McCleary, Col. F.J. Miles, Rev. Ken Miles, Rev. J. Raymond, Rev. Jack Scott, Rev. W.H. Lee Spratt, Rev. A. Telford

The Wives of many of the above worked tirelessly by assisting as Camp Mothers, housekeepers, kitchen assistants and planners.

Intermediate Children and Youth Camp Executive Mr. Frank Andrews, Pastor H. Gooderham, Mr. Austin Sime, Mr. George Sim, Miss Mildred Robinson, Mrs. A.G. Shelson, Miss Elsie Barrow, Mrs. George Sim, Miss Sarah Womack, Rev. T.L. White, Miss Clara Johnson, Mr. A. Williams and many others.

Chapter 11

1947 to 1954 ~ RENEWAL OF STRENGTH

This was a period of recovery from the pressures imposed by World War II. M.B.C. welcomed home its service personnel, including two of our Canadian Chaplains, John F. Holliday and Jack Scott. It was a year of anticipation and construction. Plans were laid to resume the ministry to Teens in the summer of next year.

At a cost of $6000. our first pump, reservoir and water system was built during the spring time. What an asset to have washroom buildings with *cold* running water . . . located near each of the accommodation buildings. Luxury, indeed !

On **May 24, 1950** the Fellowship Baptist Young Peoples' Association decided by a vote of its annual convention to transfer the property of Muskoka Baptist Camp to their 'parent organization', the Fellowship of Independent Baptist Churches. In **1951** the name Muskoka Baptist Camp changed to *Muskoka Baptist Conference*. In **1953** the name of the 'parent organization' became *The Fellowship of Evangelical Baptist Churches in Canada*.

In this interval of the early fifties, there was a major <u>transfer of property</u> bounding Mary Lake and the Muskoka River. By the good will of Ralph and Minnie Knight, the cost of the acreage was a mere $200. The shoreline of lake and river measured well over 1000 feet. The Knight's cottage was moved to the tree-lined edge of the Thompson Sugar Bush. In the next few years, a survey was made by Ewart Page of Fairbank Baptist, Toronto. The plan included a subdivision of 18 cottage lots on part of the river frontage. It was all recorded in the Muskoka Registry Office.

The conference property was strengthened by the construction of <u>4 new family cabins</u> One was funded by Benton Street Baptist Church, and named "Benton" in its honour.

These were the summers when . . .

- the <u>Loveday men</u> challenged "the rest of the world" on the baseball diamond.

- we drove to Skeleton Bay for a devotional, lunch and then, a <u>beautiful lake cruise</u> to Canadian Keswick Conference.

- <u>inventive hats</u> were a ticket of admission to the supper meal and <u>skits</u> followed in the Fellowship Centre.

- <u>handymen</u> doubled as pot boys and potato peelers, the worst chore being the scrubbing of pans used for scalloped potatoes !

- our pretty <u>young waitresses</u> waited on the tables and then rolled up their sleeves to wash all the dishes by hand.

- we thought <u>spring water</u> was absolutely pure and daily carried milk cans of spring water to the kitchen for making the tea.

- week night <u>chapel services</u> were followed by refreshments at <u>the Hub</u>, contending with mosquitoes, crowding together to keep warm.

- Sunday evenings after Chapel featured inspiring hymn sings and free refreshments in <u>Fellowship Centre</u>. (nothing was <u>sold</u> on Sunday !)

- we enjoyed wonderful <u>piano duets</u> by Dad Lawson and his son Ed. (brother of Roy). The less spiritual friends of Ed often succeeded in bribing him to introduce a few minor chords here and there . . . to the frustration of his father and the enjoyment of his brother and others.

- meals were great and cooks served with joy. ~ Jack Adams, Una Edwards, Don and Ross Holliday, Dorothy Mitchell, Alice Snider, Olive Wilhelm and more.

- <u>manners</u> were taught in the dining room by singing, *Keep your elbows off the table Mr. Jones. We have seen you do it twice and it isn't very nice . . .*

- people loved to hear <u>Stan Hunt</u> sing his incredible "My Didn't It Rain". We will never forget Noah and his Ark.

- we enjoyed <u>'dubious' sporting events</u> - flying the pyjamas of Camp Director, Rev. Ridley Latimer from the flag pole. - lifting the Austin car of our dignified speaker into Fellowship Centre and removing the keys. (Dr. James N. Bedford, President of London Bible College). The reason that young rowdies would do such things was rooted in the closeness and appreciation which they felt for these men of God. It was <u>Dr. Bedford</u> who penned **"THE PROPHET'S PRAYER"** . . .

My needs are great, my flesh is weak,
My mind, it needs Thy power.
Be thou my strength, my grace,
My all . . . and help me in this hour.

Thou hast the message in Thy Word
To meet man's every need.
Unveil that portion to my heart,
My hungry soul to feed.

And as I stand before lost men,
The living Word to give,
Infuse my soul, unloose my tongue,
That they may hear and live.

There's naught in pulpits nor in man
To meet the soul's deep need.
Wilt Thou, dear Lord, take full control
The hungry hearts to feed.

<u>Bears</u> were a nuisance challenge in Muskoka. An unnamed staff member regularly walked to the old Camp Gate to collect the daily bundle of newspapers. Early one morning, he was surprised by a giant mother bear which stood up in the ditch beside him. He beat "Bannister's mile" back to the camp (without the newspapers!)   The great hunters, RDH and RWL, who protected M.B.C. from night-time marauding bears at the dump, took positions on two sides of the garbage pit. They shared and antique 22 calibre firearm. The only animals to appear were skunks and raccoons.

<u>Camp Fires</u> were great. Remember the camp fire that was prepared by setting kindling around a derelict wooden boat. The Program Director, whose name begins with Roy, decided to soak it with gasoline. He escaped with his life to the glee of all present, but minus his eyebrows. These camp fires were known for three features: great hymn sings, great testimonies and the amazing ballads recited by Frank Andrews.

CHALLENGES OF THE 40's and 50's ~ Dorothy (Roblin) Mitchell

My introduction to Muskoka Baptist Camp began as we arrived in our "Hudson Teraplane" car. I watched my father, Pastor Leander Roblin and Pastor DeLoss Scott, the Camp Director, shake hands as the sun was setting. We spent our holidays that year in one of the river cabins ~ all five of us !

These early days in the forties and fifties were quite a challenge. The MBC kitchen had an old wood burning stove and a coal -fired hot water heater. This meant an early start to get the fires going to cook breakfast and to heat water tanks so we could wash the dishes! Mrs. Olive Wilhelm was our Cook "extra-ordinaire". She made wonderful graham cracker pies ! Her husband Clayton was a "Man of All Trades". Their living quarters were in a corner of the Millar dining room and kitchen.

Keeping food cold was another challenge. Blocks of ice were harvested from the lake in the winter and stored in sawdust in the "ice house" for summer use. Ralph Keen, our handyman, daily carried 25-50 lb blocks of ice up a 6' ladder to the ice box in the frig. No electric refrigeration! The day did come when a room size walk-in refrigerator came to Camp! Now we could make jello salads! When Don Holliday was Chef he treated us to a breakfast of pancakes on top of Blueberry Mountain. Great !

There were days when the Cooks and the Staff worked AND prayed. The Camp Committee called one of the pot boys "up on the carpet". EACH worker was very important. We did not want anyone sent home for misdemeanors ! God answered our prayers !

Sabbath Day Journey ~ Sunday was the day for worship, fellowship and our Old Testament one mile walk. Along the first Camp Road past the sign reading *"My presence shall go with thee....."*. In July, campers were asked to pick at least one cup of raspberries for a special dessert at supper. God is good, how delicious His provision. Remember the "Backward Suppers" when folk dressed backward, walked to their table backward and started their meal with dessert ! We did have fun !

The first camp road was quite a roller coaster. Do you remember? Meeting a car on the road was treacherous. Going over the huge boulders and, hopefully, safely down the other side! In my father's Hudson Teraplane car, we would flash the car lights, blow the horn, then slowly inch up the huge boulder into the night sky, squealing with delight as the road below came into view !

Boat trip days were very popular. We left the camp right after breakfast to catch the Algonquin Steamer at the Huntsville Dock . This took us to Peninsula Lake where we rode the little steam train to Lake of Bays. There was a relaxing picnic lunch sent along by the cook at camp. We enjoyed hymn sings and a devotional as we returned to Huntsville Dock. Great!

Do you remember Cabin Inspection by the Camp Nurse and Director? This particular time was during World War II when sugar cubes were a very precious item. On one inspection day I remember that Pastor Roblin left a note for the inspectors:

TAKE MY WIFE,
TAKE MY CHILDREN
BUT PLEASE DO NOT TAKE MY SUGAR !

This little "dittie" was recorded in the Camp Newspaper and read in the dining room, along with many more "secrets"! The MBC Newspaper Reporter and Editor were very active in discovering any news, romantic or otherwise.

Some thought that Camp dress was becoming much too formal at Chapel. A few young people decided to "borrow" all Pastor Jim Boyd's neckties so he would be casual. Pastor Boyd arrived in the pulpit that night with a lovely red satin tie. Mrs. Boyd had loaned him her satin housecoat sash !

Did you know . . . Camp staff were very busy Sunday evenings? We sang and gave our testimonies in area churches of Pastor and Mrs. Gordon Rendle, Pastor and Mrs. Fred Bell, and Pastor and Mrs. Jack Adams. These congregations would come into camp for the Wednesday and Sunday night services. We also had great baseball games together!

There was the witness and challenge of the baptismal services in Mary Lake. This was *a time of encouragement* to area missionaries such as Pastor Fred Bell and later Pastor Jack Adams. These times included young people from the area churches and from camp.

Oh, the memories of Chapel time Bible studies in the mornings and evenings. The musical piano artistry of Pastor Norman Pipe, Pastor Lawson Sr., Eddie Lawson, Nan Loveday, and many others, along with great hymn sings. Our hearts were stirred when Don Holliday sang "Ship Ahoy". How the Gospel echoed around the hills and across the river to the people living there ! All of this as we coped with giant Muskoka mosquitoes, while sitting on wooden benches with minimal back support. Sing songs down by the river after Chapel sent the gospel wafting over the hills, up and down the river and into the hearts of listeners. What great memories!

RECIPE . . . from 1950's cook, Dorothy (Roblin) Mitchell

<u>Chicken Divan</u>

4-10 oz pkgs frozen broccoli spears – or equivalent fresh/partially cooked	1 – ½ cup mayonnaise
	1 ½ tsp lemon juice
4 uncooked chicken breasts (w/o bone) Cut into medium pieces	¾ tsp curry power
	1 cup shredded cheddar cheese
3 - 10 ½ oz cream of chicken soup, undiluted	1 cup soft bread crumbs
	3 tbsp. melted butter

Method – Cook broccoli until slighty done. (drain). Arrange on bottom of 9x12x2 pan. Put chicken on top. Combine soup, mayo, lemon juice & curry powder. Pour over chicken, sprinkle with cheese.

Combine crumbs/butter. Spread over all

Bake at 350 for 45 mins. Serves 12. Great!

Principal Speakers – 1947 to 1954 (additions to the previous listing)

Rev. John Armstrong, Rev. Jack Adams, Rev. James N. Bedford, Rev. Jack Boehmer, Rev. Robert E. Brackstone, Rev. W. Gordon Brown, Rev. George Darby, Rev. Robert Guthrie, Rev. Morley, R. Hall, Rev. Clarence B. Hayden, Dr. E.R. Hooper, Rev. Geo. Hunt, Rev. H.A. Keithley, Rev. E. Sydney Kerr, Dr. L. Sale-Harrison, Rev. J.E. Hartill, Rev. Hugh Horner, Rev. Hal McBain, Rev. Ridley Latimer, Rev. Ken Muck, Rev. Leander Roblin, Rev. Norman Rowan, Dr. H.H. Savage,

Rev. Clarence Walker, Rev. Jack Watt, Rev. R.W. Wighton, and some listed earlier.

The Camp Committee at this time: Chairman, Rev. Don Loveday, Treas. Sydney White, Members ~ Rev. Frank Holliday, Rev. Sid Kerr, Rev. Jack Watt, Rev. Bob Snider, Charlie Hare, Rev. Bob Guthrie, Rev. George Simpson, Rev. Jack Adams, Art Fitkin.

Chapter 12

1955 to 1965 ~ BUILDING ON FIRM FOUNDATIONS

The development of affordable accommodations for families and retreat ministry was felt to be essential for growth and financial stability. In our Silver Anniversary year . . . 1955, the first masonry building was constructed. A winter and spring appeal, generated $10,000. of the $12,000. cost. Spring construction of the **8 room Lakeview Motel** gave us the first accommodation with electric heating, en-suite 2-piece washrooms and a commanding view of Mary Lake. Guests enjoyed the attractive new furnishings.

Mid 1961 an offer to purchase was made to a neighbor who was the non-resident owner of 100 acres of **adjacent woodlands**. Mr. Earl C. Thompson showed a genuine interest in the conference. He had a sign painted and displayed beside our original conference access road. It was a poem quoted by King George VI in 1939 . . .

> *I said to the man who stood at the gate of the year,*
> *'Give me a light that I may tread safely into the unknown';*
> *And he replied, 'Go into the darkness*
> *and put your hand into the hand of God.*
> *That shall be to you better than a light*
> *and safer than a known way.*

The Thompson property was a sugar bush with a small production shanty. The transaction was agreed in 1961 by a down payment. Taxes were paid through the next 5 years. The balance owing completed the sale in 1966. The total paid was $6450. This newly acquired nature preserve was destined to have four valuable functions:

-It would provide miles of trails for walking and horse rides.

-It became our major center for the development of the M.B.C. Trailer Park.

-Its western boundary became the new conference entrance through the 41 site   subdivision later registered as M.B.C. Acres.

-It became the heart of a popular <u>maple sugar</u> operation

In the spiraling economy of the 1960's, <u>camping vacations</u> had become a way of life for many families. Planning commenced to provide attractive camp sites to serve Christian families at the lowest possible rates.

The Chapel of 1936 was filled to capacity and inadequate for present demands.   In the spring of **1961** the second Chapel was built at a cost of $16,000. Contractor Jim Simms, was assisted by many volunteers. One of these was Bruce Davidson, who laid the tile floor. The new structure had a capacity seating of 400. The picture windows on both sides gave every attendant the sense of beautiful surroundings. At the Dedication Service of **August 6, 1961** the building was identified as **our *Memorial Chapel*.** The plan was to list and honour the names of godly men and women who have *walked with the Lord Jesus beside the shore of Mary Lake.* Instead of major repairs, it was necessary to demolish our Chapel of twenty-five years. The cedar pulpit was moved to the new place of worship.

A HEAVEN-SENT REVIVAL began at Pastors' Conference in June 1961. Dr. Jack Hyles was the guest preacher . . . pastor of First Baptist Church in Hammond, Indiana. More than 100 were present. Group photo, top of page #208 includes five Hollidays . . . Frank (center of row two)and top left . . . Dick, Don, Paul and brother-in-law missionary Jack Simmonds. The opening session on Monday evening was followed by spontaneous prayer groups in many parts of the central area. The daily recreation and meal schedules were adjusted to give priority time for prayer and extra preaching. There was a deep moving of the Holy Spirit:

-    The challenge for personal <u>godliness</u>.

-    A commitment for the <u>Lordship of Jesus Christ.</u>

-    A burden to <u>preach</u> the whole counsel of God.

-    A passion to rescue the perishing with <u>compassionate</u> hearts of love.

Many refer to those precious days as a *"time of refreshing from the presence of the Lord"*. It strengthened all in their service for the Master.

Viewing the needs of this 21st Century, our hearts should cry out, *"O Lord, wilt thou not REVIVE US AGAIN. In the midst of the years, make known Thy mighty power"*(Acts 3:19).

Summer leadership continued under such Directors as ~ Ridley Latimer, Don Holliday, Jack and Gwen Bell, Jim and Joan Youngson, John Coyle, Ted and Margaret Barton, Chuck and Olive Tipp, Paul and Nelda Holliday, Dr. Bob and Belva Foster

Through much of this period, grounds oversight was strengthened by year to year experienced personnel. Rev. DeLoss Scott, the 1931 "handyman and pop shop manager", served for decades in program, music and preaching ministry. He and his wife, Jennie, gave years of dedicated service.

General Hostess and Equipment Manager ~ For many years **Len and Ness Aylett** instilled a touch of warmth and excellence of care. These characteristics endeared them to the hearts of both staff and guests. Ness served on the first Ladies' Conference Committee (1967). With Len, they were on the M.B.C. Commission for a number of years. Len was present every week-end, always busy with maintenance and mechanical operations. They left in 1967, supporting themselves for 13 years of missionary service in Zambia, Africa. Upon return Ness and Len lived in their own home on M.B.C. Acres. They continued to serve in the Bookroom, and Len as maintenance foreman. This was their joy until the Lord took them home to Heaven.

Ministry of the Word included many previously identified. Other names added to the roster: Rev. Eric Crichton, Rev. Allan Crawford, Rev. Fred Davison, Rev. Harold Hindry, Dr. Jack Hyles, Dr. William Kerr,Rev. Allan Lewis, Dr. Robert McCaul, Dr. Arthur Pyke, Rev. Ray Reed, Rev. Gordon Searle

Teens' Camp and Youth Week The program for younger children occupied the first two weeks of each July. Youth Week filled the last week of the summer. The last week continued under the leadership of High Park Baptist Church and then FBYPA. As time progressed, Roy Lawson, assisting Pastor J.F. Holliday at Waverly Rd. Baptist Church and Bob Irvin of High Park, became the popular MBC duo identified as "Chief" and "Skip".

"MBC has had a major impact on my life" ~ **by Bruce Aylett**

I attended my first teens camp in 1950. This same year, my sister Marilyn was working at MBC as a waitress. I remember Norman Hare coming to our house to drive her up to the camp .

My mother and father, Len and Ness Aylett, were both members of Fairbank Baptist Church in Toronto, long before they were married. My father was part of the group attending Fisher's Glen in 1930. Rev and Mrs. J. F. Holliday were pastoring at Fairbank Church. Thus begins our MBC story. From that time we were linked to MBC.

Fay's mother and dad, Lorne and Jean Garner, used their car to drive campers to MBC during the 1940's, when gas was rationed and vehicles were scarce. DeLoss & Jennie Scott were early campers. He was the first Pop Shop manager and later a camp director. For a number of months, he lived with the Garners, during his evangelistic ministry.

I attended teen's camp for 3 years (1950-52). During that time I was able to get into a number of problem situations. It was lucky for me Rev. & Mrs. J.F. Holliday had been our former pastor and wife. They came to my defense more than once, helping to bail me out of my scrapes. I wasn't fortunate enough to stay in the Roundhouse, but I did stay in both Harmony Row and Holliday Lodge. There used to be pump water fire extinguishers on the verandas. You can imagine the fun we had with those! Bed inspection was a daily nightmare. It was just like a boot camp! We remember fun times in the dining room (Millar Hall) with the oil cloth, table covers. We would create a gutter and pour water along into some poor, unsuspecting person's lap.

Some of the great moments were at the campfires. When we stirred up enough courage, we would give our testimonies. We all enjoyed listening to Frank Andrews recite his many poems, the most famous being, "The Cremation of Sam McGee". It seemed that it took him about 30 minutes to recite that poem. It always amazed us. We always went for a Sunday walk . . . a "Sabbath Days Journey". Many times this led us up Blueberry Mountain, other days through the Sugar Bush.

In 1953 I took a job as a Counselor in Training (CIT) at the Kiwanis Camp north of Huntsville. When training was completed, my mother, Ness Aylett, picked me up. She was the dining room hostess. As we drove into the MBC grounds there was a blonde girl sitting on the rock outside the HUB. I said, "*WOW who is that?*" She replied, "*Oh, that is Fay Garner, one of my waitresses*" I fell in love on the spot and chased Fay the rest of the summer, to no avail. That fall Dick Holliday and I took a car trip to Florida. I sent Fay a small souvenir box of oranges. This must have really dazzled her. The next summer I was a handyman at MBC. Fay was working in the HUB. We started going together right away. Fay & I were married in 1958. Now 52 years later, we still come back to MBC every year. My mother was Hostess during a lot of the 50's – 60's. My father handled many of the maintenance duties. During this time he was a member of the board. My mother was the first lady on the MBC Board of Directors.

I worked as handyman for the next 3 summers. Week-ends in the years following, I helped my father with maintenance chores. It seems as though it was always a septic or pumping problem. I sat for many hours nursing the old Myers pump, replacing rubber gaskets to stop the leaking and to keep the prime. We pulled our water out of the river in those days and chlorinated it. There were times when the mixture was too strong !!

In those days the cook bought gallon pails of peanut butter. One morning we discovered that the lid of the pail was partially off. A mouse was drowning in the peanut butter! We felt badly for the mouse. We washed him off and let him go. We didn't throw out the peanut butter either.

In the spring of 1956 my father was asked to replace the MBC Entrance Sign. The owner of Artistic Signs, Len Attenborough, was a member of our Fairbank Church. Dad asked if he would design and paint a new entrance sign for the Conference. The name had been recently changed from Camp to Conference and the signage was old. My father and I spent weekends in May and June pouring the concrete foundation. We cut and stripped the pine support logs and erected the support poles. The whole time we worked with netting over our heads to ward off the black flies. The sign was beautiful and was in place for years. It is still shown on many bulletins.

When the river lots were subdivided in the early 1950's, my father purchased a 100' lot. We built a boathouse with a living room on the side and enjoyed many great years at that location. Mr. & Mrs. Chris Taylor had a cottage on the lake. Their two sons Ralph and David were my good friends. Ralph and I worked as handymen in the 50's and we continued our friendship. One day, he came, in his father's boat, to visit me at the boathouse. When Ralph was leaving from the river deck to head back home, I heard a huge "Roar". I looked over and saw that the transom of his boat was torn off. The motor, gas line and tank were disappearing into the bottom of the river. We were flabbergasted. Ralph's Dad arranged for a diver to search the bottom for the motor.

Through Doraine Ross, my mother and father were aware of the need for short term workers at the Mukinge Hill Hospital Station in Zambia, Africa. In 1967 they went as volunteer missionaries with AEF. Doraine was Matron at the hospital. They actually served there, with furlough times, over a period of thirteen years. The Lord was able to use them in a variety of ways. Their years at the Conference were great preparation for service on a mission station. They enjoyed this ministry experience immensely.

In 1967 Fay and I decided to move to Florida. Later, my Dad sold the MBC river property to pastor Bruce Woods. Fay and I have two daughters, Andrea and Shari. Andrea worked at MBC as a waitress during the summer of 1980. We continued coming north on vacations, but not every year, until my parents returned from Africa in 1980. Both our girls and all 7 grandchildren now make the annual summer trek to MBC for the month of July. Andrea has a cottage on the river, one of the old Spinster Row locations. They love the speakers, programming and socializing with Christian relatives and friends. MBC was the catalyst for bringing many of my mother's family to MBC and getting their lives right with the Lord. Her three brothers Albert, Syd and Ed Smith all worked on projects. Now my cousins are long time attendees and trailer park owners . . . Steve & Sandra McLean, Doug & Karen Smith and Glen & Heather Wilson families.

My brother-in-law, Richard Holliday, was asked to become the General Director of MBC in the fall of 1970. Dick and Marilyn accepted that challenge, working tirelessly for 20 years to improve on the operation of MBC. They expanded the land and buildings, changed the roads, water system, sewage system, developed a campground, trailer park, MBC Acres, Marina and Lake Waterfront, plus much more. The ministry pattern changed from using primarily local speakers to including well-known leaders from the US and Britain. The conference grew from a smaller operation, during the first 40 years, to a larger, thriving Bible Conference during the twenty years under their direction.

I believe all of us, that have been a part of MBC for a number of years, have a deep love for the ministry, the people and the place. MBC has had a major impact on my life. I was fortunate to grow up in a Christian home. The continuing influence of MBC on my life has made a strong imprint. The region of Muskoka, and particularly MBC, has become a part of my life. The friendships made, become lasting relationships. I find myself thinking about MBC throughout the year. Fay and I long for the summer. Then we, and our family, can return once again to enjoy the great speakers and re-connect with Christian friends.

Bruce and Fay Aylett
MBC Acres

Buddies Holliday & White
at Fisher's Glen 1930

1930 Brochure

1930 Campers

Entrance

Chapel built 1936

Farm house – dining room/chapel

1931 tuck shop

MBC Panorama - 1932-1935

Ralph and Minnie Ralph Knight

Rev. J.N. Millar

Rev. & Mrs. Fred Bell, Ken/Betty

Elsie Andrews (nee Barrow)

First Chapel

Gathering for supper

Early 1930's includes drive shed

Packed for travel

"Prophet's Chamber" Colonel Miles

Blueberry Mtn Hike with Colonel Miles

New Millar Hall – 1938

Millar Hall – Dining Room/Kitchen

Tent City – 30's L-Rev. A.J. Loveday, A. Glass, Nurse E. Bevis,
"Mom" Ruby Gonder, Pastor/Mrs. Lawrence, J.F. Holliday

BAPTISMS

3 by Rev. DeLoss Scott

Ken Page by J.F. Holliday, 1958

1980's

J.F. Holliday – 1949

1950- Counsellors in Training

Hub – 1955

1940's Committeee
D. Scott, D. Lovedays, S.L. White, F. Bell. C. P. Van Duzens

River Wharf 1930's

Departure Sign

Round House – Boys Dorm

'55 staff girls/ Hostess, Mrs. Ness Aylett   *1971 summer staff*

Counsellors 1961 with R.W. Lawson and Bob Irvin

Blueberry Mtn trek, August 1954

Ness Aylett/ Smorgasbord Night 1954

1971 waitresses with
Director R.D. Holliday

Fall scene with Len and Ness Aylett

1961 Director Rev. Chas/Olive Tipp

Pot Boys, R.D. Holliday/R.W. Lawson
with Cook Dorothy Mitchell (nee Roblin)

C. VanDuzen, D. Scott, D. Loveday

DeLoss Scott on Algonquin Cruise Ship

Morning Call, Director Ridley Latimer

Teens Camp 1951

Chapter 13

1966 to 1969 ~ PROGRAM EXPANSION

The Lord delights to accomplish his purposes through godly, prayerful men and women.

Dr. Donald A. Loveday served as Board Chairman from 1962 to 1964. He inherited a zest for the Muskoka ministry from his father, Rev. A.J. Loveday. With his wife, Nan, and his sports loving sons, they spent much time through the years in ministry involvement at M.B.C. Through the 1980's he led in the arrangements and programming of Fall Retreats for Seniors. His wife Nan was a favourite pianist and a gracious encourager of young people.

For 8 years, (1965 to 1972), **Arthur Fitkin** was <u>Chairman</u> of the Camp Committee and a <u>member</u> of the committee for additional years before 1965 and after 1972. His experience in business, advertising, professional sports and church growth enabled him to lead the Committee with great focus. Art and Nancy were both as cheerful souls as you could ever meet. Nancy would often join the waitresses in the staff kitchen as they washed the dishes. Her voice would lead the team in happy singing.

From the very first, **Sydney White** was at ease in whatever role needed his expertise. If not chairman of the Board, his responsibilities would be treasurer, secretary or just a member of the board. He was a master of draughting documents and the ways to achieve goals.

In 1969 Mr. White served without remuneration as the summer Business Manager. Under his guidance strong emphasis was placed on the **"Planning and Development Committee"** The men involved were John Bonham, Frank Bowman, Fred Butler, Earl Heron, Dick Holliday. Their particular responsibilities:

- launch plans for the development of a cottage subdivision named "MBC Acres"

- beginning years of MBC's Trailer Park complete with septic tank washrooms

- opening up a new MBC entrance off the Hood Road

NEW JUNE RETREATS Creative ministry teams led in the formation of new programs for ladies, pastor's wives, laymen and pastors.

- **Laymen's Conference**, their first in 1965.

- **Pastors' Conference** started in 1966.

- **Ladies' Conference** began in 1967. It was a June week-end event. Mrs. Vince Trimmer was the speaker, Mary Porcheron the violinist, and Nan Loveday the pianist. In the next years, the program expanded to 2 week-ends. By the 1970's, they were running 4 Ladies' Conferences in June: two on week-ends, a third from Monday supper to Thursday breakfast, and a fourth was "Conference For A Day" on the Thursday.

- **Pastors' Wives Conference** began in 1968 with 48 attending Monday to Thursday.

FULL SUMMER CAMPING FOR CHILDREN AND YOUTH

It was recognized by all that we needed to plan for a full camping program on a dedicated site. Until now the family conference accommodations were being used for children and teens. A Youth Camp Investigation Committee was appointed by the Board. The members were instructed to examine possible properties in other locations, as well as the feasibility of developing an unused part of MBC grounds. Several years passed with only one suggestion. In 1967 a Planning Meeting was called for board members to meet at M.B.C. on a particular summer Saturday at 10 a.m. Some felt we might be able to squeeze a "small Youth Camp" into the side of the property through which the old spring and stream flowed to the river.

M   Early on the morning of the committee meeting, the river quietly beckoned for a sunrise canoe ride. From the boathouse, the writer crossed the river for a morning greeting with Mr. Wallace. He was the owner of the 2.5 acre parcel of land called Arcadia. It was on the south bank of the river in plain view of the conference. It had been a small resort comprised of a two-story hotel lodge, staff quarters, a utility building and river frontage with a wharf.

Mr. Wallace was discouraged . . . working alone, trying to refloat a 1937 "Ditchburn" launch. He had acquired it with the purchase of the resort, several years before. We had talked on previous occasions, but that day, he said: "I've decided to sell the whole place ... including the boat. In fact, I'm going to see the real estate people at noon today!"

We talked! I asked him to wait until our committee could cross the river for a visit with him <u>before</u> his Huntsville appointment. "Maybe we can arrange a purchase which will eliminate real estate fees".

At 10:00 a.m. the committee members met: Chairman Art Fitkin Sr., Secretary Syd White, Treasurer John Bonham, Property Manager Len Aylett, Development Chair Dick Holliday, and Youth Camp Rep. Rev. Stuart Silvester. By 11 a.m. we rowed across the river and discussed with Mr. Wallace the property and the buildings. $32,000. was confirmed as the price. On the promise of interest free financing by one of our committee members, a $20,000. deposit was agreed and provided in due course. Upon "closing" the full amount was paid by M.B.C.

Walking back towards the river, Stuart Silvester and this writer stopped to take a look at "the Old Ditchburn". Even though mired in the clay, Stuart noticed the eye-catching Ditchburn plaque. As reported in the Huntsville "<u>MUSKOKAN, Thursday, July 9, 2009</u>" . . . *Being distantly related to the Ditchburn family, he was later encouraged by his father to claim the boat. 'The deal was, if I could get it out of the mud, I could have the boat'. On a rainy November morning I borrowed a tractor from a nearby farmer and, with the help of my brother and a friend, we hauled the boat to Burk's Falls, where it sat in a garage for a year. In 1970-71 I restored the boat for about $100.* A complete rebuilding through more recent years has made it a Collector's Item, now making appearances in such shows as the one held by the Gravenhurst Antique and Classic Boat Society. Other award winning shows include the Port Carling and Baysville boat shows. *Because the old Ditchburn has been "remade, reborn and totally made new", its new name is now inscribed as, "BORN AGAIN".* Pastor Silvester, the former pioneer and builder of Bramalea

Baptist Church, has been a long-time encourager of the ministries of M.B.C. The acquisition of 2 ½ acres and the story of an aged water-logged boat remind us of the exhortation, "despise not the day of small things".

The**1968** Camp season was to be MBC's **first full summer of ministry for children and youth.** The camp committee received various name suggestions, (Koinonia, MBC Youth Camp), however, the name chosen was "Camp Widjiitiwin". It was the native area word meaning "togetherness" or "fellowship". Committee members during the later 1960's included Frank Gill, Tom Cowan, Les Gilbert, Sam Reynolds, Bob Page, Connie Hanthorn, Rev. John Roberts, Rev. Warren Kimball, Rev. Jim Clemens, Miss M. Card., Marie Potz, B. Ambrous, Bill Curry, J. Marquis, Lorne Helwig.

April 25, 1968 - Mr. S.L. White moved and Rev. G. Simpson seconded the motion: *the proposal to dedicate 'Arcadia Lodge' during Pastors' Conference on June 18th, be accepted and that Rev. John Roberts and Rev. Dick Holliday arrange the service.* A full effort by volunteers prepared the property for its first summers. Camp Widjiitiwin operated for 9 busy seasons on its new 2.5 acres.

Camp leaders for the first years included Directors Ralph and Carol Cossitt, Abe and Vicki Dueck, Program Director Lee Mitchell, Waterfront Director Marie Potz, Counsellors for 1969 . . . Joyce Lambie, Susan Epworth, Patricia Page, Janice Potz, Nora Lee Oltman, Bruce Woodford, Susan Marchand, Dorothy Brown, Nancy Lupton, Valerie Stiff and Terry Hooton.

Chapter 14

ORGANIZATIONAL CHANGES BUT UNCHANGED PURPOSE AND POWER

by Sidney L. White

After the formation of the Fellowship of Evangelical Baptist Churches in Canada (FEBCC) in 1953, Muskoka Baptist Conference (MBC) was <u>administered by a committee</u> . . . appointed by the Executive Council of the parent body.

Among the instructions given to the committee at that time was the requirement that MBC, be operated on a profitable basis, and that the rates be such that the average member of our churches could afford to attend.

This concept, which was also <u>that of the founders</u> of M.B.C., meant that funds for capital expenditures of any size had to be secured through other sources than operating revenue. At the same time conditions were such in the early days of our Fellowship that it <u>seemed</u> imperative to restrict M.B.C. from making general widespread appeals throughout the Fellowship for capital items. Such capital projects as were accomplished were largely financed through a ***Sponsors Club.*** Its members pledged $50. each for a period of three years. Many supporters contributed in this way, as well as by giving special gifts on special occasions. Other funds, as noted in chapter 7, were raised by the sale of river-front lots. It was continually realized that other methods would be essential for larger projects.

During the decade of 1960-70 the record shows many submissions to the Executive Council of the Fellowship. Many official minutes show that these submissions were considered, discussed at length at the Executive Council level as well as by the Executive Committee and Finance Committee.

Capital needs became more pressing. It was deemed necessary to update and increase our facilities. A comprehensive review of the work was prepared and presented to the Executive Council on November 28, 1968. One result of this was the removal of a restriction on M.B.C. spending more than $500. for capital purposes without Executive Council approval. The main problem, however, was unresolved.

Soon after, this question was raised: ***Can the Fellowship afford M.B.C. ?*** A detailed spiritual and financial review was written to answer this question. In it we asked for a firm financial base upon which we could develop and grow through the use of Fellowship funds. Early in 1970, the M.B.C. Commission had to make a special private appeal, among its friends, for an urgently needed amount of $2500. This was to keep our Teens' Camp operating, as assistance by the Fellowship had been withdrawn. We succeeded in raising an amount of $1730.60, but upon examination found that the greater part of this came from members of the M.B.C. Commission, indicating that there was little general support at this time.

It was thus becoming apparent to all concerned that some decisive action was needed on the part of the Executive Council, to place M.B.C. on a different and firm basis. Later that spring the Executive Council took action by appointing an M.B.C. Evaluation Committee. It's responsibility was to make an in-depth study of M.B.C. and bring recommendations regarding its future ministry, finances and organization as it related to the Fellowship. The Rev. J. K. Pequegnat was appointed chairman of this committee.

The Committee laboured faithfully, and on August 25, 1970, produced their report. This went to the Executive Council meeting of September 3, 1970. The report itself is too lengthy to give here, but may be summarized briefly by the following points:

1. M.B.C. should be transferred to a new body eventually elected at a convention of Fellowship Baptists called for that purpose;

2. That funds realized from the leasing of the subdivision, M.B.C. Acres, shall go to the Fellowship in full payment of all indebtedness. Thus *the property shall be*

transferred on a debt free basis.

3.   Conditions of transfer to the new body would be:

(a) *A Christian Conference be maintained*

(b) *An Evangelical Baptist emphasis be retained*

(c) *The Conference be operated in a business-like fashion under capable leaders.*

This report was received by the Executive Council, and by motion, referred to the M.B.C. Commission for their consideration.

For some years it was apparent that our procedure of <u>appointing a Director for an</u> <u>operating season</u> of about three months each year was <u>far from ideal</u>. Usually it was a different person each year. Although we recognized the need, the problem would not be solved until we were able to appoint a man on a year round basis and support him accordingly. While we were confident that having such a man devoting his time to promotion all year would enable us to finance appropriately, we realized that this might take one or two years to accomplish. In other words, the revenue from a short operating season would <u>not</u> be sufficient *We could not greatly expand our operation without the services of a **full time Managing Director**.*

However, at this time we had commenced the development and leasing of lots on a wooded section of our property now known as *M.B.C. Acres*. It had been stipulated that the net revenue from this project would be remitted to the Fellowship to apply on advances made by them through the years.

After discussing this problem with the Executive Council, they authorized us to make such an appointment. We would be allowed to draw upon the funds received from leases, as found necessary, for a period of three years. Acting upon this, the appointment of Rev. R. D. Holliday as Managing Director was made. <u>He commenced his duties in the fall of</u> **1970.**

Now let us continue the story of the <u>*Evaluation Committee* and its report</u>. This was presented at a meeting of the M.B.C. Commission on September 19, 1970. Following a brief discussion, copies of the report, were ordered sent to all members for detailed consideration. In several subsequent meetings, it was evident that there was considerable hesitation as to whether the present members or others would be prepared to accept the responsibilities outlined on the report. Finally, on February 11, 1971, they recommended to M.B.C. that we inform the Executive Council of *endorsement in principle with further details to be worked out*. It was also indicated that M.B.C. was prepared to have its sub-committee meet the Evaluation Committee to work out these details. On August 26, 1971 the Executive Council approved the agreement in principle and then advised the Evaluation Committee of their desire that M.B.C. should work with them on details. Immediately a series of meetings were begun to this end.

As negotiations proceeded, it became apparent that the report of the Evaluation Committee was not completely acceptable to some of the Fellowship officers, and revisions were made accordingly. These resulted in an increased amount to be paid by M.B.C. to the Fellowship. It was felt by the Conference committee, however, that the commitments already made on the basis of the original agreement were such that they could not be terminated, but must be carried to completion. Therefore, the Muskoka Baptist Conference Committee decided to accept the revised terms.

During this time, also, such items as Provisional Bylaws, Incorporation, Directors, Bond Issue, New Lodge, etc., were given careful consideration.

On Wednesday morning, **October 25, 1972**, the Annual Convention of F.E.B.C.C. discussed and passed a resolution, which we feel must be recorded in full here because of its historic significance.

It was as follows:

Motion regarding MUSKOKA BAPTIST CONFERENCE –

HAVING been informed of the consultations that were held between the Executive Council of the Fellowship of Evangelical Baptist Churches in Canada and the Muskoka Baptist Conference Commission through the M.B.C. Evaluation Committee, and HAVING received the recommendation of the Finance Committee and the Council, I MOVE THAT the Executive Council of the Fellowship of Evangelical Baptist Churches in

Canada, be authorized to transfer all assets of Muskoka Baptist Conference from the Fellowship of Evangelical Baptist Churches in Canada, to the Muskoka Baptist Conference organization (to be incorporated in the Province of Ontario) in consideration of a payment to the Fellowship of Evangelical Baptist Churches in Canada of the sum of $51,000., and the assumption by the Muskoka Baptist Conference organization of an existing mortgage of $14,250. and loan of $10,000.. The payment of $51 000. shall be made to the Fellowship of Evangelical Baptist Churches in Canada as follows:

(1.) *a cash payment of $4,000. at the time of the transfer of the property,*

(2.) *a promissory note in the amount of $47,000., which shall be paid in two installments; $20,000. on December 31, 1974 and $27,000. on December 31, 1979; and further*

THAT the total agreement, shall be made with proper legal council and shall be effective December 31, 1972.

As stated elsewhere, we were busy on plans for the <u>new lodge</u>, and in order to expedite its start and completion for early 1973, we held a *Ground Breaking Service* on the site on Sunday afternoon, **October 8, 1972.**

Following Convention approval, plans for the organization and the building were accelerated. **Fifteen provisional directors** were named and officers appointed.

During the events recited above, Mr. A.L. Fitkin had served effectively as the Chairman of the M.B.C. Commission and Mr. S.L. White as Chairman of the Structural Committee in charge of negotiations, legal, organizational matters, bond issue, etc. When the new organization was formed Mr. Arthur L. Fitkin requested that he be relieved of his responsibilities so the officers then appointed were:

President	– S.L. White
Vice Presidents	– A.L. Fitkin & Rev. M.O. Wedge
Secretary	– F.W. Bowman
Treasurer	– R.R. Hartwick

Provisional Directors: C.A. Borrowman, R. Cripps, E.A. Faris, J.A. Feren, G.H. Hallett, E.T. Heron, H.L. Ireland, D.S. Irwin, R.W. Thompson, W.F. Wilkie, also present R. D. Holliday, Managing Director and Mrs. Harold (Ruth) Attrell, Recording Secretary

Incorporation under the laws of Ontario was granted on December 12, 1972 and we proceeded to negotiate a formal agreement with the Fellowship. There were delays caused by legal questions and property transfer matters before the agreement could be completed. We had to modify some of our concepts and plans because of corporation laws, The Convention Resolution but eventually a legal agreement was complete –

Summarized, this included the following items:

(a) recital of events preceding the agreement

(b) Restriction of members and directors to members of Fellowship churches

(c) Details of and procedure re: financial items and a very important Section #7 which we quote in full –

All parties to this agreement are desirous of making it entirely clear that this action (in creating a new incorporation) is not intended to, nor does it constitute, a separation of the F.E.B.C. in Canada and Muskoka Baptist Conference, but rather a structural reorganization that it is believed will make for greater flexibility and greater operating efficiency.

The First Annual Convention of MUSKOKA BAPTIST CONFERENCE was held on April 25, 1974 in Willowdale Baptist Church, Toronto, with afternoon and evening sessions. At the business session, complete operating and financial reports, duly audited, were given. The Operating Statement revealed an operating profit for the year of approximately $22, 000. The balance Sheet showed total Assets of $586,000. and total Liabilities of $356,000., so that the Surplus was $230,000. In considering these figures, however, it must be remembered that all assets are listed at cost, including *Land* at nearly $42,000. Present day values are many times that figure. Thus, we were able to praise God for His good hand upon us in a financial as well as in all other ways.

The Convention elected fifteen directors and these appointed officers for the year 1974-5. They were –

- President   -   Rev. D.S. Irwin
- Vice-Presidents   -   Rev. M.W. Wedge , Mr. R. Cripps
- Secretary   -   Mr. F.W. Bowman
- Treasurer   -   Mr. R.R.G. Hartwick

Our second Annual Convention was held on April 24, 1975 and again our gathering together was a time of inspiration and blessing.

Throughout the forty-five years of our history, buildings have been erected, parcels of land acquired on seven or eight occasions. Many persons have given of their best and some have passed on to their reward. We could say: *Change . . . in all around I see.*

One thing has not changed, and that is the original purpose of M.B.C. as stated by its founders. The purpose is that it might be a place of blessing and inspiration through the teaching of the Word of God and the witness of His people, in order that many may turn to accept life eternal through the Lord Jesus Christ.

Chapter 15

1970 to 1990 ~ DEVELOPMENT YEARS

MIRACLES THAT PROVIDED NEW FRIENDS AND NEW FACILITIES

His compassions fail not. They are NEW every morning. Great is Thy faithfulness

The years from 1970 have been filled with *new things*. The great faithfulness of the Lord has made possible improvements, which have added comfort, efficiency and new dimensions of ministry. This chapter could not begin to contain the full testimony of that which God has accomplished through prayer-partners, stewards, churches and hundreds of workers.

It was a **Board-venture of faith to appoint Richard D. Holliday as the first full-time managing director**. In his fifth year as Pastor of Emmanuel Church in Barrie, it was not easy to think of resignation when approached by Chairman Arthur Fitkin. The church, the MBC Board and interested friends all felt that God's hand was leading. When the resignation was submitted, the church very graciously voted to continue to pay part of my salary, for an initial period, because the Conference is an extension of the local church. Many of the initial helpers in the transition time were part of the Emmanuel Church family. With others, there was an encouraging response to the development challenge. <u>Farmers</u> helped to establish a ranch as a youth attraction. <u>Carpenters</u>, <u>electricians</u>, <u>painters</u> and <u>carpet layers</u> refurbished buildings. Spring and fall retreats stretched the Conference operating season from two and one-half to four and a half months.

What a Fellowship !   What A Joy Divine!
...*Leaning on The Everlasting Arms.*

"It's too bad you've left the ministry!" This was the reaction expressed by some of my pastor friends, when it was announced that this writer was to be the first full-time employee . . . the Managing Director of Muskoka Baptist Conference. Though they were truly friends, and appreciated the strong testimony of MBC, they were conscious that it was only a <u>summer</u> season activity. Financially, its operating budget had only reached an all time high of $55,885. in 1969. There was no criticism of the decision, but surprise that it could ever be a full-orbed vocational service for a pastor.

"Be careful that MBC does not drain our churches of needed financial loyalty!" This reaction was a natural concern for the primacy of the local church. In actual fact, it implied that our receiving offerings might limit the extent of Divine resources. Quite the opposite is true. Muskoka Baptist Conference has been one of the greatest ministries of a whole century for the strengthening of the cause of Christ across Canada and beyond.

God has done "a new thing". Many of "like precious faith" have prayed and worked and given. God has blessed because believers of all ages have been "leaning on the everlasting arms".

M   The new "Managing Director" took up residence at MBC in the very cool and quiet month of May 1971. **Mr. Mansel,** a painter and "Mr. Fix-it" from Owen Sound, Ontario, was willing to come as the only second pair of hands. Each day began with toast, eggs and bacon, served up by Dick Holliday. After breakfast . . . morning devotions for <u>all two men</u> present. *"Brother Mansel, we have some serious wiring problems. We need to pray together for an <u>experienced electrical person</u> who is <u>available</u> and <u>affordable</u>".* We read a Scripture promise passage, and then we each prayed. In mid-prayer, we heard a sound at the door, but paid no heed . . . except for the prayer subject on our hearts. When we said, "Amen", we were surprised by the voice a man leaning against the refrigerator, near the kitchen entrance. His smiling greeting . . . "Well, I guess I'm the answer to your prayer!". It was **Fred Moulton**, from Bracebridge. He had spent years as Electrical Engineer for the International Nickle Corporation in Sudbury, Ontario. He had resigned from that firm, to open his own electrical business in Bracebridge. A heart attack had stopped him in that endeavour. Having had months to recover, he came up that early morning to ask if he could be any help to us. WOW! A master of his trade . . . he started that day and served with us gratuitously almost twenty years.   Some years after his beloved wife, Ruth, went to be with the Lord, this writer married Fred to one of our wonderful cooks, **Charlotte Buder.**

M   Another breakfast morning with Mr. Mansel! After our eggs and bacon and coffee. . . Bible reading and prayer! It was <u>the last May Monday</u> before our first arriving guests for Laymen's Conference. *"Brother Mansel, we still have those big rolls of floor carpet sitting on the front porch of Lakeview Motel. You and I cannot lay the carpet. We need someone with big muscles, plus the know-how. Today, let's pray for carpet layers!"* We had been offered top quality carpet for $1.00 per running yard. After reading our Bible promise for the day, we began to pray. While Mr. Mansel was praying, the telephone rang. With only one telephone on the grounds, and being the only one present to answer, this writer tip-toed to the pantry wall phone. *"Who is speaking?"* *"My name is **Lorne Helwig**, and I own a drapery and carpet business in Kitchener. I was just wondering if we could be any help to you this week?"* *"Did you say, 'a carpet business?' Do you mean, a carpet <u>laying</u> business?"*

While the Laymen were moving into the rooms at one end of Lakeview Motel, the carpet layers were finishing the floor of the last room at the other end.

M   In mid June, Mr. Mansel went to his room in the old Staff house building. He put on his pyjamas and went to bed for an afternoon snooze. He had worked so hard, and certainly needed a good rest. The rain began to fall. The thunder rolled and the lightening flashed. Mr. Mansel was wakened from his sleep by the torrents of rain, the rolls of thunder and the howling wind. He finally got up, made his bed and folded his pyjamas... placing them in the center on top of the blanket. As he turned to the closet for his shirt and trousers, a lightning bolt with accompanying thunder tore a hole through the roof and through the bed and through the floor. His pyjamas were just a few shreds around the hole in the bed. Mr. Mansel made haste to dress. As staff members appeared to see if there was damage anywhere, our painter called for some men to *"come and look"* . . . NOT at the hole in the roof . . . or the hole in the floor . . . or the hole in the bed. *"Look at my brand new pyjamas ! They're ruined!"* Just minutes before he would have been <u>in</u> them . . . and would have been a part of 'the hole thing'. He was irritated <u>until</u> we <u>all</u> realized the miracle of preservation. *"You compass my path and my lying down, and are acquainted with all my ways"* Psalm 139:3.

M   It was in the weeks before our first June Retreats, **Cook Una Edwards** went down to the kitchen from her cabin on the hill. The Hollidays following some distance behind were surprised by a distress call. Una exited from the kitchen with her hands in the air. ***"I've lost my wedding ring!"*** She knew it was on her hand when she left her room, but it was nowhere to be found. As we stood together in the tall grass of the hillside, the question was asked, *"can you show us where you walked?"* Having pointed to the route of her steps, we bowed for prayer. As we began to search individually, it seemed hopeless, because there was just nothing but knee-high grass. Suddenly, Una cried out, "THERE!" . . . pointing excitedly into the grass. As we came to her, we could see a glimmer reflected from the sun. It was the ring, deeply surrounded by the grass. What an encouragement that the Lord answers prayer for "the little things of life".

M   When an August cold-spell prompted the ordering of a long-delayed furnace for the chapel, a family that had not been aware of the need reported their intention to donate the tithe of a legacy. **The cost** of the furnace was **$859.95**. The amount of **the gift** was **$860.00**.

1972 SUMMER IMPROVEMENTS

The Tent and Trailer Park was expanded by completion of an underground <u>water and electric service</u>. <u>New pumping equipment</u> and two miles of water pipes were installed under the voluntary supervision and hard work of a retired plumbing contractor, Cyril Hemmings. <u>Aged</u> <u>vehicles</u> were replaced by the gift of a more up-to date <u>truck</u> from the Smith family of Oakwood Baptist Church. As Conference meal-service multiplied, an entire new <u>set of fine china dinnerware</u> was donated by Ross and Evelyn Thompson, from Emmanuel Church in Barrie. Plans for landscaping were realized by the unsolicited gift of a <u>ride-on tractor mower</u> by Hutchinson Farm supply of Stouffville. Concern for quality in musical ministry was matched by the <u>annual loan of a full-sized organ</u> from the Buffalo Christian Center. We were thankful for the consecrated talent of both Mrs. Larry (Marg) Taylor and Ken Baer for their valued assistance on the instruments.

M   It was an early Sunday evening in **May 1972**. Dick Holliday was preaching at a televised service in Crestwicke Baptist church, Guelph. A note was handed to him just before the sermon . . . *Tamarack Cottage has been hit by lightning and is on fire !* Five short words were answered to the usher. . . *the Lord answered by fire. Please convey this message to the person on the phone.* It was Betty Garner who had called. She was greatly distressed that the building was burning to the ground. She was the only person on staff when I was away. Tamarack Cottage was one of four, summer only, accommodations. Within seventeen days of the fire the cottage was rebuilt by the continuous double-shift and round-the-clock service of a Christian contractor, Gordon Habermehl. The new building consisted of two suites instead of one, each including a balcony, two bedrooms, living room, three-piece bathroom, electric heat, wall-to-wall carpeting, completely winterized and soundproof. Guests moved into M.B.C.'s best accommodation while its final water connections were being made. When such guest accommodation was needed, *The Lord answered by fire*.

"Preparation for the road I would follow" ~ **by Betty (Garner) Munson**

My MBC experience began when I was a child. I spent time with my big sister Fay (Garner-Aylett) while she worked on staff in the 1950's. I thought it was the greatest place in the world and wanted to follow in her footsteps when I grew up. Her favorite job was the laundry. Visiting Fay, while she was working, included chores in the laundry. We pulled many long sheets through the rollers of the old machine. Through various stages of my life and MBC's growth, I spent seven years helping in almost every imaginable way. Little did I know that I would be doing similar things for the rest of my life in our own smaller group retreat center. It is called Mountain Lake Ranch in the Smoky Mountains of East Tennessee.

Waitressing was my first job. We were still using the old "Millar Hall" dining building. I well remember being there when camp was empty. Entering the kitchen one early morning I found a skunk had arrived ahead of me. She was checking out the menu for the day! Needless to say, I did my best to stay out of her way (must have been a "her", after all, she was in the kitchen!). I tried to be very quiet. Eventually, she went out the back door and all was well. Those were the days when the "Hub" building was situated beside the most photographed rock ever. The old Fellowship Center was always a fun place.

Some years later, I was offered the job of heading up the Tea Room. At one stage it was called the "Honey Pot". I was not crazy about that name because some would call me "Miss Honey Pot". Mr. and Mrs. Aylett were in charge at the conference that year. I wanted so much to please them since they were also my sister's in laws! Wouldn't you know, the next morning after my arrival, my very first day on the job, I slept in! It was so embarrassing! A capable girl named Sherry, who had been working there for a while, must have thought "what a dud! ... am I supposed to work with her ?" After that I made sure my alarm clock was set. I never slept in again !

I loved working at MBC. It taught me responsibility, interaction with people and how to show hospitality. Always being quite shy, this was a great growing period for me. I enjoyed the ordering of supplies, the displaying of a great variety of items and even the cooking! We made pizzas and hot dogs. We scooped different kinds of ice cream treats, made shakes, sundaes and floats. Learned all those important things everyone should know!

A few years later, just after the construction of the new conference center with the beautiful orange carpet and the big rock fireplace, I was back. (1972) This was the greatest time of my life. It probably gave me the most preparation for my future. Being there year round I enjoyed the hustle and bustle of winter week-ends. I particularly enjoyed the quietness when everyone was gone. We had beautiful scenery and often several feet of snow to enjoy on our own. Having received patient instruction from Marilyn (Holliday) who would come up on week-ends, I would prepare meals for our groups coming in on Friday. It was awesome working in that big kitchen making spaghetti, salads and pies! I had never made pies before and in such quantity. It felt like being a chef! That's the only time in my life I felt like a chef. Cooking has not been my greatest skill. It is a good thing our retreat center in Tennessee is a "Do it Yourself" deal. We do not do the cooking! During the week I would clean rooms. THAT is something I have been doing ever since! Our place is not as large as MBC, but, when it comes to cleaning, it is big enough!

My room at MBC was in the accommodation level of the "new" lodge. I will never forget the winter beauty and the thrill of those rides on the snowmobile across the lake. We could hear the cracking sound of the ice. I will also never forget the night a young fellow rode his snowmobile too close to the mouth of the river. He went right in! It took a while to get the machine out. He was not one of our people. I think the alcohol, he appeared to have enjoyed, served like anti-freeze and preserved him. It was a miracle he made it.

Nothing can match the great teaching, preaching, music and fellowship that we all enjoyed at MBC. It was an honor to work with the Hollidays, Ayletts and so many others. It was such a blessing to meet the special speakers and guests whose paths we crossed. I doubt that there is any one thing that influenced or *prepared me for the road I would follow*, quite as much as my years at Muskoka Baptist Conference.

- Betty "Garner" Munson,   Mountain Lake Ranch,

Christian Retreat and Campground, Dandridge, Tennessee, 37725

NEED OF A WINTERIZED COMPLEX

How could we ever afford a new kitchen and dining room ? This would be the largest undertaking in the history of the Conference. We had no hidden supply of funds. All officers and members of the board were present for the big discussion . . . "*how can we afford to build this central facility?*" God's man for the hour was our **Treasurer, Ron Hartwick**. He understood both financial policy and the dangers of fiscal irresponsibility. He gave a detailed projection of the future of MBC if we decided <u>not</u> to build. Then he gave an equally detailed projection, if we <u>decided</u> to proceed. The conclusion demonstrated the absolute necessity that we proceed by faith and with meticulous care. His reasons:

- financial stability

- program enjoyment

- guest satisfaction

- year round service and ministry.

His counsel prompted a unanimous vote, followed by a season of prayer.

One hundred children, young people, and adults signed as <u>Sponsors</u>. This indicated their intention to contribute $100. each for three years. By faith the directors voted to proceed as God supplied the need. In September we were immersed in detailed planning concerning construction of a new Lodge building. Contacts through our board members led us to **a godly contractor, Les Harris** of Welcon Construction, Guelph, ON. His position as chairman of the board of Guelph Bible Conference made him the most understanding individual we could have found. M.B.C. entered into a contract with Welcon Construction for a new complex at a basic price of $225,000, including working drawings plus $19,000. for kitchen mechanical outfitting.

On Thanksgiving Sunday, M.B.C.'s founders were the **guests of honour**: Sydney and Helen White and Frank and Luella Holliday. Hundreds watched while every commission member turned one shovel of sod, followed by some bulldozer excavating with the building chairman, Earl Heron at the controls.

M   **Adequate electrical supply** was a great concern. We only had Ontario Hydro <u>single phase</u> supply. As Fall 1972 progressed we engaged in much negotiation with Hydro. They offered to bring in the new three-phase service, a distance of three miles. This would be done at <u>MBC's</u> expense. Then came a surprise, last minute offer. The required service would be free of charge if we went "completely electric" in the new complex. Agreed !

M.B.C. Lodge: ~ December 1, 1972 to June 1973 opening

$5000. was in the bank as construction began. Approximately $30,000. was needed on the ninth of January, and each month thereafter, to meet progress payments. Would gifts and bonds be forthcoming? How could we afford the furnishings? What outfitting should we order? Would the Province adhere to stipulations for an elaborate mechanical sewage system estimated to cost $150,000?

M   God's provisions for M.B.C.'s major building programs have been *miracles*. When the initial $30,000. was required in January, receipts exceeded the need. In February, March, April, and May, gifts or bond sales continued to provide the large monthly payments. March furnished a vivid example of Divine punctuality. The treasurer was about to leave on vacation. The fund lacked $9,000., but <u>the full amount arrived that day</u>. **Treasurer, Ron Hartwick**, added a second level of counsel concerning the extent of our project. *"Our one great fault in the scope of this contract, is that we should be providing three times the number of guest rooms. We cannot cover operating costs unless we have adequate accommodation."* His foresight and financial leadership was the Lord's provision through busy years.

The <u>modern kitchen</u> was completely outfitted. Some equipment was acquired at an auction in Windsor, Ontario. Many of the valuable modern restaurant appliances were secured through deacon **Walter Abraham**, of Westside Baptist Church in Hamilton. He was able to arrange this Hobart equipment at a fraction of even wholesale cost. In Mississauga, a government office building, pertaining to nuclear science , was to be phased out not long after its construction. The personnel food supply center included new stainless steel kitchen counters and other items. Through Walter, these were supplied to M.B.C. as a charitable gift.

Two giant fireplaces and a large outside stone wall panel were skillfully crafted. They were donated jointly by our Laymen's Conference and Len Robinson the experienced mason who produced them.

It is interesting to reflect that the natural cedar finish and functional building design, which elicit commendation from all, were first set down in drawings by Ewart Page. He was among the first campers at M.B.C. and a strong supporter through the years.

Just before the new hotel complex was opened, we experienced the worst lightning storms and flash floods of many years. These not only terrified some staff-members, but revealed problems to the capable contractor, Mr. Leslie Harris. He was able to counter the problems by including an extensive storm-sewer and flood control system. A substantial part of this safety installation was his donation.

The furnishings for the building were matters of special concern. How could quality goods be afforded? There were sixteen motel suites, a dining room to seat 375, offices, bookroom, and a spacious lounge! Added to these costs, we had to provide the full kitchen outfitting, 275 feet of floor to ceiling drapes and extensive carpeting.

M   In April 1973, two registered letters were delivered to a meeting of the M.B.C. Commission. One was a quotation of **$30,000.** for all general furnishings, with no charge for all colour coordination. The second was a notification regarding M.B.C.'s share in the legacy of **Mr. Roland Laughtenslager**. This gift amounted to **$30,006.32**. More than twenty years before the death of this faithful missionary-treasurer of Benton St. Baptist Church, Kitchener, he had consultations with his Pastor, Leander Roblin and with M.B.C. founder Frank Holliday. After preaching at a Sunday morning service in Benton Street, Pastor Holliday was entertained for lunch at the Laughtenslager home. Sitting at the dining room table they discussed the doctrinal position and practical objectives of Muskoka Baptist Camp. Frank Holliday's son Richard, was a silent teenage listener at the table. Mr. and Mrs. Laugtenslager decided that this bequest should be left to the Conference. In the providence of God our need for **outfitting of the Lodge was met right on time**, with an extra $6.32 !!!

A quality sewage system would be a legal essential for the new Lodge. A personal presentation was made at the Parliament buildings in Toronto. Extensive engineering drawings were submitted. Approval was secured for Canada's first commercial sewage system of its kind. It cost only $22,000. It had no mechanical components and was virtually maintenance free. God had led us to a builder who had installed such a system, in a simpler form, in another country years before. The savings were well over one hundred thousand dollars, based upon appraisals.

On **May 30th, 1973**, the M.B.C. Lodge opened its doors to the first guests. Though it seemed large in size, it has been packed to its capacity ever since. Its versatile facilities served as the hub of guest service in all seasons. Landscaping layout and inside foliage arrangements add to the warmth of décor and reflect the artistry of Mrs. Walter Dearden. She recommended that *in food service areas, all colours should be edible*!

In addition to meal service and guest accommodations, the Lodge had office areas, a Book Store, a lounge which doubled for smaller ministry gatherings, and half of the dining room as chapel for larger retreat groups. Evening snack times utilized the Lodge Kitchen and Serveteria. Through the next five years, this was the operational limit, until the Chapel Complex was built.

M **"We need a cook. Pray for a cook"**. That was the word of request called by a staff member to Ness Aylett. It was a weekday afternoon, as "Mrs A" was on her way to a prayer time with a few ladies. Later, Mrs. Aylett was greeted by two visitors from Mount Forest. Their names… Edmund and Sadie **OVENS** !

The talents of Sadie Ovens in the kitchen were matched by the outdoor abilities of Edmund. He was capable in all manner of grounds maintenance and animal husbandry. They were wonderful co-workers until the Lord took them home.

M   More problems! The **new dug well**, inside the Lodge, was not adequate to supply sufficient water. During the time of consultations about the problem, dishes were washed by hand eighteen hours per day. The water in the building was supplemented by a garden hose connection with a river pump. Requests to well drillers all over Ontario were refused because of extensive prior commitments. After a Sunday evening prayer meeting about the problem, the first choice firm phoned at 6:15 a.m. *Our biggest rig has finished a job early, and in four hours can be on your location if still needed.* Drilling for two days five feet from the wall of the mechanical room, ten feet into bed-rock, at the 142 foot depth, an underground stream of pure water was tapped, with supply adequate for a town of ten thousand people. The cost of drilling and all the equipment installed: $2800. The hundreds present gave *praise to God for water from the rock.*

With more extensive use and a greatly enlarged area, communications for staff and guests became a pressing need. **The Ladies' Conferences of 1973** provided much of the funding as their part in a telephone/public address system. Electronic engineer Allan Knight, and telephone specialist Peter Culp donated hundreds of hours and untiring labour to make possible the two systems. These enabled us to hear or be heard on all major parts of the Conference. By simple switching, the office could pipe music or paging to all points. For hundreds outside of the crowded chapel, the loudspeakers enabled all to hear the Word of God. Late arriving guests in the camping area or in conference accommodation, could use a *ground telephone* which would even ring at the Director's bedside.

Chapter 16

EXPANDING THE FULL YEAR MINISTRIES

From 1973 to 1975 many retreat groups established a place in our yearly schedule. It was a ten day camp at Fisher's Glen in 1930. The time was extended to two beautiful Muskoka weeks in 1931. M.B.C. now operates programming throughout the year and serves the interests of a significant number of evangelical ministries.

Africa Inland Mission	Huntley Street Staff
Bible Science Association	Ontario Bible College
Christian Business Men's Committee	Salvation Army Officers and Wives
Christian Legal Fellowship of Canada	Sudan Interior Mission
Christian Biker's Association	The Navigators
Central Baptist Seminary	Word of Life Club

MBC RETREATS AND SPECIAL CONFERENCES were developed to meet particular objectives.

- ☒ Snow Conference,

- ☒ Weddings and Receptions

- ☒ Homebuilders, Fall Festivals and bus tours

- ☒ Sweetheart's Conference - for pastors and wives.

- ☒ Single Again - for Bible teaching and interaction to encourage whole families in which a spouse had died or left their household.

- ☒ Conferences for ladies, pastors, pastor's wives, laymen, college-careers, seniors, youth

1975 *What do you do with all that property?* It is interesting that each portion of the total 260 acres has developed its own particular identity. A central triangle includes the Chapel, the Lodge, and the Hub, with gardens, sitting areas, lighted paths, pond and waterfall. Just beyond, are family cottages and a motel. A Sports Area and children's *MacDonald's Farm* occupy the 1936 chapel location and staff-house areas. The former dining building, Millar Hall and Fellowship Centre, served as chapels for the children. There was an aggregate attendance of 2000 for July and August. The Beach, the Marina: each parcel of ground was developed according to a master plan. In all the use of property, the beauty of unspoiled nature was being preserved. Natural finish, rocks, trees, and all evidence of undisturbed nature have been kept in mind. Horse trails and footpaths now give leisurely access to parts of the grounds hitherto rarely visited.

Trailer Park: During the early 1970's there were new washrooms, shower buildings, roads, barbecue pits, picnic tables, water supply, electricity, and a reception building. All of these, plus involvement in the Conference program, gave any camping vacation *that extra touch.* Groceries, home baking, and laundry facilities are some of the services provided. John and Helen Patterson of St. Catharines, became the first overseers of M.B.C. Tent and Trailer Park.

M   In 1973 - a <u>NEW</u> CAMPING AREA OFFICE. We attempted to move the old building which had been M.B.C.'s Hub and then office. We put the building on two long logs and began to pull with a bulldozer. We were hoping to move it for use as the Trailer Park Office. It could not make the journey up the hill. While this writer and dozer owner Don Cottrill, were working on the project in the quiet spring day, a truck pulled up beside me. It was Howard Ratcliff of Century Mill, Stouffville. *Dick Holliday, whatever are you trying to do with that pile of junk?* Together we drove up the hill to look at the desired Trailer Park entry site. The need: a reception office, storage area and a grocery store. Howard said, *my carpenter, George Barrett will start next week.* All the manpower and materials were donated for the erection of an attractive new building, serving every Trailer Park guest. This proved to be an invaluable asset.

A family friend of many years, Howard Ratcliff had a sensitive heart for the developing needs of MBC. The supply of building materials and the "hands-on" involvement of himself and other craftsmen resulted in major improvement of the waterfront, many buildings and wisdom around the Board table for many years.

By 1975, growth of the trailer park under John Patterson's management resulted in a shortage of sites. Some had to park their units in the "holding area" . . . usually reserved for storage. By 1977 we added 58 new sites equipped with water, hydro and septic sewer connections. During the same time, we constructed a large new building outfitted with public washrooms, showers, a coin laundry and a workshop. Electrical improvements were made by Fred Moulton. Two years later, we had added 20 new seasonal sites, but the waiting list had grown to 76 by 1979.

1980 was the year for completing a 10 year development program for MBC's Tent and Trailer Park. Several hundred people laid 3000 yards of nursery sod and assisted in many beautification projects. Three contractors were involved plus the volunteer labourers. In 1985 and 1986 a total of 63 new sites were developed. A new camper store was added and equipped. A high volume well was drilled to improve pressure in the Trailer Park and upper elevation buildings. As we came to the end of the 1988, receipts had increased by 25%. This increase was primarily due to the 52 new sites added in 1987. During the same period, costs relating to municipal requirements for road improvements, engineering, maintenance and personnel had substantially outpaced our income for this one year. The Trailer Park Store sales doubled from 1986 to 1988. Income from the store, Patio and Nibble Nook helped to increase revenue to $18,500.

Trailer Park Chaplain

Dr. E. S. Kerr came as a vacationing resident to the Trailer Park. His caring interest in people soon gave him the title of "Trailer Park Chaplain". He made himself available to chat and pray with any of his trailer park families.

MBC ACRES: *Who would ever build a cottage on the roads so far from the lake?* The question was asked by a number of people when the cottage-lease community was envisaged. M.B.C. Acres began when Larry Taylor and Development Chairman, Dick Holliday measured forty-one lots. They marked out roads, and drove galvanized pipes into the ground as stakes. An official survey was completed and later registered as the Site Plan. The men of Emmanuel Baptist Church of Barrie, working under the direction of Deacon Lorne Sommers, cleared the roadways.

In spite of almost unbelievable difficulties, all legal arrangements were made, and cottages have now transformed an unused bush land into a rustic forest haven for Christian families. A total of 86 privately owned or leased lots now circle the conference and provide a stability of interest and prayer support, which has been invaluable.

SUGAR BUSH BENEFITS 1966 was the year in which the Conference took full possession of the 100 acre hard maple forest. The land transaction included an old decrepit sugar shanty. What a sweet temptation to challenge the skills of the men on staff! This was the natural domain of **Howard Wadge**, who beautified our grounds. He also took the run to town for the mail, produce and any other supplies. He would meet arriving guests at the bus or train station. His love of the outdoors was matched by a heritage which included maple syrup production. Howard and some of his MBC friends arranged the purchase of a large evaporator, and brought it from Quebec. All of this at their own expense. It had a busy life in the late winter seasons. Pails were better than pipe lines because the animals could intercept the flowing sap from the tubing. Howard was the manager. **Don Lively**, his son-in-law was his assistant. (Don was MBC's Assistant Director). **David Hartwick**, a long time staff man and two cottagers, **Jim Bushby** and **Howard Ratcliff** completed the team. The objective each season was to collect 2000 gallons of sap for a yield 100 gallons of maple syrup. When bottled and labeled, it was sold in the bookroom to benefit the income of MBC. Genuine Muskoka sweetness!

MBC RANCH: We were encouraged by farmers to begin a horsemanship program for children and adults. This would serve both the conference guests, campers from Widjiitiwin, and all others who visited. Two ponies and four horses were donated in 1971. Use on our grounds was enjoyed, but wintering the horses in Orangeville presented serious problems. In 1974, the Board authorized the construction of a barn on condition that it would not involve a cash outlay. Six days later, fifty-two cottagers and friends began work at 7 a.m. All marveled at the way in which Lloyd Ward, from Emmanuel, Barrie, could run back and forth on top of the walls to set the rafters in place. What a balancing act! The day ended with the completion of the **barn-raising** at 7 p.m. All materials were donated or conveyed from two southern Ontario barns which had been given to us for demolition. Volunteer teams collected the siding and beams. The "Toronto barn" involved a crowd of more than 40 men and women. A similar group dismantled the "Tillsonburg barn".

M   THE BARN: Well we remember how the barn was completely **filled with hay**. We took four trucks and a long farm hay wagon from M.B.C. to Ottawa. **Howard Harris** and his wife **Grace (Harmer) Harris** were our cordial host and hostess for overnight and meals. Grace was a camper from the early years of MBC. Howard had offered *all the hay you can carry back to your new M.B.C. barn*. We loaded each vehicle and the wagon to the full 12 ½ foot height ! Great lodging, happy travelers, we waved a warm farewell as we left the farm. On the dual highway through Ottawa, the big load on the hay wagon shifted . . . and fell crossways, building a high wall from the truck at the shoulder to the centre median steel rail. Police cars came ! *If this was anybody other than you M.B.C. guys, it would be 'driving with an insecure load'. Move it as quickly as possible, while we go* for *our morning coffee.* (I had preached recently in his Alta Vista Baptist Church). What a traffic jam, but we moved it quickly. Reloaded . . . SECURELY. Mission accomplished . . . except that one vehicle *ground to a halt* an hour from home. Fortunately, its driver was our Master Mechanic, Len Aylett. He returned the next morning, to tow it home.

A barn full of hay was important to us. By this time we had a full line of riding horses and a few ponies and pony carts. Our Ranch included a "democrat" carriage and draught horse. These were the gift of our Benton St. Kitchener driver, **Elmer Filsinger**. He also donated a large hay wagon complete with safety bars for the children. In its first month of use it carried 3000 children. Twice each year a truck load of feed pellets would arrive from **Grand Valley Fortifiers** in Cambridge. Board Member Jim Ross made sure that we have the best of feed for our horses and ponies.

The riding program was one of the most practical tools of instruction. It taught children a discipline and respect for animals. They also learned how to overcome fear and to maintain balance. Our staff became very adept at care for the animals and equipment, as well as the instruction for all ages of riders. It was one of our most popular recreational services for both conference guests, Widjiitiwin campers and all on the grounds.

A Laundry, Carpentry Shop, Mechanical Shop, Boy's Dorm, Storage ! ! !

How ever do you excite interest in financial support of such mundane facilities ? Help Lord !

M   It was about 1933 that Frank Holliday performed the marriage of Mr. & Mrs. Page of Faith Baptist Church, Toronto. Soon after the wedding, Mr. Page was transferred by the Canadian National Railway to the Montreal office. There was virtually no contact with Frank Holliday until that pastor's son, Dick Holliday, was preaching in several Montreal churches on an Easter week-end. There had been preaching assignments every night for several weeks. The week-end included meetings twice on Good Friday, a Youth Rally on Saturday and two church services on Sunday.

Mr. and Mrs. Page invited this writer to dinner on Saturday evening. That day I had a fever, and had no appetite. I tried to cancel the dinner engagement but the couple insisted. A trip to a doctor resulted in an injection of penicillin. Within an hour I was red, weak and desperately itchy all over. Returning to the physician, he gave a neutralizing shot and warned me concerning an evident allergy to penicillin. I was the most reluctant visitor at that evening meal with the Pages. Now at retirement, they wanted to discuss two subjects: **Question: #1** *"Where should we live when we retire? We want to move out to the west coast".* I suggested our Baptist senior's homes in the Vancouver area. Later they made the move. This became their home until the Lord took them to heaven.

Question: #2 *"What practical financial help do you need at MBC, that other people don't supply?"*

Soon thereafter, they paid for the new **Maintenance and Services building** ~ The motor mechanics shop, carpentry shop, store room, laundry, male staff accommodation and all utilities. This included a new drilled well for the heat pump which supplied all with low cost year-round heating.

Those dear servants of the Lord never saw the fruits of their MBC investment, but it has been a most incredible help every day to this present hour.

BEACH DEVELOPMENT and **waterfront-reclamation** were undertaken in **1975**. All members of cottage and trailer park families worked as "Trojans" and finished the job. They called it *MBC's Rock Festival.* This <u>M.B.C. family community</u> contributed immeasurably to the progress of God's work in the Muskoka Hills. . . .

- The impetus by prayer-support

- financial backing for site improvements and efficiency

- allowing overflow use of cottages/trailers during June Retreats

- communication of expert professional advice

- supply of material and manpower

- enthusiastic involvement in recreation events and chapel ministry

MIRACLES OF PROVIDENTIAL CARE

M   In 1976 the care of the grounds in all four seasons was a major concern. Lawns, roads, snow removal, mechanical systems, all of these needed special equipment. The reporting of the year includes some of God's provisions. Air conditioning for the Lodge building, a large electric food mixer, a commercial refrigerator, a children's climbing play center, a high-speed copier for Chapel recordings, a half-ton truck, a station wagon, 2 heavy dump trucks, a commercial clothes dryer, beautiful hand-made quilts, aprons, curtains for guest rooms, all the plants for our gardens . . . and then there was the road and grounds care. Through the gracious stewardship of the Keith Hutchinsons of Stouffville, the following John Deere equipment was provided with only the warranties, **but not an invoice**:

- one diesel tractor with twin snow-blower, heated cab and a front-end loader;

- one lawn and garden tractor with a mower and a power blade;

- three hand powered mowers.

The Hutchinsons were always quiet and gentle, but so sensitive to the work of God and so generous to use **"Hutchinson's Farm Supply"** for the service of the Master.

PEOPLE WITH SERVANT HEARTS

Every June from 1971 to 1977, **Keith Wood** of Emmanuel Baptist Church in Barrie,   used his cube truck to travel with Dick Holliday to pick up the Hammond Organ from the Buffalo Christian Center. Director **Alan Forbes** loaned it to us for summer use in the Chapel. After loading the organ, we would proceed to the Stouffville area to meet with **Charlie Ratcliff.** He would help us load various farm animals which he had chosen for our "MacDonald's Farm" at MBC. The list of creatures which Charlie was donating, usually included chickens, ducks, a turkey, rabbits, a calf, a lamb, goats and only one time, a rooster. Keith was a most gracious chauffeur. He paid for the fuel and provided the truck, the energy and the disinfecting clean-up!

Vic Jackson from Emmanuel, Barrie spent much time every June riding our mower to groom the lawns for the summer conferences.

Lorne Sommers of Emmanuel, Barrie owned a septic tank supply business. From 1965 to 1976, on approximately thirty occasions he delivered one or two giant concrete tanks for our septic systems. It was always his practice to charge just the cost of materials, without adding delivery or labour. What a tremendous helper for a very mundane necessity. **Graham Sommers** and family, (**Ron and Bill Crane**) were carpenters. They built most of the cabins at the enlarged river property of Camp Widjiitiwin. It was a long cold winter of hard work.

Ron and Violet Cripps were long-time friends and MBC campers. Ron served on the Board, most years from the time of incorporation. They also were part of MBC Acres. Ron knew that vehicles are necessary but costly. For two decades he supplied a "people mover" van for Conference use. When its mileage reached a certain peak, the vehicle was replaced by a new model. As President of Aiken Motors in Simcoe, he has used his company to help MBC in a very practical way.

Communication with the public has been greatly assisted by the skills and generosity of photographers. Pictures taken have been used for publications, church promotion and the portrayal of MBC's history. Literally thousands of pictures are now being converted to digital format. One of our first photographers was **Elsie (Barrow) Andrews.** Her delight was to capture themes of beauty, often entertaining conference guests with the marvels of God's handiwork in nature. **Jack Harrison** from Guelph was a gifted professional. Jack and **Ed Smith** focused on individuals and groups. Ed Smith delighted in following construction projects from the sod turning to finished landscaping. By a special camera, he was able to produce the panorama views. Some of his modern technology makes it possible to have a versatile library to illustrate what God has done.

Len and Myrtle Klinck, Oakwood Baptist, Toronto helped in ways that were not noticed by the public. Myrtle always had an eye and heart sensitive for counseling ladies. She served for many years on our Ladies' Conference Committee. Len, being involved in emergency health services, was our key provider of first aid supplies and emergency equipment. His oxygen tanks were the practical instruments of not only saving the life of Pastor Sugden but also our Auditor Mr. Dick Wyse and winter accident victims rescued from the frigid waters of Mary Lake.

Chapter 17

MEETING NEEDS BECAUSE WE CARE

Every soul on earth is important to God. Our service for Him must show the love of our Saviour. John chapter 5 demonstrates how to show that love.

Jesus visited a pool called Bethesda   (House of Mercy)

    ☒   There lay *a great multitude* of helpless people

    ☐   *A certain man* was there . . . 38 years.

    ☒   NOTE: *"Jesus saw him lying there . . . and knew . . .*

    ☐   **Jesus never loses sight of the individual in a crowd !**

This objective has continued from the beginning of MBC. Leaders have sought to touch individuals with the love of Christ.

We remember foster parents, Mr. and Mrs. Pike. They brought five, six and more children for a week or two weeks, for a number of years. Each of the children had some form of physical or personality problem. They had been assigned to the Pikes by the Children's Aid. They came for the first time when meals were served in Millar Hall. In the new Lodge dining room we arranged a waitress to provide special attention for their table.   For many years the Pikes and their foster children felt that MBC was the greatest place on earth. After 20 years looking after children with special needs, Mrs. Pike was honoured as "Ontario's Mother of the Year".

The new MBC Lodge and other fully winterized accommodations made it possible to meet many personalized needs. At each June Pastor's Conference from 1975 onward, it was duly announced that any pastor and wife needing a mid-week day or two of rest and respite, could just phone ahead and come. Such a brief time of care was not charged, but treated as part of ministry.

TIMES OF TRAUMA AND STRESS

In an age of pressure, home fragmentation and spiritual decline, the exhortation of the Saviour has never been more needful: ***Come ye yourselves apart, and rest a while.*** We remember the wise paraphrase by Dr. Vance Havner

> ***. . . if you don't come apart, you'll come apart!***

"A Place to be quiet" ~ recollections by Allison Fish

I accepted Christ at a young age with the guidance of Dr. Roy Lawson, sitting in the old Honey Pot on the grounds of MBC. I had a Christian home, loving parents and a strong Bible teaching church to help me in my spiritual walk with the Lord. We attended Wortley Baptist Church with Rev. Robert Wilson as senior pastor, during my early years. He was followed by Dr. Donald Launstein who completed his time there by officiating at my wedding. Besides the strong Bible teaching I received from the pulpit each week, Wortley had a wonderful youth program complete with Bible study and fun fellowship events. It was comprised of youth leaders under the supervision of adult sponsors, who acted as mentors. I enjoyed being involved in the leadership of the group, learning to serve others.

An end-of-summer event was scheduled for the beach, late August 1981. As we assembled at the church, threatening clouds prompted cancellation of the bus and postponement of the event. Word from the beach then assured us of good weather, so we scrambled cars and enjoyed an amazing day of sunshine and fun. At dusk, the caravan of cars headed home.

Half-way home, the car I was in moved awkwardly from the gravel to the pavement. The wheels caught, pitching the car on its side, and then on to the roof. I became aware that I was hanging upside down. Everything was quiet. In the dim light I saw that my hand was severely injured. Assisted by others, I crawled through the opening where the windshield had been, and I sat beside the road. I was really concerned to keep pressure on my hand to stop the bleeding there. It was later, at the hospital, that I found out that I had an open gash on my elbow and had suffered a fracture there as well.

My parents came with what seemed a host of others, cramming into the waiting room. Each person from the car was examined that evening, and all the others released with bumps, bruises and a few stitches. Near midnight, I was taken to the operating room. Two specialists worked for four hours to treat the damage and to repair what could be fixed. They completed a partial amputation of my right index finger.

The next day, as I surveyed my heavily bandaged arm and hand, I was grateful that I still had my remaining badly bruised fingers. I was released six days later, after celebrating my 17th birthday in my hospital bed.

The next four months were a challenge . . . the demands of school without the ability to write with my right hand! I would rotate the subjects for my daily work because my left hand was slow. Homework had to wait until after dinner. Four days each week I spent in physiotherapy to regain use of my elbow and my hand. It was work, sweat and tears. I surpassed my surgeon's expectations by having almost full range of elbow movement and a good function of my hand. There was a question about further surgery on the hand, for better appearance and the functioning of the remaining fingers. No one could make the decision for me. My decision was to proceed during the Christmas break of my senior year. As the surgery time neared, elbow pain increased and feeling and movement of the fingers decreased. Further investigation of the elbow determined that nerve compression from scar tissue seemed to be the problem. Elbow surgery would be added to the December work on the hand.

Challenges continued with school work and rehabilitation. My objective was to graduate with good grades that spring. I hoped that recovering from this final round of surgeries, I could move ahead with the future. God used my experience during this period to spark a desire to pursue a career in physiotherapy. With the encouragement of the therapists who worked with me, I applied. Through people, and circumstances God made it very clear and possible for me to be accepted into the Mohawk-McMaster physiotherapy program. I left home that fall excited about starting this new chapter of life, confident that I was where God wanted me to be, fully healed from the past and ready to move forward.

Within 8 weeks, pain signaled trouble, first at my elbow and then in the nerves of my hand. Phantom pain had always been present to a degree, the missing injured digit still imprinted on my brain. Troublesome neuromas were responsible for the added pain, and surgery was needed to try to correct the problem. A few months later, scar tissue would need to be dealt with and this would become a pattern over the next three years. University studies did not stop. Work had to be completed and surgeries were scheduled during study breaks. Five trips to the operating room for procedures on my hand, elbow or both, made life a struggle. Questions started to arise, within myself as well as from those around me. *How could all this be part of what God had for me? Had I been wrong about becoming a physiotherapist? Would I have to quit?* I struggled to see how this painful condition and repeated surgery, could be part of a loving God's plan.

I had made my commitment to Christ at MBC and through yearly <u>family vacations</u> to the trailer park there, as well as numerous youth retreats and college retreats, I had formed a close relationship with the director Rev. Richard Holliday and his wife Marilyn. Whenever I was on the grounds, Pastor Holliday would make the time to catch up on the news and follow my journey with its ups and downs. My third year at school was the most trying time, and the pressure to make it through, was made extremely difficult because of the pain. It was a challenge to sleep. The physical work during clinical placements caused a great deal of pain. No medication was available, and surgery would have to wait until exams were over. I recalled an open invitation that Pastor Holliday had given me the last time I had seen him and decided to make the trip north for a week-end. I know God does not reside in any one place, yet **MBC had been *a place for me to be quiet* and hear from God.** Besides making my decision for Christ, I had been blessed to sit under some amazing Bible teachers, growing spiritually and being challenged to join in teen foreign missions at camp, all on the grounds at MBC. When I arrived I found a warm welcome and a place to rest and meditate on God rather than my circumstances. I was free to stroll the grounds and revisit the places that reminded me of God's leading. I needed the reality of God's past faithfulness to renew my faith in what He planned for my future. Despite my weakness, He was able to carry me through, and if He had set this as my path He would not abandon me. I left that week-end still bearing the pain, still facing exams and surgery, yet with a renewed sense that it was all possible with God.

I did not know about the cost to MBC for those days, I am not even sure I asked. I was hurting and needed a place to heal my soul's concerns and find rest for my physical body. Pastor Holliday had seen my need and opened the conference space for me. **I do know that it was a blessing to me, a pivotal time that made a difference.** I went on to successfully complete my degree, graduating in 1987, working as a physiotherapist for 13 years. I have returned for several additional surgeries in recent years. The pain continues, daily, but the God who walked with me on the grounds of MBC still walks with me today. His promises never fail.

Allison (Milligan) Fish, Calgary, Alberta

MIRACLES ALL THE YEAR ROUND

An excerpt from the 1974 Annual Report   ~

☐   **The First Convention of Muskoka Baptist Conference, Incorporated**

Blessings __NEW__ every morning! In the Fall months of 1971 – 1972, the season was extended to Thanksgiving. Construction heaters were used in the dining room for guest comfort on cold days. Church retreats, Homebuilder's Conference for couples, Fall Folliage Festival for families. These were NEW features of the Colour Capital of Muskoka.

*NEW RETREATS: From the Fall of 1973, retreat ministry continued without missing a beat. Fears of how to handle heavy winter snows were dissolved by Deacon Keith Hutchinson's gift of a **NEW** **Diesel tractor** complete with cab, power steering, front-end loader, grader, blade and snow blower. A Christmas Snow Conference was followed by the winter retreats and more than one hundred professions of salvation and decisions for life dedication were recorded. Skating on the lake, a giant ice-slide for use with truck inner tubes, skiing, tobogganing, and the two new (gifted) snowmobiles . . . These were all firsts for M.B.C. programming. The Retreat groups include Bible schools, churches, and missionary agencies with ministry to couples, families, youth, pastors, and deacons, ladies, and men.

*<u>NEW</u> SERVICES: The Lodge made possible an ideal wedding banquet setting and accommodated twelve honeymoon couples in the fall of 1974.

*<u>NEW</u> BANQUET MINISTRY: Groups of Christian Business Men, "Ladies Only Please" church picnics, and community ministry functions.

*<u>NEW</u> BUS MINISTRY: Again during 1974, eight churches chartered buses to bring senior citizens on spring and fall Muskoka tours. The three to four hour stop at M.B.C. included a meal, recreation, cruises and ministry. These were "high days" for most responsive groups of people.

*<u>NEW</u> AIR-CONDITIONING: thanks to Laymen's Conference of 1974. They provided financing for the Lodge dining room cooling system. While only two-thirds of the total installation could be afforded in 1974, dining room temperatures were kept below the outside heat.

*<u>NEW</u> GRAND PIANO: The June'74 Ladies' and Pastors' Wives Conferences received special offerings, which made possible the purchase of a first quality used instrument. What a blessing throughout the year! The dedication of the Chapel piano was in memory of Mrs. Donald ("Nan") Loveday.

*<u>NEW</u> ROOT CELLAR: Most people have never seen it! It is 14 feet wide, by 40 feet long, by 9 feet high. It is buried fourteen feet below the ground. The professional Christian farmers who suggested building it, have also been key suppliers of fresh product. This enables the Conference to have better control of food costs and quality. This helps to keep rates down. Contributions included 12 000 pounds of potatoes, 700 head of cabbage, 800 loaves of bread, carrots, onions, turnips, a butchered hog . . . even a farmer who shears M.B.C.'s sheep and donates the money from the sale of the wool.

*NEW BARN: Our first winter use of the horses was an instant success in 1975. Materials for the barn and many 1974-75 projects were made available at tremendous savings through the interest of Ratcliff Lumber personnel.

M *NEW WELL AND PUMP: A change was needed to eliminate many mechanical problems and a chlorination system. A new drilled well could now serve pure water to everyone on M.B.C. property. The entire cost was less than one summer's supply of chlorine. The engineer supplying the operational equipment could not understand why the electronic "on-off" switch of the pump would not work. He came back to supply a second electronic switch . . . which also did not work.

Finally, a test of the water led to the conclusion, *there is no mineral content in the water for conductivity to turn the electronic switch on and off.* The engineer's comment, **this is the first time that I have ever experienced a well with virtually PURE WATER.** The switch we finally installed . . . a common toilet tank float control (about $5). When the level of the water is low, the float triggers the pump to operate and replenish the reservoir supply. When the float is pressed up by the replenished water, it shuts the pump off.

FIVE WELLS ~ WATER FROM THE ROCK: Between 1973 and 1981 five wells were drilled at MBC. The <u>first</u> was by the wall, just outside the Lodge building, on a lower shelf of soil over bed rock. It was good water, but, sufficient for the Lodge building only. It was not adequate for the increasing demands of "a small town", and too far away from Camp Widjiitiwin's new site.

Our well driller explained, *"when God made the world, he fashioned great reservoirs of water under the earth. Do you want to find them? Go to the <u>high</u> grounds, where it seems that the rock structure has been pressed upward. That's where the water will be held. We'll <u>drill from the high ground</u> and find the water in those upward folds of the solid rock. Sure enough".* Any one of our four subsequent drilled wells had a virtually unlimited supply of pure water. They were our "high ground" wells... at the Conference and at Camp Widjiitiwin.

*NEW LAKEVIEW MOTEL: In our first winter of programming we discovered that accommodation had to be provided, not only for guests but for all staff members, as well. None of the staff owned their own local residence. Popular demand pressed winter facilities two-thirds beyond Lodge capacity. Something had to be done before a second winter. Our treasurer, Ron Hartwick demonstrated the importance of winter use. The combined accommodation needed to be adequate for at least one hundred and fifty.

By gifts and loans, a rush program was made possible to enlarge, refit, and winterize M.B.C.'s oldest existing guest accommodation. This was the 1955 masonry "Lakeview Motel". After the renovation was completed, only the roof and one quarter of each partition wall remained of the original rooms. The square footage of the rooms was doubled. Four-piece tiled bathrooms, patio doors, large windows, and an easy parking lot entrance were added. Complete with drapes, spreads, two new double beds, wall-to-wall carpeting, each of these became a choice suite. While making the change, the electric and water supplies were made adequate for future expansion of this building. Well used even at the end of 1974, the rooms were ready for full continuous occupancy from January 1ˢᵗ, 1975.

*NEW STAFF ACCOMMODATION BUILDING: With winter accommodation at a premium, there was a need to house senior and a few other full time staff. *Summerset House* was a two-family dwelling overlooking the Conference grounds. A fully winterized building, it has been a key to meeting needs relating to year-round ministry. Howard and Gladys Ratcliff made this building possible.

*NEW SUMMER SPECIAL FOR LADIES: Every Thursday afternoon during July and August, large gatherings of ladies now enjoy "Tea" with a craft demonstration and Bible study time. Mrs. Lorraine MacGregor, and Mrs. "Eli" Foster established this feature.

***NEW** OUTREACH** by the Managing Director. In 1974 pastor friends assisted in contacts for an extensive itinerary involving Dick Holliday with Dr. Earl Hallonquist. He was the Chief of Scientific Research of McMillan-Bloedel of B.C. At each session, the subject introduction was a film about the scientific reliability of scriptures. It was followed by Dr. Hallonquist and then questions from the audience. In just over three weeks, we ministered in 81 sessions . . . churches, high school assemblies, colleges and universities . . . from Windsor U. to

McGill. The intensity and resulting appreciative responses were thrilling to say the least ! Many positive letters were a refreshing encouragement.

Every year from 1971 to 1990 this writer was privileged to represent the Conference and Camp Widjiitiwn by preaching and teaching in churches throughout all of Ontario, other provinces from Quebec to B.C., in the USA and beyond. Mid-weeks and week-ends from Fall to Spring were opportunities to share the Word in Sunday Schools, preaching services, rallies and other events. Usually the number of occasions ranged from 20 to 40 and sometimes more churches.

As the Conference grew, other Christian agencies asked for discussion and reaction in a forum of consultation. Some of these would meet with us at MBC for a day or two of interaction concerning policies and practices. In most cases, there was a site visit and meetings with the respective management and boards. We usually filed reports of site analysis, equipment, staff, organization, finance and ministry. The following had at least two or three contacts over a period of years.

Bird River Bible Camp, Manitoba	Pleasant Bay Camp, Consecon, ON
Camp des Bouleaux, & 2 others in Quebec	Point Roberts Salvation Army Camp/Conf
Camp Canbay, London, ON	New Life Camp, Bluewater Association
Dalesville Baptist Lodge, Quebec	Sault Ste Marie Campference, ON & MI
Fairhavens Bible Conference	Sunnybrae Bible Camp, B.C
Muskoka Woods, Rosseau	Camp Quanoes, Crofton, B.C.

*NEW CONFERENCE FOR SWEETHEARTS: Pastors and wives filled our accommodations in February and March mid-weeks. This proved to be good relaxation and times of precious spiritual refreshment.

*NEW SUNDAY NIGHT SINGS: Summer Sundays after Chapel feature a "family song-time" with refreshments. Every week the Lodge is packed to capacity. As in all our summer programming from 1972, Rev. Roy W. Lawson engenders much joyful exuberance. There is a pointed and heart-warming spiritual thrust. What a thrill to know of seven who professed faith in Christ during 1974. The response was prompted by the happiness and testimonies of M.B.C. staff.

*<u>NEW</u> WATER-SKI PROGRAMME: With boating equipment and a large floating wharf, M.B.C. operated a very successful water-ski training program in 1974. Both Conference guests and Camp Widjitiiwin were under the supervision of Mr. Cameron McArthur. As senior Men's Waterskiing Champion for Canada, he led the ski program for college and career groups. It was in 1973 that God spoke to Cameron at an M.B.C. retreat. After Cameron, Pete Mallory of Emmanuel in Barrie led the program for 7 years.

*<u>NEW</u> ELECTRICAL INSTALLATION: *The Lord sent out a great wind!* It caused a tree to fall on a transformer pole, which supplied electricity to the original buildings of the Conference. When the Ontario Hydro investigated, they would not permit reconstruction of the original out-of-date system. Insurance funds covered the cost of removal of five meters. They were willing to write-off the cost of a new supply centre. It included the provision of a greatly increased and more efficient installation. This will be adequate for years to come. Electrical engineer, Fred Moulton has for many years assisted the Conference with our wiring concerns. He contributed both extensive "know how" and his own labour, as a volunteer, in the expansion of these facilities.

*A <u>NEW</u> STAFF EACH YEAR: In addition to a few who serve throughout the year, close to one hundred are selected annually from many applications, and usually represent more than sixty churches of various provinces and a few foreign countries. To list all the volunteers, part-time, and full-time partners on the M.B.C. team would make a lengthy catalogue. The greater the emphasis upon high Biblical standards, the greater the spirit of joy and oneness felt by participants, and evident to guests.

Perhaps the greatest accomplishment of the <u>early 1970's</u> is that basic facilities were developed to serve Bible-believing churches throughout the year. The spiritual dividends were thrilling, and volumes could be written about those personal testimonies. All who have witnessed the blessing of God upon the Muskoka Baptist Conference must surely be moved to echo: "Great is Thy Faithfulness".

☐ **1974 ~ THE FIRST CONVENTION** of Muskoka Baptist Conference, Inc.

It was held at ~ Willowdale Baptist Church

☒ Speaker - Dr. A.V. Henderson

☒ Song Service led by Rev. Martin Wedge

☒ Music by the Choir of Emmanuel, Barrie and The Ken Baer family, Instrumentalists

Elected as the Board of Directors:

President – Rev. D.S. Irwin

Vice Presidents – Rev. M.O. Wedge and Mr. Ron Cripps

Secretary – Mr. F.W. Bowman,

Treasurer - Mr. R.R. Hartwick

Members: Mr. R. Bickle, Mr. C.A. Borrowman, Mr. E.A. Faris, Mr. J.A. Feren, Mr. G.R. Hallett, Mr. H.L. Ireland, Rev. A. Larson, Mr. H. Ratcliff, Mr. R.W. Thompson,   Mr. S.L. White

Building Committee Chairman - Earl T. Heron

SUMMER SPEAKERS ~ 1973 to 1975

Dr. D. Allen, Calvary Baptist, Hazel Pk. MI

Dr. J. R. Armstrong, Mt. Pleasant, Toronto

Dr. J. Balyo, Grand Rapids Baptist Col, MI

Rev. R.E.J. Brackstone, Chatham

Bible Authority & Modern Science
Drs. H.M. Morris, D. Gish, H. Slusher

Rev. A.T. Forbes, Buffalo Christian Center

Dr. A.V. Henderson, Newcastle, DE

Dr. J.F. Holliday, Second Markham Baptist

Dr. D.S. Irwin, Central Baptist, Brantford

Dr. D. Jennings, Calvary, Ypsilanti, MI

Dr. M. Jackson, Calvary, Muskegon, MI

Rev. E.G. Kennedy, Forward, Cambridge

Rev. A. Larson, Calvary Baptist, Oshawa

Dr. K. Moon, Northside, St. Petersburg, FL

Dr. E. Pickering, Baptist Bible College, PA

Dr. J.M. Stowell II, Grand Rapids, MI

Dr. Jack Scott, Central Baptist Seminary

Dr. H. F. Sugden, South Baptist Lansing, MI

Dr. G.B. Vick, Temple Baptist, Detroit, MI

Dr. W. Welch, Grand Rapids Baptist, MI

Dr. S. Wemp, Lynchburg, Virginia

1973 Ribbon Cutting of Lodge Building
Dick/Marilyn Holliday, S.L. White

Lodge Dedication Stone -Rom. 1:16

Lodge building

Sunday Eve. Staff Sing 1975

"Must be Thursday!"

Smorgasbord

1973 – packed dining rooms!

Cook – Charlotte Moulton
Known for her butter tarts!

Sandra Strongman (nee Hiltz)
Faithful cook for 8 years!

Waitresses 1976

2 "Chefs", Roy Lawson/Dick Holliday

'75 Ladies' Committee:K. Norris, F.Pengilly, A. Wilkie, B. Sheppard, M.Eberlee,
SpeakerMarj.VanderPuy,V. Hartwick, P.Strathdee, M.Klinck

Ladies' Committee: Speaker, I. Allen, Ev Thompson (Chair), D. Stouffer, M.
Stephenson, B. Sheppard,Kinsinger, L. Wood, (absent- S. Kernohan)

1972 Ladies' Conference

'75 Pastors' Wives Conference

'72 Laymen's Conference Committee

'72 Laymen's Conference

First full summer – Camp Widjiitiwin 1968, the Board Chairman was Art Fitkin

Camp Widjiitiwin Craft Center

1968 Waterfront - Director, Marie Potz

Widjiitiwin Directors: Abe/Vicki Dueck   *Hillside*

Archery

"Tabins"   *Pup Tents*

Canoe "Camp-Outs"

Lee Mitchell leading campers

"Warriors" arriving for baseball

Widjiitiwin Counsellors

Widjiitiwin versus Conference

Professional engraver, Walter Dancy

Dedication of Cabin #1, Elsie Andrews

Widjiitiwin property dedication '77
Board, Staff, Directors. Intro by R.W. Lawson

New Widjiitiwin'78 - tents for temporary meals & meetings

"Trading Post" for snacking campers

Beloved Director, "Mrs. Mac" (Lorraine MacGregor)

Board Chairman, Bill Havercroft with Graham Sommers, builder of 18 cabins

1984 Widjiitiwin Longhouse: George Hayes, Lorraine MacGregor, Jim Youngson

Widjiitiwin Campers visiting Conference…. Andy/Lorraine MacGregor at right

Longhouse nears completion

Welcome to 1988 campers

1989 Camper Group

Widjiitiwin Waterfront

Widjiitiwin waterfront program

Chapter 18

MEMORIAL CHAPEL 1978

Exalting His Name Together . . .

Every summer Sunday of the 1970's our Memorial Chapel of 1961 was crowded beyond capacity. As time went along there were more outside than inside. The urgent need for more space would be met in accordance with the Lord's supply.

M **The Bickle brothers** of Cobourg and **Howard Ratcliff** of Century Mill, Stouffville had supplied a large quantity of logs for a major waterfront project of the City of Toronto. These men knew that much of the timber was left over and available for their pick-up. The logs had been cut in half lengthwise. They brought them to M.B.C. With their own equipment they made the concrete cradles, placing one at each end of a log. They were arranged like a large amphitheatre in the field outside the Chapel. The entry wall of the Chapel was made into moveable panels, and a large platform built outside. Every Sunday morning, the Chapel service was convened in the open air. **RAIN?** . . . sometimes in Port Sydney, Huntsville, Baysville or even across the river, but <u>never once on a summer Sunday morning</u> until our third Chapel was dedicated in 1978.

M In 1977 special gifts and pledges, including the memorial gift from Langstaff Baptist, amounted to a total of $75,000. Construction began in November. God laid our need on the heart of the Stephenson brothers. (David Stephenson, President). They donated the services of skilled foreman Jim Williams and extensive engineering, equipment and supervision. The contractor's fee...an official **$1.00 !** The giant trusses for the roof and the many smaller piles of metal and wooden parts were piled carefully on the ground, spread over about half an acre, beside the site. The possibility of winter snow was cause for concern. The snow did not begin in earnest until mid-December. By then, **W.A. Stephenson Construction** of Willowdale had the roof in place and closed in. Then the deep snows came. The work neared completion by

April 1978, at which time **Contractor Don Wilson** of Lindsay undertook his part by building the **Tea room and Book Store**. What a great team ! Our total constituency was giving firm support. As time moved on our finances would demonstrate this fact.

Dedication of the new Memorial Chapel took place on July 2, 1978. There was heart-stirring gratitude to God for the gifts and services which had made it possible. The large gift from **Langstaff Baptist Church** came to us at just the right time. There were many sacrificial gifts in memory of some of God's special servants. Churches loaned 1000 chairs. Ever since it opened, the building has been fully used, often to overflowing. It is conducive for preaching, excellent in acoustics and has a simple, natural elegance to assist the ministry impact. Hundreds of decisions have been made to trust and follow the Lord. MBC is a BIBLE conference. We preach the Word and believe the Gospel to be "the power of God unto salvation". Growth has paralleled our emphasis upon preaching and teaching. The design of the building included a large overflow seating area, covered by a custom canopy. This was installed as a gift from **Jim and Bev Jepson**. Jim was a Member of Parliament for London and a valued member of our Board of Directors for the years 1983 and 1989. The Lord took him home on November 29, 1989 at age 47.

"THY WORD IS A LAMP"

"Vacation With A Purpose". From its inception, the Word of God has been the central theme and focus of Muskoka Baptist Conference. It is not only the conviction of those who labour behind the scenes, but it is the main desire of all those invited to preach and teach. Each one is unique.

Dr. Roy W. Lawson has carried a number of responsibilities and ministered in many parts of our country and beyond, but virtually every year since his teens, he has returned to MBC. While a Pastor, a leader of the of FBYPA and then as General Secretary of our Fellowship of Evangelical Baptist Churches, Roy maintained ministry contact with the Conference and Camp Widjiitiwin. Though he usually had other mid-week duties, he helped us by shouldering much responsibility for leadership of the platform and program. It was his second home. Because of his infectious humor he lifted the spirits of all present.

After speaking at a retreat in the mid-eighties, he was leaving after the morning service. Whenever this happened, the kitchen would make him a bag lunch to conserve his time. He picked it up from the staff dining room and hopped into his car. He never admitted how far he drove before discovering that he had mistakenly taken a bag of garbage instead of his bag lunch! Passing busy staff members at their morning chores, he was often heard to say, *"Are you under the spout where the glory flows out!"*

He was first and foremost a man of the Word, with an application that challenged all ages. Joan Lawson was always a helpful co-worker, serving wherever she was needed. Her preference was the bookroom. Their boys, Dan, Dave and Doug were all helpers on summer staff at various times.

Every mid-week and on vacation times from High Park Baptist in Toronto, **George and Joan Shuttleworth** occupied the tiniest trailer in our park.   Their 1960 honeymoon included a week at a river cottage, where disturbing MBC neighbours treated them to a noisy Shivaree. They loved being in the trailer park. Through many years, George was a favourite song leader. His arms spread wide earned him the nick name *"MBC's 747"*. Some days each mid-week, when Roy Lawson was occupied by responsibilities in the Fellowship Office, George was in charge of platform. He encouraged all in the joy of the Lord. His technique was detailed, prayerful preparation so that people could experience the great truths of the hymns and songs being sung.

Dr. Howard F. Sugden and Lucille were role models for any pastor or pastor's wife. He went up and down the aisles for half and hour before each service to warmly greet everyone possible and share just a gentle word of encouragement. All knew that he loved them.

A feature much appreciated was the "Little Red Box" after each mid-week morning chapel. People would submit their questions in advance. Mrs. Sugden would read the questions and Pastor Howard give the answer . . .except those frequent times when Lucille Sugden exercised her right to give the answer first. What an insightful pair and what tremendous enthusiasm. Their succinct Bible answers to 226 questions have been typed by several volunteer MBC secretaries and recorded in the book - -

"What Does The Bible Say About. .?" Kregel Publications of Grand Rapids, MI.

A sample question . . . #144 - - *"What does it mean to know Him and the power of His resurrection ?"* Dr. Sugden answered: *"I think it means exactly what it says. When Paul wrote this in Philippians 3:10 he was talking about the power that raised Jesus Christ from the dead. He is saying to me today that the same power indwells me as a Christian as that which raised Jesus Christ from the dead. If you want to see something of the mightiness of the power of God, come and see an empty tomb. Understand there is a risen Christ. And then understand that the same power that raised Christ from the dead lives in you. He is in you --- that same power!"*

M   Returning to his room after preaching one evening, Pastor Sugden came to the top of the long stairway in the Lodge. A young lady was sitting on the bottom step reading her Bible while waiting for the public telephone to be free. Dr. Sugden's foot caught the edge of the top step. He pitched forward into the stair opening, and literally accomplished a "front roll", landing in a sitting position on the bottom step, beside the young lady. Though shaken, he immediately said to her, *"I'm sorry to drop in on you like this"*. We were thankful there were no injuries.

M   During the three week ministry of another summer, Mrs. Sugden made a 1 a.m. call to this writer. She said, *"I think Pastor is unwell and needs a doctor"*. By the time I reached the car, my nurse daughter, Kimberly, was opening the opposite door. As we arrived at the accommodation building I picked up the First Aid Kit and Kimberly the oxygen equipment and stretcher. It was immediately determined that his heart was in serious difficulty. With the help of Roy Lawson, whose room was nearby, we carried him by stretcher to the car. While I drove, Kimberly administered oxygen all the way to the hospital. The next day the doctor stated, *"if you had not given him oxygen on the way, he never would have made it"*. While a patient in Huntsville Hospital for two weeks, he ministered to staff and patients. His roommate was deeply moved and Pastor Sugden had the joy of leading him to faith in Christ. When arranging discharge from the hospital, it was co-ordinated with his church family in Lansing, Michigan. A member of South Baptist Church was a pilot and owned his own plane. He flew up with Dr. Suk Chang, Pastor's Sugden's physician, together with a Deacon. We drove the Sugdens to meet the plane at Muskoka Airport. They had a safe trip home and returned for preaching ministry every summer, including 1990.

M   **Dr. Jerry Falwell** came to preach at Pastor's Conference. It was at the height of tension by those who disliked his emphasis on practical Christian living. The police informed the writer that we must plan security protection from the time he landed at Muskoka Airport. I arranged for off-duty police officers to assist us. We met before the plane was due at the airport. As it turned out, the plane was two hours late, but it was still afternoon, so he would not be tardy.

The policemen were interested in Dr. Falwell. "*Why does he need protection? What does he believe?*" For an hour I had opportunity to explain God's plan of salvation. One of the officers prayed, asking the Lord to come into His life. The other prayed brokenly that "*some day*" he would be able to be a Christian. I struggled with the reluctant man, but he affirmed, "*I know I need God. My home is a mess. I just can't do it now*".

Not long after, the first officer was baptized and became a member of the Baptist Church in Bracebridge. The other officer committed suicide three weeks later. It was some months before the believing man called to tell me about the outcome of that afternoon in the airport. Dr. Falwell's ministry really stirred the hearts of Pastors. He had been accompanied on the plane by one of his faculty members, **Dr. Elmer Towns**. Dear Elmer stayed with us when Dr. Falwell left. He ministered the next week and many summers thereafter.

After two of his preaching weeks in the MBC Chapel the sermon series was published. The book was entitled "The Names of Jesus". It was a study of encouragement about the "*700 names of Jesus which help us really know the Lord we love*". Its forward, "*the chapters in this book were preached as twelve messages at Muskoka Baptist Conference Canada during the summer of 1986. Appreciation is extended . . . for giving me the opportunity to minister the Word of God to over 1000 people each summer".*

Dr. J. Donald Jennings and his wife Doris came from busy ministry responsibilities in the northern States, as Minister at Large for the ABWE and as Pastor of Temple Baptist Church in Tennessee. Doris was one of our Ladies` Conference speakers. Pastor Jennings had an interesting facet in every sermon introduction. It was a quotation about the Word of God. A favourite sample . . . **THE PRECIOUS BIBLE**

Though the cover is worn and the pages are torn, and though places bear traces of tears,

Yet more precious than gold is the book, worn and old that can shatter and scatter my fears.

When I prayerfully look in the precious old Book, many pleasures and treasures I see;

Many tokens of love from the Father above, Who is nearest and dearest to me.

This old Book is my guide, `tis a friend by my side, it will lighten and brighten my way;

And each promise I find soothes and gladdens my mind as I read it and heed it today.

Dr. Paul and Pat Dixon, President of Cedarville University, Ohio

The Dixons were role models of one of his book titles, *The JOY of Discipleship*. Through their ministry at MBC we had many responses of life commitment to Christ from young people. Some of these were our own staff members. In addition to his morning and evening full Chapel sessions, and an extra ``Christian Leaders`` teaching workshop each morning at 11 a.m., he conducted our early staff devotions. What an impact on all ages.

Missionary, Dr. Viggo Olsen . . . Diplomat of the American Board of Surgery, Pioneer builder of a modern hospital in Bangladesh, honoured by the State of Bangladesh with Visa #001. People were greatly moved by his testimony of conversion (summarized in the 71 page booklet, *The Agnostic Who Dared To Search,* Moody Press). The full missionary story is included in the larger volume, *Daktar.* We heard that testimony in personal communication and praise God for many who responded to the invitation of the Gospel.

Dr. John Blanchard is one of our world's greatest evangelical apologists both in printed works and his depth of practical teaching. His times of ministry in our Chapel stirred hearts with the authority of Scripture and the necessity of a life changed by commitment to Christ. The wide range of book subjects and the high quality of presentation always resulted in a large volume of sales for personal study and witnessing. One of the most popular titles continues to be ``Ultimate Questions``. *The ultimate questions are about God and your relationship to Him. Nothing in life is more important than this.* These were some of the greatest to strengthen personal confidence in the Word and practical for all to witness.

Sermons From Science was one of our most spectacular, but spiritually rewarding ministry times. **Dean C. Ortner's** background as a military test pilot, scientist and associate in Moody Institute of Science, led him to life-time service in reaching all ages with the importance of submission to the laws of God, both the physical law and *the law of the Lord.*

What an amazing sight to see over 500 people on our hillside listening and responding to **Dr. John White** of Calvary Baptist, Grand Rapids, MI. He was the author of the teaching format, ``*A Walk Through The Bible*``. No one will forget the hazards of being in the last group of Israelites while journeying towards Canaan.

We had some **great** <u>**father-and-son**</u> **preaching weeks**, (probably unique experiences)

> Dr. James and Dr. David Jeremiah
>
> Dr. Lehman and Dr. Richard Strauss
>
> Dr. Joseph Stowell II (GARB) and Dr. Joseph Stowell III (Detroit & MBI).

The enthusiasm, hilarious stories and mutual ministry respect reinforced some of the greatest weeks of Bible preaching.

"CALL TO ME, AND I WILL ANSWER" . . . *Jeremiah 33:3*

Through every Conference season , **"Morning Watch"** took place in Fellowship Center, then in the 1961 Chapel, and finally in either the Hub or the Lounge. There were always some who gathered each morning at about 7:30, for Bible reading and earnest prayer. This maintained a bond of dependence and expectation, the key to spiritual victories and divine providence.

ANNOUNCEMENTS ! ! ! In the first summer of Dick Holliday's years as Managing Director, Dr. Jack Wyrtzen invited the Hollidays to spend time in residence at Word of Life, Schroon Life, N.Y. They lived in the accommodation next door to the Wyrtzens. What a great opportunity for fellowship and learning. It was a time of observing every operation and camp program on their properties. One comment by the "Dean" of camps and conferences: *"I am often criticized for making announcements. The single, most important reason for the growth and blessing of God upon the whole Word of Life ministry, is my commitment to tell people some specific blessing which God has given that day"*.

Looking back on his years from 1971, Dick Holliday feels the same. It was a commitment to the Lord to keep people informed. Through summers and other public services in the Chapel, every mid-week evening and on Sundays, he was on the platform. He usually gave a facet of the vision of MBC, AND a testimony of some particular blessing, or people saved that day. The concern was to communicate what God was doing. As with Jack Wytzen, such "announcements" elicited both appreciation and some jibes of humour. In reality, no other exercise resulted in a stronger impact for praise, prayer and support.

SOME OF OUR FAVOURITE MUSICIANS

"let us sing unto the LORD; let us make a joyful noise to the rock of our salvation" Ps. 95:1

Music can be one of life's greatest expressions of the range of emotions in the Christian life. We are exhorted to *"exalt His name TOGETHER"*. What a thrill to sit under the inspiring music of gifted singers and instrumentalists! What a preparation by the Holy Spirit when hearts are spiritually focused and ready for the preaching of the Word!

> Des Bell, Frank Boggs, Crowning Brass, Vicki Dueck, Michael Faircloth, Don Holliday and George Shuttleworth, Kurt Kaiser, Lloyd Knight, Burt Kettinger, Liberty Singers, Mathews Bros., Miles and Webb, John Moore, Bob Nagel, Parshauer Sisters, Bill Pearce, Jim Reese, Springers/Jordans of HCJB, Lenny Seidel, Diane Susek, George Beverly Shea, Jack and Sarah Warren, Johnny Rae Watson, Tim Zimmerman Family Groups – Black/Birnies, Greiners, Phil Collins, Elliotsons, Greiners, Kreigers

MBC PUBLICATIONS

Through the 1970's and 1980's music and printed materials were featured for those who wanted take a little bit of MBC with them.

"MBC Echoes" (1973) a 78 rpm record featuring favourite Conference artists . . . Jim Reese, Conquerors Baptist Bible College Quartette, Tenor- Lloyd Knight, the Ken Baer family, Vicki Dueck, Dixie Dean, the MBC Trio (Grace Bowman, Sandra Kernohan, Phyllis Stewart), Violin by Nelda Holliday, Don Howard/Bruce Scott and Soloist-Desmond Bell.

"What's Cookin' at the Manse", a 66 page cook book with favourite recipes. This was a project of the 1975 Pastor's Wives Committee of MBC. . . . *"a Bible vacation center featuring the finest in dining plus the nourishment of the Word of God".*

"My Favourite Recipes", another cook book. The recipes were gathered by *The Happy Wanderers*. The retreat began as a quiet week-end, for two ladies, who wanted to escape to a peaceful MBC . Instead, it resulted in a bus load. Within three years, it was a large winter retreat, with extensive creative planning and always a financial project to provide some outfitting for Camp Widjiitiwin. They even prepared in advance by crafting unusual quilts for décor and cosy beds.

Many booklets and other publications were helpful tools for Christian families:

"57 Reasons Why I Believe The Bible Is the Word of God" authored and widely circulated by Dr. Fred John Meldau. He was one of seven rebel teens, including DeLoss Scott, who was saved under the faithful preaching of Pastor A.J. Loveday. He attended MBC in its early years. This copyright was passed on to us.

Tracts and booklets by such titles as, *"The End of the Journey"* by J.F. Holliday, *"The Breath of God, (Lines About Christmas)"* by Paul T. Holliday

Words and Music, *"It is I", the Master Calleth,* by Paul Holliday and Sandra Kernohan.

LABOURERS TOGETHER

In 1975 a letter was sent to **Howard and Alice Wadge** of Timmins. It was a request that they would sell their business and their house and come to help us at MBC. They were members of First Baptist Church in Timmins and owners of Kenogamissi Lodge. The Lodge was located 30 miles into the forest and the last 5 miles by boat. Howard was a resourceful, outdoors person with a master's touch in gardening and mechanical skills. They operated the hunting and fishing lodge as a family, attracting guests from many parts of the USA and Canada. Alice was a professional bookkeeper and secretary, working in a real estate office each winter.

The letter of request was prompted by the need of someone to develop the gardens and landscaping of the conference and assist in the daily run for produce selection and Huntsville business. For Alice, it was our need of office and bookkeeping skills. In the spring of 1976 they came ! With some assistance they pulled two little cabins together and developed their own residence in the trees between the Conference and the Trailer Park. Additions added comfort and space in the late 1970's. They served sacrificially and faithfully for more than twenty-five years.

The attractive pond and fountain system which graces the entrance to the conference property was developed and maintained as a gift. Howard provided, planted and maintained such gardens as the front of the Lodge and Chapel. He even had a secret vegetable garden!

In the summer of 1976, **Don and Linda Lively** came from Bethel Baptist Church in Simcoe, to share the on-site business duties Assistant to the Director. Linda was dining room hostess and assisted in the office. They had been in our church in Timmins, Linda being the oldest daughter of Howard and Alice Wadge. They gave invaluable service for four years. They fitted in wherever there was a need. Their children, Bruce and Kerri, were close to the Holliday children in age. They had chores in the Ranch and grew in service routines.

Through the 1970's when Ron Hartwick was our Treasurer and chief financial counselor, his wife **Vi Hartwick** was very helpful to the practical function of our accounting system. Off grounds, she maintained the bookkeeping routines, including the payment of all accounts. It was not until Alice Wadge was established in the office, that Vi was able to transfer these operations to the Conference.

Late in 1979 Don Lively accepted a call to Bethel Baptist, Strathroy. As 1979 drew to a close, **Dave and Joyce Findlay** came to fulfill the same type of responsibilities. Their background with HCJB missions proved most helpful. Staff administration and the nursing skills of Joyce maintained smooth oversight in the rapidly growing retreat seasons and large summer attendance. Along with their son Peter and daughter Patti, they were wonderful co-workers.

After four years (1983), Dave Findlay was asked to oversee a property transition time for the Fellowship Baptist Office. Jack and Shirley Janes came at the end of 1983, overlapping Dave and Joyce Findlay by three months. God provided the exceptional skill and dedication of this well-experienced couple and their daughter, Janice. Jack was a great help to Len Aylett and the Conference office through the period of required mechanical upgrades. Those improvements involved the water supply, the sewage pumping system and the building of 7 acres of lagoons. Just as prior staff leaders had done, Shirley and Janice Janes worked capably in the dining room, the office, the bookroom or Hub . . . where-ever the need was greatest.

Earl Heron and his family have carried a full load of responsibilities through the full stretch of conference growth. He was a valued part of the Development and Planning Committee in the 1960's, on the Camp Widjiitiwin Committee and on the Board of Directors. He has been an encouragement, counselor and helper in many major projects . . . always soft spoken, but knowledgeable and hard working. One of our summer staff couples even stored their household goods in his Dad's barn!!! That was a little beyond the call of duty!! Earl was the best of Christian character in heavy duty work boots.

VALIANT 'PEOPLE' WENT WITH HIM, WHOSE HEARTS GOD HAD TOUCHED ~ I Sam.10:26

Through the 70's and 80's God gave us a great company of experienced full-time staff and volunteers. It is not possible to recount the full story or to describe the value of services rendered.   These indeed were valiant people, sensitive to the will of God, serving for Heaven's reward. Some carried very large responsibilities. This listing is just a sample and should include pages of those already mentioned elsewhere, and others also, whose hearts God touched to share the responsibilities of a great work.

Elsie Andrews, Ruth Barnett, Lyle and Ruth Ann Beckett, Charlotte Buder, Jim and Flo Bushby, Paul Collins, Bruce and Margaret Davidson, Rhoda Gilmour, Harold and Rowena Hamilton, Dave and Barb Hartwick, Ted and Corrine Hiltz, Scott Hisey, Bob and Madeleine Hood, Andy and Olive Hutchinson, Bruce Lothian, Miles and Wilma McBrearty, Shirley Morrison, Fred Moulton, Susan Myers, Edmund and Sadie Ovens, John and Helen Patterson, Harry and Joy Percy, Murray and Mary Pipe, Rev. Wm. Piper, Elmer and Marie Potz, Gerry Quickfall, Howard, Don and Charles Ratcliff and their families, Joan Saunders, Doris Schweitzer, Gord and Marilyn Stephenson, Doris Switzer, Dave and Edna Stephenson, Sandra (Hiltz) Strongman, the Stirlings, Larry and Marg Taylor, Murray and Blanche Taylor, Don and Edith Thompson, the Warrens, the Wattersons, Mrs. Phyllis White, Maisie Wyse . . . indeed all our staff, trailer park, MBC Acres and other area residents.

A "MEMORIAL CHAPEL" INDEED !

The chapel constructed in 1961 had been designated "Memorial Chapel" in honour of many who had a vision and sacrificial share in the work of MBC. This spirit of gratitude was applied to the new building. **THE GRAND PIANO** had been donated by the Ladies' and Pastors' Wives Conferences of 1974. It was given in memory of Nan Loveday, the beloved wife of Rev. Donald A. Loveday. She was a member of Fairbank Baptist Church when she first attended Muskoka Baptist Camp. Her husband was one of the earliest handymen and later a Pastor who preached many summers at the Camp. He served as a Board Member and frequently as chairman.

A new **ORGAN** was dedicated in memory of <u>Mrs. Charlie (Iva) Ratcliff</u> and <u>Mr. Keith Ross.</u>   Iva loved the Lord, thrilled to the great hymns and was an earnest witness to friends and strangers. Keith Ross was the husband of Marg Ross (a sister of Ness Aylett). Keith also loved the hymns and was a strong witness as a Civic Councilor in the city of Oshawa. Both families had a deep love for MBC. as evidenced by the involvement of succeeding generations. The instrument was chosen for quality tone, versatility, and easy maintenance. It would not be affected by humidity changes.

God gave us the dedicated service of many **talented musicians**. The typical brief instrumental prelude before Sunday and evening services soon lengthened. People enjoyed twenty minutes to half an hour of favourite hymns. These were often requested by the crowd which gathered early. The musicians who shared in this ministry did so as volunteers through each summer. They were always full of joy and responsive to both the congregation and the speakers of the week. The most frequent pair was <u>Marg Taylor</u> of Calvary, Oshawa and <u>Ken Baer</u> of Willowdale Baptist, Toronto. Other favourites included <u>Bill McGilvray</u>, Springvale, <u>Carol Millar</u> of Willowdale, <u>Dorothy Davis</u> of Benton, Kitchener, <u>Marlene Taylor</u> of Windsor, Ivy Waite, Marg Beney and Paul Kerr.

The gift of permanent **Chapel seating** was partially funded from the Memorial Service of <u>Rev. Dr. Paul T. Holliday</u>, President of Central Baptist Seminary. He died on September 7, 1979 at the age of 49. The balance of the seating installation included memorial gifts from other friends. Paul loved MBC and had served in many capacities, including summer director and preacher. The Chapel seating was designed so that attendees would move in from the aisle and have cushioned comfort and good back support. This was very welcome after years of wooden benches and chairs. Paul was a scholar in literature and Bible languages, a great communicator. He had many published works in blank verse and poetry. His thesis was in poetic format, the first such ever received by the University of Toronto. It was an exegesis of Amos . . . *The Herdsman of Tekoa.*

O WORSHIP THE LORD IN THE BEAUTY OF HOLINESS.

This Scripture admonition was prepared to occupy the centre of the platform, near the ceiling. In **1980**, two side panels of velvet draperies were added. This gave a touch of warmth. On the side walls **Rev. Earl Clemens** designed two murals. These depicted parables of our Lord. The one who *hears the Word and the one who sows the seed. The good ground is he that heareth the Word (Matt. 13:23)* and the other mural . . . *We shall reap if we faint not (Galatians 6:9)*

The **CHAPEL BELL** located by the walkway, near the entrance was placed there in memory of **Larry Waun.** He was a teenager under the ministry of Pastor Roy Lawson. "Larry became a Christian when he was nine years old. At twelve he was obedient to His Lord in believer's baptism and became an active member of Bethel Baptist in Strathroy. He served faithfully in the Baptist Youth Fellowship of his church. He went to be with Christ on March 30, 1960".

THE HUB AND BOOKROOM

This building adjoining the Chapel became a wonderful place for fellowship. It had a most commanding, panoramic view of Mary Lake. It has been a continuous magnet for gatherings for mornings studies, times of prayer, afternoon inspiration for laymen, ladies, pastors, and young people. It has been our second most important center for meal service. It is common to see people sitting around the fireside enjoying the sense of warmth and relaxation. When the young people came to the pastor of Fairbank Baptist Church, requesting "a Baptist Camp for youth", one of the young men in the church at that time was Mr. Jim Ross Sr. In his memory, the family provided the lovely bronze fireplace. The room was carefully decorated under the hand of Rev. Earl Clemens. Artifacts, up to 200 years in age, were collected from many parts of Canada, USA and foreign mission fields. They were mounted on walls and plate rails surrounding the room.

With the building of the Memorial Chapel, a small bookroom was moved from the Lodge to occupy a more adequate area adjacent to the Hub. The availability of helpful Christian literature and the books and music of ministry personnel have made it the hub of interest and service.

HONEY FROM MISSIONARY BEES

Would you to sell honey to support the Christians in Columbia? The words of missionary Don Whiteside. With Rachel and his children, they had established a new business to help the nationals who had lost their jobs because of their faith. Don had helped many to develop hives and learn the skills of producing a wonderful product. The little creatures involved produced "morning glory honey". Don had been a friend during Seminary days and had shared his personal testimony of God's grace and power in each of the churches which I had pastored. How could I say "No" to my friend and his new Columbia believers? "HOW MUCH HONEY?" The missionary response . . . "Oh, just a barrel or two". When the barrels came off the ship at Montreal Harbor, several months had passed. Clearing customs and delivery involved another month. **19 barrels, each weighing approximately 1000 pounds,** arrived at MBC.

How do you sell 9 ½ tons of Morning Glory Honey? First, Mrs. Elsie Andrews had to bottle it - - - carefully, hygienically, and with labels according to government standard . One little problem was that the time in transit had caused the content of the barrels to solidify. Mrs. Andrews needed the help of staff men to warm the barrels over an outside fire, suspended from the forklift of a tractor. Some barrels were delivered directly to institutions such as residences for seniors. We even supplied a little trestle in which the respective places could set the barrel. The Managing Director promoted the availability of the honey during announcements in the dining room, in the Chapel services and around the province. . . . it seemed, for years! All that said . . . IT WAS <u>DELICIOUS</u> HONEY! At the Conference grounds, many were able to recite the little lunch time story about "Missionary Bees and the Morning Glory flowers in Columbia, S.A." Any still needing honey? Ask Missionary Don Whiteside directly !!

CAROUSEL

The ice cream parlour and ministry centre for teens was the gift of a faithful couple. It solved the after chapel line-ups in the tea room and was a most popular attraction. It proved to be very helpful to care for overflow guest and staff dining. The attractive yellow canopy was provided by Raymond Brothers Company . . .the personal gift of Jim and Bev Jepson, London.

"GOD'S FAITHFULNESS IS NOT MEA-SURED BY A YEAR OR TWO"

~ S.L. White

From the beginning days of M.B.C. there have been those who have given of their time and labours to support the ministry. It is His work and a testimony of His faithfulness in supplying His workers and His material provision for His testimony on MBC grounds. We hereby record our gratitude and praise for His abundant provision throughout the years and for His unfailing mercy and blessing upon us.

"He owns the cattle on a thousand hills, the wealth in every mine . . . ."

ESTATES DESIGNATED FOR THE CHAPEL AND MINISTRY ~ 1970 to 1990

Langstaff Baptist Church	Rev. DeLoss and Mrs. Jennie Scott
Miss Ellen Becker	Mr. Sydney L. White
Mrs. L. Bickle	Mrs. Hazel Bowie
Mr. Duncan and Dorothy Cuthell	Mrs. Dora Hallam
Mr. Elgin and Doris Mullin	Mrs. Irma Harding

MEMORIAL GIFTS ~ THE CHAPEL AND MINISTRY

Mr. Arthur R. and Mary Alloway
Mr. Richard Alexander
Mr. Frank Andrews
Mr. and Mrs. N.G. Baer
Miss Constance Baldwin
Rev. George Bell Sr.
Mr. Thomas Broadhurst
Mr. Fred Butler
Mrs. Maureen Clemens
Mrs. Lillian Coffin
Mrs. Violet Cripps
Mr. and Mrs. Adam Davidson
Mr. Charles Hare
Mr. Gordon Eagleson
Mr. Elmer Filsinger
Mrs. Reta Gillmore
Mr. Kenneth Gould
Mr. Arnold Hamilton
Mr. "Mac" Harris
Mr. Cyril and Betty Hemmings
Mr. Angus Hills
Mrs. Luella Holliday
Dr. Paul T. Holliday
Mr. and Mrs. Hood Sr.
Mrs. Mabel Irvin
Mr. Don Jackman
Mr. James Jepson
Rev. and Mrs. Len Jones
Mr. J.A. Keith
Mr. August and Bella Kemper
Ms. Willie Kirkconnell
Mr. Ralph and Minnie Knight
Rev. and Mrs. Roy F. Lawson
Mr. James Lind
Mr. L. Lively
Mrs. Nan Loveday
Mr. Russell Lunney
Mr. Jack Macdonald
Rev. and Mrs. Victor McCleary
Mr. "Pappy" Meyers
Ms. Mary Miller

Rev. James Nichol Millar
Mr. and Mrs. Harold Mitchell
Mr. Harold Neal
Mrs. Helen M. Newman
Mr. Ralph and Minnie Knight
Mr. George Nix
Mrs. Sadie Ovens
Mr. Ewart Page
Mr. C.F. Parker
Mr. Robert Patterson
Mr. and Mrs. G.S. Peters
Mr. and Mrs. C.T. Raham
Mr. J.A. Rayburn
Grant Reynolds
Rev. and Mrs. Norman Rowan
Mr. James B. Rhodes
Rev. DeLoss and Jennie Scott
Dr. Jack Scott
Mr. and Mrs. George Simpson
Mr. George Sinclair
Mrs. Onah Sinclair
Mrs. Claire Smith
Mrs. Barbara Smith
Mr. Edwin Smith
Rev. and Mrs. Harold Stainton
Mr. Hubert Stanley
Mr. David Stevenson
Mrs. Carolyn Taylor
Mr. Chris Taylor
Mr. Don Thompson
Mr. John ten Pas
Miss Grace Tims
Mr. Bruce Vance
Mr. Nickle (Nick) Waite
Mr. J.W. Waite
Larry Waun (17)
Rev. Thomas and Phyllis White
Mr. and Mrs. Wylie
Miss Maizie Wyse
Pastor and Mrs. Whitelaw Sr.

THE SAMARITAN FUND Without promotion, there were sensitive hearts which expressed interest in funding time at MBC for needy people. As the fund grew, we endeavoured to utilize just the interest. The Lorene Bickle Estate provided $10,000. to establish a fund for use by Camp Widjiitiwin. It was used to sponsor 10 needy campers every year. Another foundation gift was used to bring a large number of children from the Six Nation Reserve near Brantford. Pastor Melchie Henry co-ordinated the boys and girls and the transportation to complete the arrangements. What a testimony to their neighbours.

MUSKOKA BAPTIST CONFERENCE INCORPORATED

Year	Income	Capital Donations
1968	50,515	
1969	55,885	
1970	57,465	
1971	73,620	
1972	133,524	
1973	251,366	
1974	258,876	
1975	318,396	
1976	438,038	
1977	428,162	135,538
1978	539,524	301,428
1979	613,478	178,593
1980	684,174	199,222
1981	809,700	200,722
1982	893,966	164,543
1983	1,032,864	179,382
1984	1,141,430	189,547
1985	1,191,221	343,333
1986	1,259,244	389,171
1987	1,415,891	397,967
1988	1,538,947	412,351
1989	1,730,368	224,578
1990	1,871,649	146,063

Capital Donations from 1977-1990 = 3,492,438

(this includes $30,000 from Lautenschlager Estate)

Chapter 19

1978 ~ THREE GREAT STRIDES

#1 Camp Widjiitiwin ... new property

We have watched as Camp Widjiitiwin opened on its new, enlarged site. The number of summer camper weeks grew from 712 to 1265. It gave space and safety for all manner of sports. Much of the work of grounds preparation and the construction of buildings involved a high percentage of volunteer labour.

#2 The 1978 Chapel complex.

We rejoiced in the Dedication of the new Chapel with its overflow capability. Everyone loved the cosy Tea Room and Book Room. What an easing of space from the crowded programming during the past five years. The Lodge was the multi-purpose cold weather Chapel, Bookroom, Hub, and indoor activity center. People commented on a sense of reverence and attentiveness to the music and preaching felt in the new building. The original cedar pulpit seemed to fit as a central feature on the platform.

#3 The MBC Inn.

The Muskoka Lodge was a popular, secular resort from the days before World War I. It was owned by Sam Ginsberg and his two brothers. Sam was interested in the growth of MBC and on occasion visited. His property covered well over 600 acres. It included a large Lodge building, motel, boathouse, barn and two houses along the Pt. Sydney Road. There was considerable frontage on Mary Lake and a land-locked lake a quarter mile across country from the central Lodge building. After much consultation and research, Charlie and Iva Ratcliff personally arranged the purchase of the land and buildings and signed them over as a gift to MBC. The property is located just 2 miles distant. (by road or boat). In the time period from August to December 1978 **"The MBC Inn"** became a reality. Two of the small parcels of land were sold, soon after.

On Thanksgiving Sunday several hundred gathered for an afternoon dedication service involving the founders, Frank Holliday and Syd White. The board of directors was present and participated. President Bill Wilkie accepted the keys of entry. MBC's assets increased more in 1978 than in the previous five years combined.

The first steps toward the practical use of the MBC Inn included a complete rebuilding of the 12 room motel. The structure was gutted and refurbished. It was fully winterized, including instant hot water supply, new carpets and furnishings. This proved to be a great help in caring for our main conference guest overflow. We could use it throughout the year. Two professional quality tennis courts were constructed, including the high fencing. All costs for reconstruction and improvement of the property were cared for by the donors.

1982 the **MBC Inn** 12 room motel was ready for use. According to the Annual Report of 1986, use of this accommodation generated an income of $100,000. every year. Though at a two mile distance from the main conference, it was quiet and boasted its own beach and tennis courts.

MBC ISLAND It is one acre of land surrounded by Mary Lake, just two miles straight west from MBC's beach. The name registered is "Lawrence Island". This was purchased and given to MBC by Charles and Iva Ratcliff. Camp Widjiitiwn uses it for an overnight, wilderness, camp-out experience. Intermediate and Senior Campers enjoy the excellent sloping shoreline which helps their lessons in scuba diving.

Two years later, **Board President, Don Reynolds**, wisely observed . . . *"our constituency should be aware that accommodations in the senior conference only number 32 winterized units. There is a continual strain to fit in those who want to come. The winterized rooms are really those which cover the major operating costs. The comparative low number of rooms limits those who would otherwise see and feel challenged to support the ministry of the conference. Your directors have set themselves to the only realistic solution . . broaden our accommodation base for registered guests by increasing the number of rooms. This will have a dramatic affect upon both operational efficiency and debt retirement".*

LAKEVIEW VILLA The need for increased winterized accommodation led to the planning of Lakeview Villa. It was decided that we should add a new building attached to Lakeview Motel. By a contract with Ratcliff Lumber, construction began at the end of **1982**. Facilities included twelve large family rooms, two outfitted for handicapped people. Mrs. Chris Allemang counseled about use by the handicapped

The lower level included 4 guest suites and a large meeting room. This was complemented by the antique décor by Rev. Earl Clemens. The outfitting consisted of a piano, organ, lovely new chairs, pulpit and shelving. It was funded in memory of <u>Jim Lind</u> of London. Personalized gifts were given by other friends for the accommodation rooms. They are <u>in memory of</u> Dr. Jack Scott, Mrs. Luella Holliday, Mrs. Violet Cripps, Mr. Arnold Hamilton, Mr. August and Bella Kemper, Mr. Edwin Smith, Mrs. Barbara Smith, Mr. J.W. Waite, Mr. Chris Taylor, Mr. L. Lively, Mary Miller and Willie Kirkonnell. The Dedication for the Lakeview Villa was in June of **1983.**

M   THE LAKEVIEW MANOR A beautiful, new, 12 room motel was constructed, furnished and landscaped as a gift, by the Jim Ross family. It was ready for use in **1986.** The sacrificial investment was prompted by a deep concern that MBC should have <u>enough accommodations to pay its operating costs</u> and retire all debt. The carpet laying was the gift of another friend of MBC. Ceiling fans were donated and installed to eliminate dampness and distribute the room temperature.

M   TREE TOPS DORM Another work bee! We needed a year round staff house for girls. Under the leadership of contractor Jack Serez (Willowdale Baptist, Toronto) and Pastor Ted Baker (Central Baptist, Brantford), 40 strong volunteers gathered to do the almost impossible. The 3500 square foot dormitory included a dorm parent's suite and a large lounge suitable for devotionals and relaxation. The labour and all materials were donated. After the major construction Ted Baker, Jim Sinclair and Carl Brandon added the trim and all finished carpentry. Dan and JoAnn Kerr, the 1988 Dorm parents, looked after the inside painting and homey atmosphere.

SUMMER SPEAKERS 1984 to 1987

Dr. W.E. Anderson, FL	Dr. Hal MacBain
Dr. Manley Beasley	Dr. John Moore, Evangelistic Crusades
Dr. Ron Blue, Dallas Theol. Seminary	Dr. Stephen Olford
Dr. Bruce Dunn, Peoria, IL	Dr. Oswald Sanders, O.M.F.
Dr. G.E. Gardner, Grand Rapids, MI	Dr. J.M. Stowell III, Detroit, MI
Dr. Jesse Hendley, Evangelist	Dr. Lehman Strauss, CA
Dr. Terry Hulbert, Columbia B. College	Dr. Howard F. Sugden, Lansing, MI
Dr. D. Jennings, Tacoma, WA	Dr. E. Towns, Liberty Baptist College
Dr. David Jeremiah, CA	Dr. C.E. Weinhauer, Vancouver,B.C.
Dr. R.W. Lawson	Dr. Warren Wiersbe, Lincoln, NE
Dr. Vernon McGee, CA	Dr. John White, Grand Rapids, MI

MINISTRIES TO CHILDREN AND YOUTH

"Suffer the little children to come unto me". Camp Widjiitiwin was "up and running", but a wonderful new door of opportunity was opening. Ministry to the children of conference guests, trailer park families and an expanding cottage community. Fellowship Centre was the meeting place for boys and girls.

From the beginning of M.B.C. there was a strong focus on the younger generation. In the early decades of ministry on Mary Lake, Harry and Penelope Taylor were great encouragers of the founders. When Frank Holliday was Pastor of Charlton Avenue Baptist Church in Hamilton they used time and finances to help strengthen the ministry. At M.B.C. Penelope Taylor used her Bible story visual aids to impress upon young hearts the basic truths of the Word of God. She was involved in conference interests until her home going in the early 1970's. She was an avid exercise and health foods fan. . . founder of Canadian Health Aids. A morning swim and collecting boulders for the waterfront were regular enjoyments. Her full woolen bathing suit must have kept her warm on cold swim days during the spring and fall. She came to this writer one day, very apologetic. During the winter, moths had eaten some holes in the posterior of her swim attire. She had not noticed it until after her swim !!! It was difficult to keep a straight face while assuring her that all who knew her were well aware of her standards of decorum.

She was a regular attender at summer Morning Watch. It did cause her concern that people who gathered for prayer, would inflict damage to the body by drinking the offered cup of coffee.

Her properties, adjacent to M.B.C., were willed to the conference. Subsequently they were purchased by Christian families associated with M.B.C. The proceeds became helpful support for ongoing projects. Their Hamilton home was given to Foreign Missions by the suggestion of this MBC Director and Dr. Hal McBain (FEBC Missions Chairman).

Children's programming during chapel times has had the love and expertise of many great helpers. We remember the first of the 1970's when Shirley Morrison and her daughter Cheryl, as well as Joan Lawson, assisted by sons Dan and David, led the boys and girls in singing, competitions and Bible stories. It is difficult to remember the sequence of time and the names when so many served. **Many of our cottagers and trailer park families helped in this way**. Some of our chosen summer staff were designated to work with the children in the evenings,

From 1972 to 1982 **Margaret Davidson**, assisted by her daughter **Lois (Earl)** headed up the Monday to Friday morning program for 6 to 12 year olds. In very creative ways they used a current VBS theme and the Bible stories came alive to the boys and girls. For five years, 1979-1984 on Wednesday nights they used the theme that Dr. Frank Holliday had chosen for the summer. *One year, we were sailors and all the Bible stories had to do with the sea, then cowboys, or princes and princesses in God's kingdom.* Dr. Holliday Sr. was known as *Captain John, Cowboy John* and used appropriate hats to tie in with the theme. Sandi Kernohan, Lori and Lynnie helped with these children's programs. Sandi also wrote theme songs and taught the Bible stories.

Gladys Harrison, assisted by Steve and Jackie conducted programs for 3-5 year olds in Millar Hall. What was first accommodated in Fellowship Centre grew to a second age group located in Millar Hall. Others who made the Bible stories come alive included Children's Evangelist, Dr. Frank Wellington and missionaries Rev. Harry Percy and Judy Wadge.

Those working with children from 1978 to 1987 were Marilyn Alton, Gladys Harrison, Margaret Davidson, Jack and June Cox, Mrs. Ken Derksen and Wally Rourke (our M.B.C. favourite magician). In 1984 there were more than 60 professions of faith in Christ. In 1986, Miss Lorraine Dick and Miss Heather Ross had a staff of more than 20 for age-graded ministry programs. 1987 Mrs. Joy Percy cared for 2,849 babies, bringing her total to 9,478 since 1982 ! Daily morning and evening ministry in all our children's departments pointed more than 70 children to faith in Christ in 1987.

Report for Children's Ministry

1975 – 3556 aggregate for 8 weeks.

1976 - 4500

1978 - 5000

1982 - 7668

1983 – 10,568

1984 – 12,397

1987 – 15,000 + an aggregate of 2,849 babies in the Nursery

There was a signal of concern expressed in the 1984 Annual Report. "We have accommodations, Dining Rooms, and Chapels – but no indoor areas for group recreation. We need activity facilities for mud and snow months. Founder's Hall is an urgent need . . . a large winterized building capable of use for a multi-sports program, three areas of VBS, carpeted space for sit-on-the-floor" informal ministry".

Chapter 20

CAMP WIDJIITIWIN

1969 to 1977 the Children and Teens Camp operated on the north side of the Muskoka River.   It was very satisfactory to see a camp for boys and girls on its own location with an extended season. Very capable leadership gave direction during the nine years. Tents and then "Tabins" were used for accommodation. Regularly the leaders would bring the campers across the river to have competitive ball games and other sports on the larger field available at the main conference. Sometimes they would arrive in native costume looking ready for battle !

Though the first Camp Widjiitiwin property was adequate for a small group of children and limited programming, it was a great beginning. **Vice President, Ross Thompson**, gave a committee report to the directors, October 16, 1973. It observed that the present site was <u>not suitable for the long term</u>. After investigation, it had been learned that 24.5 acre property was available below market pricing. It had been owned by Christian friends, the Truemans, and was located nearby, on the conference side of the river.

The new M.B.C. lodge building had just been completed. It was a major financial outlay. Mr. Thompson presented an option that he and others could proceed with the purchase of the property on behalf of M.B.C.   They would hold the property until M.B.C. was ready to assume the responsibility. This report was tabled for further discussion. The Youth Camp Property Committee (R.W. Thompson, R.W. Lawson, E. Heron, W. Wilkie and R.D. Holliday) met to discuss the feasibility of acquiring and developing the site, while still operating at the present 2.5 acre location. The recommendation was made to the full board at its December 13th meeting with a closing date of January 2, 1974. President W. F. Wilkie said "THANK YOU" to the legion of the Lord's special workers . . . Ross Thompson and the ten men who helped MBC buy the land in 1973".

1975 saw a "**GAP MAN**" = *God Always Provides* offering. The $10,000 objective provided the site plans and road development for the new Camp Widjiitiwn location. By the personal sacrifice and hard work of a number, all arrangements were confirmed.   The physical work of road building was the special project of "the Smith brothers" from Ennerdale and Wishing Well churches and other volunteers.

1976 the youth camp still operated on the north side of the river. There was an increase of 20% to 712 camper weeks. Drawings for the cabins were completed and the architect was working on the drawings for the main building planned for the new site.

CREATING A ROAD AND THE NEW CAMP GROUNDS

The 24.5 acres was a forest. Half way down a steep hill there was a deep gully and flowing stream. It needed to be transformed into a sports field. The Smith Brothers (Albert, Syd and Ed), Charlie Ratcliff and other volunteers had created a road. They cut the trees from the main conference property to the new Widjiitiwin site. **The Bickle brothers** from Cobourg arrived with an immense mobile rig with huge wheels. They also had their flatbed transporter and a large dump truck. Their first task was to cut down all trees where the playing field and lodge would be developed. They also needed to clear the site for each of the 22 camper cabins and washrooms. Having felled the trees, branches were cut off and the trunks sawed into long lengths. The big machine scooped the logs into transportable "belly loads" and put them on the transporter. The same machine excavated each stump and loaded it onto the dump truck. We are still waiting for an invoice !!! What an unseen, but essential task from these unusual servants.

Al Stephenson and his brothers arrived with a bulldozer and backhoe. They worked for weeks to level ground and dig where neces- sary to develop the whole site and waterfront for use in programming. It has become a breathtaking experience to drive the new road and view the property.

A deep gully and flowing stream was transformed into a great sports field in 1983. Gifts and forty volunteer workmen created a beautiful assembly area, welcoming the arriving guests and campers.

1977 camp was operated for the last time on the old site. This property had been sold for $40,000. Under the direction of **Gord Stephenson** the new camp was taking shape. The first cabin was ready at the new site. Materials were supplied by Brian Langtree of Century Mill, Bala and construction by Contractor, Lyle Habermehl. The dedication of the new Widjiitiwin property took place on Labour Day week-end . During the Fall and Winter of 1977/1978 Ron and Graham Sommers, and Bill Crane of Emmanuel Baptist Church in Barrie, constructed 18 of the 22 buildings. Hydro lines were installed and a new well drilled. Extensive work was done by Stephenson Construction on site development and a new marina for camper use in 1978.

Widjiitiwin's first site was across the river from the Conference. Its size, buildings and waterfront were not ideal but God set His seal of blessing upon those 9 years. We thanked the Lord that the youth camp grew from 200 to 700 in three years and had maintained that 700 for the next three years.

1978 was the first year for campers on the new property. A large tent was erected for the Chapel and Dining room. A temporary wooden building was created as a kitchen. These were indeed pioneer years with people of vision and perseverance.

M   **George Hayes** was a dedicated and faithful chairman of Camp Widjiitiwin from 1975 through 1990 and beyond. Retirement as a Toronto Board of Education Supervisor was ideal preparation for the needed leadership. He was present to lead every Camp Committee meeting. He was present on "Welcome" Days when children and parents arrived at Camp. He was a strong presence in all the changes through the transition years, moving from across the river to their permanent location. He was a man of detail and personal attention. George and Nancy were blessed by children who loved the Lord. **Nancy** was part of the Willowdale musical team which ministered at the conference in the 1970's. She was always a helper and encourager.

June 1978 George reported with joy about that first year:

Prayer and divine intervention resulted in a miracle opening of Camp Widjiitiwin. Three weeks before camp was to open there was a "freeze" caused by technical and complex details. Would we be able to open? There was much prayer by many across Canada. Three days before campers were due to arrive, permission was granted. This was the signal for a host of volunteers to descend on the site. Eighteen days of work were completed in three days and nights. What an excellent demonstration of the power of prayer and the effectiveness of Christians working together. Registrations almost doubled. Ministry and programming efficiency greatly improved on the new grounds. The spiritual impact seemed much greater. One in 5 campers professed faith in Christ.

Camp Widjiitiwin Committee Members instrumental in the years of planning: D. Alexander, Rev. A. Ballantyne, L. Gilbert, C. Hines, A. MacGregor, D. Marritt, Rev. H. Stainton, G. Stephenson, M. Thorlakson, D. Towe, Ruth Troup, K. Trudgian, Rev. D. Whitelaw. The persistence and vision of <u>Chairman, George Hayes</u> kept the objectives in focus. Gordon Stephenson, P.Eng. gave many weeks of man hours as our Supervisor of all development and construction.

Volunteers from more than 50 churches helped in building, painting, wiring, plumbing, logging, road building, brushing, digging, sewing, cleaning, etc. Some churches in particular were Emmanuel, Barrie, Harrow, Mt. Forest, Central Brantford, Benton, Kitchener, Willowdale, and Ajax.

The summer camp ministry was closely knit with the senior conference program. Co-ordination for joint use of land facilities, horses, waterskiing, sailing and equipment was a key to efficiency. Purchasing, registration and office routine were all cared for by conference personnel to free the hands of Widjiitiwin staff. The **Institute of Christian Camping** conducted its second year at Widjiitiwin. This involved college level instruction by 12 camping experts. Graduation credit was given by two seminaries and two colleges. Those completing the course served at Widjiitiwin, two other Ontario Conferences and several local churches.

The **1980/1981** ministry team at Widjiitiwin (incl. - *Institute for Christian Camping)*

Dr. Frank Wellington, Rev. Wm. Curry, Rev. Don Ballantyne, Rev. A. Forbes, Pastor Bob Peckham, Rev. Paul Fawcett, Pastor S. Hamburger, Dr. J.F. Holliday, Pastor Ian Wells, Dr. R.W. Lawson, Rev. G. Wishart, Rev. Wm. Bauman, Mr. David Alexander, Mr. D.R. Findlay, Rev. R.D. Holliday, Rev. L. Baptist, Rev. H. Percy, Rev. R.D. Holmes, Mr. Sid Daniels, Mrs. Mary Fligg, R.N., Mark and Nancy Haines, Linda Schultz, Mr. Joey Allen, Pastor Malcolm Cameron.

1981 Ladies' Conference gave a gift which made possible a new 3-sided swimming pool. The sodding of the hillside which overlooks the river swim and boating area river, was provided by a faithful couple. July and August were divided into 4 two week sessions for ages 8 to 14 and one Youth Week for ages 14 to 19. These 1115 "camper weeks" proved a tremendous opportunity for Christian influence and witness. Many campers came from needy homes and were **sponsored** by individual Christians and a few by churches. For the second year a week was operated which included **deaf children**. Some of these trusted Christ as Saviour. 25 young people and staff members came for 2 weeks from the **Ray of Hope Mission**. In addition to receiving ministry and enjoying recreation, they worked for 4 to 6 hours each day. The projects included brush clearing, grounds improvements and construction of a large and valuable barn and stable for the Widjiitiwin and Conference horseback riding.

Mrs. Lorraine MacGregor, from Emmanuel Church, Barrie, was Camp Director at Widjiitiwin from 1976 to 1984. She was an outgoing, loving person very much interested in boys and girls. Her husband **Andy** served on the Youth Camp Committee. They "weathered" the transition from the limited camp property on the north side to the occupying of the new grounds.

What excitement in 1984 when they opened the "Longhouse". The leaky tents and cooking shed were exchanged for a proper kitchen, dining room, chapel and activity area. The Youth Camp was growing and the program demanding. In 1982 Rev. Keith Wiggin became Camp Administrator. He was on the property from June 1 to November supervising many projects. An excellent operational manual was prepared, outlining staff and counselor job descriptions.

Welcome to West Park Baptist Church, London. 140 children arrived in two large buses and a number of cars. Pastor Paul Fawcett and church leaders packed a great program of Bible Study and sports into the two busy weeks. It was a great example and testimony.

Jarvis Street Baptist Church under Rev. Norman Street and Rev. Rudy Wiebe hosted two great weeks for children and young people. Their Camp Saugeen was temporarily suspended to comply with new waterfront requirements. Involving our full staff team, they utilized every space and God gave a rewarding ministry response.

1984 was a landmark year for Camp Widjiitiwin. The LONG-HOUSE was completed ! *We now have a permanent building for food-service and meetings. We thank God for His goodness and we thank His people for their generous support.*

*Mr. **Gordon Stephenson, P. Eng.**, one of our committee members, devoted an enormous amount of time preparing the detailed drawings, and helping with the supervision. **Andy MacGregor**, **Dave Alexander** and MBC's Managing Director provided advice and assistance in specific areas. An engineering team of **Gordon Stephenson, Edmund Yao of Colonial Homes, Brian Langtree of Century Mill and Larry French of Bert French and Sons, contractors,** provided technical and professional information and advice. We are grateful for the support of the MBC Board of Directors. Nothing would have materialized if the Lord's people, had not responded so generously.*

The Lodge provides comfortable accommodation for meals and meetings. There is space for indoor activities on cold, rainy days. **The fireplace** was provided in **memory of Ralph and Minnie Knight**. The campers seem to have an appreciation and a pride in the new building. This is demonstrated by their deportment, care of the facility and even their attention during services. <u>This has resulted in an improved quality of ministy.</u>

M The 1984 whirlwind construction of Widjiitiwin's central building took place in May. The shell was erected in one week by 40 men under the supervision of Mr. Jack Serez of Willowdale Baptist church. The rest of the construction was completed in 7 weeks. About 100 volunteers. from many churches made this possible. Some gave direction and used trade skills . . . men such as Fred Moulton, Bracebridge, and Graham Sommers, Phil Lamb and Carl Brandon from Emmanuel Barrie.

Chairman George Hayes reported - *Lorraine MacGregor resigned as Camp Director after 9 complete summers of leadership. She will be greatly missed. We look for someone who has the same qualities – a love for children and staff, spiritual concern, discipline in programming and sacrificial giving of self and family.* Lorraine continued as Consultant and sometimes, onsite encourager.

The "**Mail Box Club**" was introduced and supervised by Rev. Harry Percy. Campers were encouraged to enroll in this correspondence Bible study course. During the summer season the **film "Widjiitiwin Days"** was produced to show the camp's activities and ministry. It was used extensively by various church groups and Bible colleges. A **Legacy** of $10,000. was received and used to **sponsor 10 needy campers** every year.

1985 to 1990 were blessed by the capable leadership of Susan Myers, Wayne Welch, Don Ballantyne, Harry Percy, Rudy Wiebe, Skip Metzler and others. Each Camp period had a ministering camp Pastor. During these years former camp director Lorraine MacGregor and her husband Andy, continued as a valued Consultants.

In **1987 and 1988,** Paul and Sue Whittingstall came as summer Directors. Paul was a former camper and 6 year staff member of Camp Widjiitiwin. He returned with experience having served as Director of Camp Quanoes in B.C. There was growth to a total enrollment of 1001 camper weeks. Widjiitiwin hosted Fall Retreats for several churches. There were 76 professions of salvation. 2 great youth weeks were the best ever attended. 18 campers attained their "Royal Life-Saving Certification" and all others upgraded their levels. Widjiitiwin Reunion the following February, was the largest on record with about 180 campers, counselors and committee members. In the two years 1987 to 1988, 150 children and young people made a profession of faith in Christ.

1987 Widjiitiwin Report it was said . . "*Cook Geraldine Quickfall is the best and most flexible possible.*   Gerry led the food Service at the youth camp for many years. In the summer she was at Widjiitiwin and in the main conference kitchen the rest of the year. She was greatly appreciated by the many young people who worked with her.

The **1988** Camp Widjiitiwin Committee members were George Hayes, Chairman and members Bill Beckner, Sid Daniels, Andy MacGregor, Harry Peters, Gord Stephenson, Paul Whitelaw, Jim Youngson. Also sitting with the committee were Widjiitiwin Director, Paul Whittingstall, Rudy Wiebe and General Director of MBC, Dick Holliday.

In 1989 Rev. Rudy Wiebe was Camp Administrator and Mr. Skip Metzler, Director of Ministry and Program. *The family members entered wholeheartedly into their work, providing an effective team.* There was a growth in registration to 1265 camper and training weeks.   44 professed salvation in the first five weeks of Junior Camp. *Many other children, particularly those older, dedicated or re-dedicated their lives to the Lord.* Skip Metzler indicated, 'the excitement and enthusiasm seen on the counselors' faces when they reported a profession of faith was indescribable'. *This certainly makes Camp Widjiitiwin worthwhile.*

A new Camp Video entitled **"A Flame That Burns Within The Heart"** was produced by Round Table Associates of Stouffville, ON (Lloyd Knight and Sons). This has been well received.

Smith Bros.(Albert, Syd and Ed) cuttingWidjiitiwin road

Jack Harrison, MBC photographer

Ed Smith, MBC photographer

Aerial view of MBC grounds by Bruce Holliday

Dedication of Inn property 1978
L to R R. D.& J.F. Holliday, C. Hare, B. Wilkie, J. Cox, C. Ratcliff,
C. Borrowman, A. Forbes, L. Taylor, R. Harwick, H. Ratcliff, L. Aylett

Trailer Park Residents

Lakeview Motel

Conference vans by Aiken Motors (Ron Cripps)

Syd White, Mr. Mercer, Dr. Jack Scott

Art and Nancy Fitkin

Trail Rides
L to R A. Forbes, J. Watt, W. Wilkie, D. Alexander,
H. Hindry, H. MacBain, R. Holliday

Pony rides

Provider of horse, buggy and the rides . . . Elmer Filsinger

Ranch Team K. Holliday, C. Rendle, L. Mitchell, J. Pipe

Teams & sleighs loaned free for winter rides

MacDonald's Farm – Sue Barnes

Kimberly Holliday and lamb

Trail ride with Jack & Doris Scott, Jack & June Cox & others

Winter trail rides ~ soft landings!

Sandi Kernohan and youth choir – '78
Front- Paul Davidson, Doug Lawson, Lynnie/Lori Kernohan, Jackie Harrison, Kathy
Pipe, Bruce Lively Back- Lisa Hiltz, Kerry Lively, Judy Pipe, Bruce Holliday, Sandi K.

Weekly Bible stories for children by "Captain John" Holliday

Hay rides for children and young people

Fellowship Centre VBS – Leader, Margaret Davidson

"Tree Tops" for preschoolers in Millar Hall –Leader, Gladys Harrison

Crafts

MacDonald's Farm enjoyed by toddlers

Crafts in the Honey Pot

Kindergarten children around Story Tree

Marina

Muskoka Queen

Water Ski Team ~ Brad Taylor, Dan Lawson

MBC Cruise Boat

'75 Rafting with Lynnie/Lori Kernohan,
Doug Lawson, Bruce Holliday

Cottagers baseball team vs the World

Lawn Bowling, Croquet and Putting Green

Bottling honey from Columbia, S.A. (Doug Smith/Dan Pengilly)

Gift of 70 LIVE turkeys !! Alb Smith & Howard Ratcliff, Ron Hartwick

*Doug and Doris Smith
work on "the birds"*

*MBC in Huntsville Parade. . . E.
Andrews, Don/Edith Thompson*

Calvary Oshawa Snowmobile Retreat

Hockey on the Marina

Starting cars after a sub-zero retreat

Boiling Sap – Dave Hartwick

Tapping maple trees

Howard Wadge/Howard Ratcliff boiling sap

*Don Lively/ Howard Ratcliff
make snow candy*

Howard Wadge checking the pails

*Bruce Holliday/Bruce Lively
with a catch of fish*

The champion fisherman . . . Dr. John Moore

Bob Lively, Don/Linda Lively, Roy
Lawson, Dick/Marilyn Holliday

Dave/Joyce Findlay, Dick/
Marilyn Holliday

Our great line-up of waitresses

What a staff team ! 1980's

Pastors' Conference 1961

Staff gals with Ness Aylett – early 60's

Sunday mornings 1974-1977

Packed in but rejoicing!

S.L. White and J.F. Holliday
50th anniversary of MBC

Frank Holliday with Roy
Lawson &Dick Holliday

Syd White/ Art Fitkin, Board Chairman

MBC stalwarts – Jim Boyds, Frank Hollidays, Syd
Whites, Ralph Knights, Roy F. Lawsons.

Syd White and Frank Holliday

*1977 sod turning for Memorial
Chapel - Earl Heron*

Construction of Memorial Chapel Winter 1977-78

Chapel building with Carousel to left

1978 chapel crowd – 1000 borrowed chairs

*Chapel Dedication – Christian leaders, government officials,
music by "His Own" (Willowdale)*

"Make His Praise Glorious"

Memorial Chapel with pews

Cedar Pulpit – built by former property owner Bert Olan

Overflow surrounding Chapel east side

Liberty Baptist musical team

HCJB Musical Team-
Springers and Jordans

Pianist . . . Marg Taylor
and memorial piano

Organist . . . Ken Baer and memorial organ

Inspecting lagoons – Eugene Felhaber, Len Aylett, Gord Stephenson, P.Eng.
with 3 district engineers in the background

Pump distribution center (L to R)   3 Rysco Engineers, Jack Janes,
Alec McDonald, Lyle Beckett, Len Aylett, Dick Holliday

1990 completion of third lagoon & spray irrigation system

MBC Board, Staff and partners 1984

MBC staff Christmas Dinner

Board of Directors 1990 plus auditor W. McMullen, R. Holliday and L. Beckett

Jim/Elaine Ross, Jim/Lil Ross Sr., Doraine Ross
Nancy, Heather and Ian Ross

Manor Motel 1986. A major gift to increase accommodation
and thus a more adequate operating revenue.

*Dick/Marilyn Holliday, Kimberly
(9), Bruce (3) - 1971*

R.D. Holliday family

Romance at MBC . . .Bruce Holliday/Melanie Roberts

1990 Holliday/Aylett family picture

*50 wonderful years for Len & Ness
Aylett in 1984 L to R – Lorne/Jean
Garner, Bruce / Fay Aylett, Len&
Ness, Marilyn, Dad Holliday and
Dick. Centre Back row – Andrea,
Shari Aylett, Kimberly Holliday*

Wall Scripture Décor by Rev. Earl Clemens

MBC 60ᵗʰ Anniversary 1990

Memorial Chapel paintings by Daisy Dunlop

Chapter 21

TWO EXPENSIVE HURDLES

Muskoka Baptist Conference has always endeavoured to conform to every stipulation of the law. *"The powers that be are ordained of God ....." Romans 13*

From the late 1960's, two levels of government initiated strong demands on MBC's time and finances.

#1 PROVINCIAL - (STANDARDS) The province had established a new regulatory department called 'The Ministry of Environment". It brought into law a greatly extended framework of standards for all Ontario **waterworks and sewage systems**. Having needs similar to a small town, steps were gradually introduced over a period of years, requiring stage by stage conformity in all of our mechanical systems.

#2 MUNICIPAL - (TAXATION OBJECTIVES) The presence of so many people on MBC property and the quality of buildings which were being erected, prompted the Municipal authorities to view the Conference as **a commercial enterprise**, with sufficient wealth to pay greatly increased taxes . . . even on the Chapel.

The First Hurdle - For the years to and including 1971, MBC received routine visits by Provincial Health Inspectors. In 1972, this inspection came under the new Ministry of the Environment. As the official licensing authority, they visited our Millar Hall dining room and kitchen regularly through the summer. Toward the end of the season, they handed us a notice that the Conference must *either decrease patronage or construct new meal service facilities.* From our perspective, churches were requesting use of the Conference beyond the seasonal capability of summer buildings. Capacity crowds necessitated double meal sittings. A winterized motel-hotel complex became an essential rather than an option. Our constituency was urged to pray.

THE RESULT: We dedicated our new Dining Room, Kitchen, Accommodations, Offices, Lounge, Bookroom . . . the Lodge Building. Compliance with regulations and standards has always been the "obvious" for MBC.   1973 to 1980 were key development years. We respected the process by securing official permits and inspections for every aspect of growth.   Storm sewers and the Lodge septic tank system, alone, cost $25,040. This of course, would not include the appeal to the Parliament Buildings in Toronto for other steps to ensure MBC's conformity with the new laws.   Every building which had one or more washrooms and every trailer site washroom connection required a permit before installation.   This included all cottages of MBC Acres, the river subdivision and existing Conference buildings which preceded 1970.

Each well, each chlorination system and septic system had its own certified approval. There were five wells. There were scores of septic tanks.   Each involved extensive time and included great generosity by such installers as Lorne Sommers, Larry French, Larry Taylor and others who volunteered their strength. Even with charitable considerations, the Conference portion of these projects involved considerable expense. So much of this work was essential but scarcely noticed by most people.

"DO EVERYTHING DECENTLY AND IN ORDER"

July 1984 – We had a few days of very heavy rain. Arriving at the Lodge building one morning , it was noted that the lovely lawn down the hill held a glaze of water. The natural spring in the hill area had gradually seeped into the large tile bed, filling it completely. It had actually become a water-course. The failure of the tile bed was in no way the result of poor workmanship or wasted funds. What do we do now ? Like it or not, you have to notify the Ministry of the Environment . . . IMMEDIATELY. The representatives arrived late morning. Their instruction, *"shut down the septic system for the Lodge and cement the intake and outlets for the tank"*. That started a trucking contract for "Honey Wagons", 6 to 10 times every day until we replaced the big septic bed. What an expensive, noisy nuisance ! !

The engineering report required that we make immediate preparation for installation of three large pump stations. These would receive all sewage from the central buildings of the conference. Each of these pump stations was equipped with 3-phase submersible equipment to force the sewage uphill to two newly crafted lagoons covering five acres. The basic contract was $259,000. The project required extensive landscaping, the supply of hundreds of truck loads of clay to line the sides and floor of the two lakes. The work continued through 1981. In the spring of 1983, six acres of spray pipes, pumps and intricate electrical work finally completed the 2-year construction schedule. This brought the total outlay to more than **$280,000.**

As the contracted firm was completing its work of building the lagoons, deficiencies were identified by the supervising firm, Rysco Engineering. An attempt to have remedial work was delayed because the contractor had immediately sold all of his equipment. This was followed by notice of bankruptcy. Any new work would be by a replacement contract.

NOT MY FAVOURITE DAY !   July 6, 1984 The Conference was filled to capacity.

#1 *A violent electrical storm* knocked out our hydro supply.

#2 Soon after, a telephone call gave us the tragic news of ***the death of our friend*** Hannah Buxbaum. This was later discovered to be by an act of violence. She was one of our helpers in the support of children and others who needed MBC's care.

#3 At that point the ***telephone was silenced*** by an area ***power failure.***

#4 As the sky was clearing, we watched as Bruce Holliday, on horseback, came galloping at full speed toward the Lodge. He was not his usual calm self ! His message was . . . . ***the stream is rising*** *down at the ranch !* Immediately, we assumed that there was a <u>real</u> problem. Len Aylett and Jack Janes responded immediately and within minutes reported that part of one side of Lagoon #1 had broken. The breached dyke allowed most of the contents of Cell #1 to flow down into the forest area. "***The earthen dam has broken*** *and we cannot use the telephone to notify the Ministry of Environment!"* We did reach them by vehicle at noon hour, however, we were later charged in court with *failure to notify immediately.* Months later, after a lengthy court, proceeding, we were exonerated.

By 5 p.m. on July 6th, ***the Canadian Press descended*** with questions of all kinds, including the false statement that raw sewage had poured out into Mary Lake. In actual fact, treated effluent, which was ready to be sprayed, had escaped into the spray area of the forest near the Port Sydney Road. Some had entered the upper water course, as witnessed by the Ranch staff. That evening, approximately forty MBC cottagers delivered a hand bill to every area cottage around the perimeter of Mary Lake. It was ***a "boil water" notice*** for 24 hours, just in case contamination would be discovered by Health Department testing. We were proud of our team and thankful that no contamination was ever discovered in the river or lake. That prompt endeavor was later cited in Supreme Court as excellent community service on the part of MBC. One lagoon had held firmly . . .the one that was still receiving sewage. The lagoon which broke had been resting for 30 days and was ready for spraying into the forest.

1987   Mr. Gordon Stephenson, P. Eng. accepted an appointment by the Directors of MBC. From that time, he has been identified as our "Professional Consultant". His counsel had been invaluable, but now it was ongoing oversight of the engineering companies and for construction on our grounds. Government regulations, the demands of professional counsel and the high costs of growth require great care to ensure good value and economy. Mr. Stephenson has been the Lord's special instrument. He has been our professional volunteer through the 1970's to the present.

COMPLETING MECHANICAL INSTALLATIONS

The work which followed the damaged Lagoon included much more than just repairing the dyke and the deficiencies of the first contractor. The five acres of the two lagoons were to be given an extra layer of special clay. The Ministry required that we extend construction by adding a third lagoon. This would expand the total lagoon area to 7 acres. The required work went beyond 1985. **The detailed diagramming** and the additional provincial work, required by the Ministry of Environment, kept contractors and staff very busy until completion in 1990.

1. <u>Waterworks</u> – a complete report of every sink tap, pipe and pump at the Conference, Trailer Park and Camp Widjiitiwin

2. <u>Electrical</u> – every panel, wire and energy use by MBC

3. <u>Storm sewers</u> – their size, depths, materials, elevations and handling of water

4. <u>Alarm systems</u> as required for safety, sewer pumps, lagoon levels, water <u>reservoirs</u> (low and high levels)… all fully engineered

5. <u>Public Address</u> and private grounds <u>telephone systems</u> for safety

6. <u>Sewage Systems</u> . . . the design and construction of a third lagoon; the installation of a larger spray irrigation system; the addition of more pumps and meters. The cost of the spray irrigation system alone, was estimated to be **$150,000**.

The work load, engineering expenses, construction and related legal costs presented a tremendous drain upon staff time and energy and funds. The information and work <u>will</u> be helpful for future staff and development. The demands stipulated completion by mid-1986. It was a busy winter !!!   Time was needed to complete the spray irrigation system near the Lagoons. This enabled us to postpone construction of the third lagoon. 1985 and 1986 were known as "the years of the engineer". Thousands of dollars were spent in studies and reports to demonstrate that all systems fully conform to Municipal and Provincial standards.

1988 MBC started the construction of a **third sewage lagoon**. The electrical and mechanical installation was deferred until 1989 as was the refurbishing of the clay liner of the two original lagoons. The new 7 acre facility has cost more than **$300,000.** to date. The value for staff efficiency and economy will be a great help. Another surprise was the requirement that we install full **duplex chlorination** systems at every well. This involved engineering, equipment acquisition, installation and Ministry certification.

Between 1986 and 1989 the only new improvements were by specifically designated gifts, or to meet the demands of intensified Ministry of Environment engineering standards. There were no spending extras! If MBC had decided to decrease the number of people on our grounds, we could have postponed some of the sewage and water works expenses. Instead, the problems have been resolved by full compliance with all the new standards.

"Every tap, trap and valve"! . . . **The water works** had to be shown on engineered drawings. All sewage works had to flow to one master disposal system. This included a series of high powered submersible pumping stations. The sewage was pumped to eventually fill a lagoon arrangement of three-ponds. Every thirty days, one of the three ponds would begin a disposal cycle which would spray all of its contents into a remote forest area. ----

The accumulated cost of all these mechanical systems and sewage works was ~ $1.8 million dollars !

- In response to a request for prayerful 1990 Christmas giving, the largest offering in Muskoka Baptist Conference history totaled **$368,000**. This was applied directly to the bank financing.

- Holding MBC in his customary high esteem, the banker was satisfied with a signature only, for the $1.2 million still outstanding, as witnessed by our treasurer of that year.

- Offers to purchase the MBC Inn property had been considered, but deferred until the new year. The policy adopted in 1989, as expressed by our President: "*the sale of our MBC Inn property, this important step will enable MBC to be debt free*".

"*God is faithful, Who will not allow you to be tested above that which you are able to bear*". The following report summary identifies Operating Income and Capital Donations. This is just one aspect of the faithfulness of our Lord's supply.

TRIBUTE TO WHOM TRIBUTE IS DUE

The Second Hurdle - In January 1987, the Sheriff delivered a supreme Court action initiated by the Municipality of Huntsville against MBC. It was an effort to multiply the taxes we pay. Even the Chapel was assessed as a commercial enterprise. In 1977 and 1978 the Supreme Court had ruled against Huntsville's effort, declaring that we had been overtaxed. Now Huntsville had retained a tax specialist Law firm from Bay Street, Toronto to *"press the charges, sparing no expense"!* *"MBC pays no taxes"* was a newspaper campaign with many letters orchestrated and published. The truth was that <u>we had</u> paid taxes regularly, including $26,262.71. in 1986.

M   It was an effort to classify the Camp and Conference as a <u>commercial enterprise</u>. If successful, an accumulated, additional levy of not less than $354,761.20 would be added to the previous year's increase in taxes. After more than two years of delays and discussions, the case came to court in 1990. In the two week trial, this writer was on the witness stand for three days of cross examination by two Crown Attorneys. As a last argument, one of the attorneys opened one of our summer brochures and asked questions about our Conference speakers. This brochure identified three scientists who would present the accuracy of Scripture in matters of history and natural science . . . Dr. Henry M. Morris, Dr. Duane Gish, Dr. Harold Slusher.

The attorney asked – *"Do these men hold degrees from <u>secular</u> universities?" The answer was, "Yes". Are they ordained <u>ministers?</u> The answer was, "No".*

The qualifications were examined in detail and then the conclusion exclaimed with excitement: *"These are men of <u>science,</u> and are <u>not</u> ordained ministers of religion ! We all know that the <u>Bible</u> and <u>religion</u> do <u>not</u> speak with authority in matters of science. This is a sample of MBC operating a <u>secular</u> commercial enterprise. Their subject is not always religion"*

To this, the writer replied, *"Sirs, if the Bible does not speak with <u>accuracy</u> in matters of history and science, it does not speak with <u>authority</u> in matters of faith and eternal destiny."*

Judge Thomas, turned his chair toward the witness stand. *"Rev. Holliday, I have always felt that if the Bible was taken into any discipline of education, and examined as to its authority, and accuracy, it would be found to be without error. I have never heard such a satisfying statement on this subject"*. For twenty minutes, the judge asked questions about the credibility and authority of the Bible. Soon after, he pronounced, *"Case dismissed"*. The proceedings completed, both prosecuting attorneys warmly congratulated the defendant and wished the Conference well. Then for two hours, by the request of Judge Thomas, we had a Bible study in his chambers, concluding in prayer together. That was quite a day !

STEERING COMMITTEE

In **1986**, a Steering Committee was appointed. Their function was to make contacts and communicate MBC's financial targets. It was felt necessary to increase knowledgable prayer partnership and informed giving. The Bond Issue of 1973, which funded the construction of the Lodge building, was due and payable on October 1, 1989. In accordance with policy and the help of this Capital Fund Committee, the $250,000 was paid in full, on time. Chairman, Bob Crichton; Members: Ron Cripps, Dr. Bob Gringmuth, Dr. Burt Harper, Bill Havercroft, Bob Hood, Bob Lowe, Bob McClintock, Tom McCormack, Paul Ratcliff, Terry Ratcliff, Jim Ross, Gill Scott, Eldon Smith.

PLANNING AND DEVELOPMENT COMMITTEE

Through the 1980's the Board has coped with continuous pressures concerning new regulations for mechanical systems. It was felt that a master schedule was needed for *"the co-ordination of all present and long-range plans"*. A Planning and Development Committee was duly **appointed in 1987**: Chairman, Jim Lucas; Members: D. Miller Alloway, Frank Henkleman and Len Klinck . Ex Officio on the team were Board President, Jim Ross, Steering Committee Chairman, Bob Crichton, General Director, Dick Holliday and Engineer, Gord Stephenson. The work of this team resulted in the first property survey since the 1950's. It led to preliminary drawings of a long discussed activity building and other future land use projections. Extensive funding was indicated, which initially looked after the costs of design-engineering work.

Leadership by Board Chairmen

Through the 1930's, the "Camp Committee" included some who assisted for a year or two, attending to ministry or duties of practical care. Five men carried the burden of Board Member leadership. Mr. Sydney White usually served as Treasurer. The other four were Rev. J. Frank Holliday, Rev. Sidney Lawrence, Rev. Tom Summers and Mr. Etric Harley. The next decade added Gordon Bigham, Charlie Hare and Rev. Donald Loveday.

Mr. White continued to serve on the Board until 1977. He was president for some of the 1930's, and 1940's, and again in 1960. From 1970 to 1972 he was Chairman of the Structural Committee which led to incorporation. He was a man of God, full of grace and corporate understanding.

Mr. Arthur Fitkin was a co-worker through some of these years. He was known for his abilities as an astute business executive, with a lifetime of ministry assistance in local churches and at MBC. Between 1965 and 1983, he was a member of the board for fourteen years, eight of them as President.

MUSKOKA BAPTIST CONFERENCE
Board Members & Officers
1970 - 1990

Mr. Walter Abraham

Mr. Alan Agnew

Mr. Ron Barnett

Rev. Ron Baxter

Mr. Ross Bickle

Mr. David Black *

Mr. Clare Borrowman **

Mr. Frank Bowman

Mr. Craig Corner

Mr. Ron Cripps **

Mr. Don Dafoe

Mr. Edmund Faris

Mr. Eugene Felhaber

Mr. Jaffre Feren

Mr Duncan Findlay ***

Mr. Arthur Fitkin *

Mr. Ted Flemming

Mr. Frank Gill

Mr. Grant Hallett

Rev. Jack Hannah

Mr. Ron Hartwick ***

Mr. Bill Havercroft *

Mr. Earl Heron

Mr. Paul Hisey

Rev. Dick Holliday (1970)

Rev. Don Howard

Mr. Chris Huehn

Mr. Howard Ireland **

Rev. David Irwin *

Mr. Jim Jepson

Rev. Art Larsen

Rev. Mark Lowrie

Mr. Murray Moffitt

Mr. Tom Putt

Mr. Howard Ratcliff

Rev. Gordon Rendle

Mr. Don Reynolds *

Mr. Ken Robertson

Mr. Jim Ross *

Mr. R.D. Rouse ***

Mr. Bruce Scott

Rev. DeLoss Scott

Mr. Gil Scott **

Rev. Ted Searle

Mr. Eldon Smith

Mr. Gord Stephenson

Mr. Larry Taylor

Mr. Bob Thompson ***

Mr. Ross Thompson **

Mr. Stuart Tyers

Rev. Martin Wedge **

Mr. Sydney L. White *

Mr. Bill Wilkie*

Presidents   *   Vice Presidents   **   Treasurers   ***

Ex Officio 1970-1990 – Managing Director, R.D. Holliday

1969 – Chair, Arthur Fitkin, Treas. John Bonham, Frank Bowman, Harry Edwards, Earl Heron, Dick Holliday, Bob Page, D. Reynolds, Al Silvester, DeLoss Scott, George Simpson, Sydney L. White

PRESIDENTS OF THE BOARD

1962 - 1964	Rev. Donald A. Loveday
1965 - 1972	Mr. Arthur Fitkin
1973	Mr. Sydney L. White
1974 - 1975	Rev. David Irwin
1976 - 1979	Mr. W.F. Wilkie
1980 - 1981	Mr. Donald A. Reynolds
1982 - 1984	Mr. William Havercroft
1985 - 1989	Mr. Jim Ross
1990 - 1993	Mr. David Black
1993 - 1994	Mr. Gil Scott
1994 - 1996	Mr. Peter Gibson
1996 - 1997	Mr. Jim Ross
1997 - 2000	Mr. Scott Martin
2000 - 2003	Rev. Paul Havercroft
2003 - 2007	Mr. Scott Martin
2007 - 2009	Mr. Mike Nichols
2009 - 2010	Mr. Donald Symons
2010 -	Mr. Cliff Topping

"The steps of a good man are 'plotted' by the Lord"

Almost every name in this list of leaders has a strong family history through parents and grandparents who brought their children to Muskoka Baptist Conference. Some met their life's partners while present on these grounds.

Chairman Bill Havercroft . . .

Muskoka Baptist Conference has been conceived and founded by men of vision to provide Christian fellowship, to spread the Gospel, to develop Christian workers and to assist churches and institutions engaged in similar activities.

Chairman Don Reynolds . . .

In 1957, when I was 13 years of age, while sitting in the old white shuttered chapel... I responded to the invitation from Pastor Ellard Corbett. That evening I was saved. When I was sixteen, I joined the staff. My assignment was "Pot Boy". My salary was $90.00 for the summer! Mrs. Grundy was the cook. During the time of my parents and now for my family, the Camp is a very large part of our lives.

A Dedicated Place ~ The Perspective of Art and Nancy Fitkin ~

"*I believe in miracles, for I believe in God*"- John Peterson's sentiment is echoed by believers all over the world. Art and Nancy Fitkin lived their thankfulness for the miracle of new life in Christ. They were committed to the miracle ministry of Muskoka Baptist Conference. They saw the value of "the camp" as a means of developing young people and helping them to grow. They felt that families needed to be refreshed by the preaching of the word. They knew people would enjoy Christian fellowship in such a place of physical beauty.

Art and Nancy were supporters of this fledgling ministry throughout the early years. Physical and financial support was rewarded by the enjoyment of vacation time with their children. When asked about his vacation plans, Art's answer was always, "Why to MBC of course." To the Fitkins, MBC was "home."

There were occasions when MBC was just where the whole family needed to be. Their beloved daughter/granddaughter, Lori was about to lose her sight because of cancer. Arthur and Nancy Fitkin and Jim, Sandi, Lynnie Kernohan found solace just walking the grounds with Lori. Each sensed the presence of the Lord, the One who would sustain them every difficult day.

In time, devotion to family prompted Lori's grandparents to move to Brantford. It meant leaving their Toronto home, their church family and many friends. The plan was to provide a home for their granddaughter, for the last 5 years of her Brantford education. This meant that Lori would no longer have to live in a special training residence. A Brantford benefit was the renewal of acquaintances with many friends from MBC.

Art and Nancy Fitkin enjoyed seeing the fulfillment of the vision of many, in the work of MBC. It was a place where the God of miracles touched lives. Salvation, restoration, families encouraged, believers learning to trust His leading . . . these were the real substance of MBC's ministry. What a grand place, our MBC ! How wonderful the sense of His presence when we are there!

by daughter, Sandra (Fitkin) Kernohan

Spiritually Strengthened at MBC ~ **by Evelyn Thompson**

My first introduction to Muskoka Baptist Camp came as a teen-ager. We travelled by train to Huntsville to attend the youth retreats at Mary Lake. Years later we were part of the church family at Emmanuel Baptist Church in Barrie. Our Pastor, Dick Holliday, resigned to become the Director of MBC. Over the next number of years we spent many Emmanuel Family Week-ends there each spring.

Ross joined the MBC Board of directors at the end of the sixties. He remained on the board, with some sabbaticals, for 20 years. MBC was always close to his heart; he was so excited to watch the conference ministry expand and see the Lord work in so many lives. He also loved children and young people. He was instrumental in bringing Camp Widjiitiwin across the river to a larger and more suitable location. Ross was thrilled to see it grow and become a very important part of MBC's ministry.

In 1978 I joined the Ladies' Conference Committee of MBC. For 18 years of 10 day conferences, it was a joy to work with great committee members. This time stretched and *strengthened me spiritually.*

Our family has been greatly involved with MBC over the years. Daughter Sandi met her husband Cliff Topping at a Youth Week. Now he is on the Board of MBC. Their daughter Megan worked on staff one summer. It was there she met her husband Josh who was in the Summit program. Our daughters Cathy and Jo spent summers working at MBC in various ministries. Later, Jo, returned as part of the office staff.

Over the years, Ross and I spent many holidays at MBC. We were blessed by the fellowship and ministry. We were so thankful for the impact it had on the lives of our girls. It has been an encouragement in each life in our family.

After almost 60 years of marriage, God called my beloved partner home. His many qualities live on in the lives of his daughters ~ his own deep faith, his humility and wisdom, his integrity and Christian example. He was a quiet man who lived his faith out loud. He was so pleased to have been a part of the work of God through the ministry of Muskoka Baptist Conference.

Evelyn Thompson
Emmanuel Baptist Church
Barrie, ON

A Family Heritage at MBC ~ by Kimberly J. Sharp (nee Holliday)

What a host of memories and reflections flood my heart and mind in this 80th Anniversary year of Muskoka Baptist Conference. My brother and I have a family heritage connection with those who worked to establish MBC in its early years. Our personal reflections primarily center on life as it was when we were growing up. This was throughout the twenty plus years in which our parents fulfilled leadership responsibilities at the conference. There were many who were a part of that history with us. As children and young adults, we lived that history in a more public way than most families. We observed the events from the inside … and were often conscious of <u>being</u> observed. Our perspectives are thus intensely personal. Our different vantage point may interest the many who also have strong ties to MBC.

The history and memories of Muskoka Baptist Conference have been an integral part of our family throughout all of my lifetime. From earliest years summers included staying at the "boat house cottage" of my maternal grandparents (Len and Ness Aylett), or the "upper" or at "lower" river cottages of my paternal grandparents (Frank and Luella Holliday). These vacation times developed a personal love for all that the conference has meant to us as a family.

Childhood memories include a long list of adventures. Most of these involved lengthy explorations of the forest. We built forts and tree houses, and went on quests to fight imaginary foes. We called ourselves by elaborate Indian names and made bows and arrows out of sticks and string, even suffering the consequences of jackknife use. We "noodled" for fish in the creeks and stalked bullfrogs in the ditches. Unauthorized visits to the "haunted house" had a tremendous allure, and we went there often. Sometimes we were chased away by angry owners. This only added to the sense of mystery and intrigue.

We crawled through the hedge to visit our neighbor, Mrs. Kemper. Her cottage (Hilarity) was nearby on the riverfront. She gave us chocolate wagon wheels to eat. We watched cigarette smoke swirl around her head as she chatted with us in her croaky voice. We felt slightly guilty, just being around someone who was smoking.

Our Uncle Paul was a wonderful story teller. We loved his gentle manner and his kindness to us as children. He was the one who taught us to "noodle". He helped us collect water lilies and other pond foliage from the swamp downriver. We were amazed by the power of swamp gas and the vastness of the secret passage networks in the swamp. Uncle Paul rewarded even our smallest acts of valour, issuing certificates to reinforce good behaviour. I remember being tremendously pleased when I was ceremoniously presented with the "order of the purple serviette". I do not recall what I did to earn so great an honour.

Swimming in the lake was great fun. We routinely commiserated with any who fell victim to the trauma of clam shell cuts or leeches. You could walk out in waist deep water for a long way, but the old saw mill had left spongy areas into which you occasionally sank if wading farther from shore. It was a particular triumph when we were big enough to climb on to the raft with the "big" kids. It was really cool to water-ski right from the dock. One staff member made history when he snagged his bathing costume on the wood and skied half way round the lake with his suit round his ankles. The river dock was known for its cold water. Brave souls would swing on a rope which was fastened high above the river bank. My biggest swimming worry was encountering the huge dock spiders that lurked under the edges of the boards of the dock, or flat against the logs near the water's edge.

Swimming or canoeing across the river enabled us to climb Blueberry Mountain and savour the sweetest blueberries you can ever taste. I loved to canoe in the evenings and watch the bats swoop across the bow of the boat. They scooped up the insects that were disturbed by the motion of the boat. Canoes were also good for "galumping." Standing with both feet on the gunnels of the canoe, you tried to bounce your opposition off the other end. This was hugely entertaining. The higher the canoe rose out of the water the louder were the cheers of the crowd. What a great triumph to be the one left standing. My Dad's sister, Dorothy Simmonds, was the best "galumper" I ever saw.

We made toast in my grandmother's two-sided "lift up" toaster. The result was usually the cremation of at least one side of the toast. We fed chipmunks from our hands and were captivated by the lonely, haunting calls of loons from across the lake. The call of the loons is the sound I miss most of all. In those years it was also still possible to hear the howl of wolves in the late evening. It added more zest to our late night story-telling. The walls of the Holliday river cottages were lined with books. I spent many happy hours reading my way through musty volumes of "The Bishop's Shadow" and The Elsie Books.

When our parents assumed full-time ministry service at MBC, our whole family became involved. My brother and I had always been close, but now as a matter of necessity we became inseparable. I helped a staff member from our church in Barrie in the care of Bruce who was not yet 4. There was a six and a half year age gap between us, but it wasn't a big issue.

My Dad's duties as Director were really a dual appointment. From the beginning Mum was an important part of the team. Through most of the years she served as a volunteer. As conference facilities grew and ministry programming stretched into the fall and spring, so grew the numbers of staff, volunteers and guests.   Jobs for family and friends included every avenue of service at MBC. Everyone "pitched in" to ensure that guests were always treated with special care and attention.

In the years before winter programming began,, we lived in the old director's cabin . It was located across from the maintenance shop. Our "central" heating consisted of one heater in the center of the sitting room. Air conditioning was an open window. We had sleeping accommodations in two rooms, with a small sitting room and a three-piece bathroom. There was no space for a kitchen. Use of an ironing board blocked all foot traffic in the cottage. I have vivid memories of that cottage. My Dad, was violently assaulted there by a disgruntled individual. I greatly admired the black eye he sported for weeks afterwards. He always proclaimed that my Mum had "decked" him.

Staff members were encouraged to respect an "FHB" policy. We knew that guests go first, so **F**amily **H**old **B**ack. My own responsibilities grew in various directions. I learned to pump gas in the marina, care for the farm animals and the ranch, take trail rides, waitress, run the dishwasher, wash (and dry) pots, operate the cash registers in the snack shop and bookroom, prepare food in the snack shops, stock pop machines, dish up food in the dining room, help with the laundry and housekeeping chores, assist with music ministry. As time went on, training found expression in responding to first aid problems, and help with office routines.

Chapel services were still in the wooden building at the top of the hill. We enjoyed the breezes that blew through the windows, while we wiggled and swiped at unspiritual mosquitoes that disturbed our concentration. The old pulpit with its sturdy logs was a familiar sight It helped to support our knocking knees when we were "encouraged" to formally participate in the music of the evening. Indeed singing was a big part of what we did at MBC. We regularly sang "Thank you Lord" as our communal grace before dinner in the old dining room. I did not even realize that this hymn had verses until recently. We had sung it as just a chorus over many years. My Uncle Don Holliday's rendition of "Ship Ahoy" made my hair stand on end. I loved to sing the second and third verses of John W. Peterson's, "Heaven Came Down." The last lines incorporate an intricate vocabulary matching the melody and the message. It is so compelling:

> *Born of the spirit with life from above,   into God's family divine,*
> *Justified fully thro' Calvary's love,   O what a standing is mine.*
> *And the transaction so quickly was made,   when as a sinner I came;*
> *Took of the offer of grace He did proffer;   He saved me, O praise His dear name!*
>
> *Now I've a hope that will surely endure,   after the passing of time;*
> *I have a future in heaven for sure,   there in those mansions sublime.*
> *And it's because of that wonderful day,   when at the cross I believed;*
> *Riches eternal and blessings supernal,   from His precious hand I received.*

We sang lustily the old hymns and choruses, and continued those sing-a-longs at campfires and firesides. When we maxed out the capacity in the Chapel, we needed to hold Sunday morning services outside. God even ordered the weather. Showers never disrupted any summer Sunday morning Chapel service. Some days the rain was all around us, but it was as though the Lord himself sheltered the Chapel on Sunday mornings.

There seemed to be more time for contemplation in those days. We did more reading, listening and singing together than we seem to do in our current age of electronics and other entertainment. We hugely enjoyed skit nights by "the rock" or in Fellowship Center with its crackling fire. The creative talents of each group and our collective sense of fun and laughter are abiding memories. One skit was entitled "big chief dirty face of the never wash tribe". I thought it was a fantastic piece of live theatre. Roy Lawson led us all in the "lion hunt" and waxed eloquent in the re-enactment of "rinse the blood off my toga". Late risers during youth week were hauled out of bed and dumped into the lake. Baseball games on the ball diamond were hotly contested. We even managed to inject some fiendish glee into the baseball games. In mid-competition, when the best slugger unsuspectingly was up to bat, a painted grapefruit would be surreptitiously substituted by the pitcher.

Laundry, food service and animal care are pervasive threads that run through all my collected memories. In the early days, we rode in the one ton truck to the spring, where large milk cans were filled with the cold water. Back at Millar Hall, there were special smorgasbord nights. Family fun meals included hat nights and a weekly lesson in "how to eat spaghetti". Meal service was family style and it helped us learn about portion control and asking permission for seconds.

Mammy and Pappy Knight were an essential part of the laundry team in the early days. I initially watched, and then learned to help them. This required the use of a stick to catch laundry in the old-style washing machines, so it could be put through the mangle. I can still hear the swish- swish of water and smell the soap. Once things were washed, we hauled big baskets of heavy wet linen up the stairs to the laundry room roof. We grasped the clothesline pulley reels, attached the dozens of sheets to the long, multiple clothes lines stretched out over several hundred feet. Drying was accomplished relatively quickly on a breezy day. Just as God ordered time to stand still in Joshua's day, so too, did God direct the weather to ensure that even the laundry needs could be met.

The increase of the number of three day special conferences meant that facilities were stretched to capacity. On each changeover day there was a scurry of activity with "all hands on deck". We gathered up laundry and cleaned rooms. We kids happily rode to Huntsville sitting on top of truckloads of pillowcases stuffed with linens. Our in-house MBC laundry service capabilities could in no way cope with the volume. There were no DVDs or Nintendos in those days. We spent countless hours stuffing machines and watching the spinning and tumbling of linens. Finally everything was folded and reloaded for the return trip.

Our family involvement was, in the true Baptist sense of the word, total immersion. It really did not occur to us to "opt out" or merely serve as observers. Our house was in Barrie, Ontario until I was able to complete grade 13. All of our non-school hours were spent in the Muskokas. Every Friday, during the school year, we became commuters, joining those heading north on highway 11 to Huntsville. We rushed to complete homework in the early evening hours. We then helped to serve a meal of spaghetti to the youth groups arriving around 11 p.m. They were "hyper" and hungry after the long drive north from Toronto or elsewhere. We fell into bed on Friday and Saturday nights, while the kids hit the tube slide, the ice rink or the snowmobile trails. We knew that the busyness of waitressing, food service, trail rides and housekeeping precluded late night entertainment for us. Sunday's routines concluded with the usual housekeeping and laundry blitz when the guests left. Then we returned to Barrie for school routines. School friends spoke of weekend social events, movies, and concerts. We felt strangely disconnected from all of that. For a number of years, our family of four, usually shared room 814, downstairs in the main lodge. This consisted of a small room with two-beds and a pull out cot and no window. Bruce and I felt it had the charm of a basic prison cell. We experienced all the noise of every enthusiastic new group. It was pitch black at all times and it was impossible to have any inkling of time of day or weather conditions. Of course when we turned on the room light, there were normal amenities.

One definite benefit of family involvement at MBC was my Dad's annual pilgrimage to our respective school teachers. He would describe the "cultural experience" which we were planning for the whole family during a school season. The reason included the fact that we all were busy during all summer and school break weeks. He always seemed to be successful in arranging that reluctant concession ! These were our family vacation times.

At the end of each winter retreat there was a strategy to help the guests navigate the steep, slippery hill. Staff would oversee the starting of frozen cars. Once they were lined up and ready,   Dad's admonition to each city driver was, "keep your momentum and greet no man by the way". If we could not launch them on their journey we would need to serve an evening meal. There were always a few cars with poor traction, for whom male staff added extra weight on the back bumper !!

There really was no part of the year that was "down" time. In the 1970's it seemed that work involved a skeleton team of dedicated aunts, uncles, cousins, friends, staff, volunteers and other special people we adopted as "family". We were a strange mix of people, bound together in a common ministry. I felt that my best friends, when growing up, were all "retired". They worked longer and harder than most young people. We laughed together and tested one another's patience. These were my role models of how God would have us live as stewards of time, talents and abilities.

Accommodations changed for us. We moved into the lower half of the cottage built by Mr. and Mrs. Howard Ratcliff. It was named "Summerset House". Bruce and I had our own affectionate names. It did have a kitchen AND windows . . . and family living space! Living there was complicated by my Dad's obsession with communication with ALL the campers and conference residents. The conference PA system was linked up to a speaker system in the cottage. This meant all his "good morning, rise and shine" and other daily greetings filled the cottage. In desperation my brother and I would try to find better and more effective ways to muffle the speaker by stuffing pillows and other things on top of it.

My love for the animals became an obsession. Some of these unofficially shared our household accommodation This was often without the official knowledge of my parents. Rudi, the <u>orphan lamb</u>, spent most of one summer with me. He went "loopy" if he was left outside. Improvising diaper arrangements proved to be a complicated challenge. <u>One snake</u>, run over by a car, needed to be washed off and sewn back together. He lived under my bed in a box until she/he (I never was quite sure) shed its skin and I was able to release it back into the bush. Orphaned raccoons, Rascal and Hoby, provided good companionship. They were tricky to round up when they wanted to explore. When the duck hatched the chicken eggs, she marched them down to the pond where they would have drowned. I lined my dresser drawer and borrowed my Mother's heating pad. The 13 baby chicks were able to stay safe and dry. I think my Dad objected most when he stepped into the shower and discovered my orphaned Canada goose sitting in our only bathtub.

My Mum's appreciation of animals was more from a distance. When all guests had gone home, she agreed, with some reservation, to go for a horseback ride. Going down the steep hill to the beach was definitely not her preferred destination. Her emphatic "Whoa Midnight, whoa Midnight" was repeated all the way down the hill, without any noticeable effect. I don't recall her riding with us again !

As I reflect upon those times, I miss the many cooks and kitchen helpers who presided over meal service. Roast beef was always served Sundays in the main dining room. Eventually chicken strips were the alternative Sunday dinner served in the Tea Room, next to the Chapel. I still dream about Cook Charlotte Moulton's butter tarts. Just thinking about them makes my mouth water! Each day of the week was a set meal plan. Thursday was always smorgasbord day. Eventually this involved separate meal service arrangements for children of the guests. The staff were required to entertain and feed the various age groups of children. They would eat burgers while their parents enjoyed the huge, colorful variety of main dishes followed by cream puffs and other delicacies. Staff dressed up in western attire. We ranch hands were tasked with hundreds of pony rides. This was my least favourite job. Games and hay rides were also part of the program. Every week we had to pick bits of hay out of our hair that had been thrown around by over-enthusiastic kiddos. In contrast, dining room staff wore long dresses. This added an air of elegance.

A highlight of the summer time was the Sunday evening sing-a-long led by Program Director, Roy Lawson. He was assisted by guitar-playing staffers. These events followed the Sunday evening service.

Guests munched on snacks and joined in the music. The camaraderie of working with people who were motivated by their love for the Lord was a living testimony for all to witness. Breakfast staff devotions were often led by my Grandfather, Leonard Aylett. These were succinct and full of practical theology. His gentle admonitions were highlighted by astute observations and Godly wisdom.

As responsibilities increased, our parents relied on the Lord's strength and guidance. There was continued blessing and growth in the ministry of MBC. Never ones to shirk any task, they were usually the first to start each day and the last to finish. We joked that our laundry machine usually went on at 11:30 pm. They had an energy and passion for the work to which God had called them. This must have been fueled by God's enabling alone. My brother and I were acutely aware of the pressures and work load. I do believe that it was God's power that sustained them through those strenuous years. We laughed about the "I'll do it" motto that was our Mother's response to every need. They truly loved the ministry and the people too. They felt the challenge of the many who came to the conference with spiritual, emotional and even physical needs.

All areas of programming and staffing need to function smoothly. The scheduling and coordination of activities included so many facets. It was a real labour of love for my parents. Mum spent hours figuring out seating plans for the dining room, ensuring compatibility between groups of people who would share tables and conversation. She was the general hostess and provided oversight for meal service routines to ensure that things went smoothly in both the dining room and the kitchen. She continued to take a personal interest in all of the special needs and backgrounds of everyone under her care. As numbers grew she was assisted by a wider hostess team. . . Lynn Mitchell, Linda Lively, Joyce Findlay, Nancy Ross, Ruth Gillott, Melanie (Roberts) Holliday, Jo Ann Kerr, Ella Mae Jones, Dorothy Budd and others.

Both my parents have phenomenal memories for names, faces and backgrounds. They remember small elements in the lives of individuals. It was this attention to detail that endeared them to all. People felt that they really listened to whatever information or needs were shared, and they did! This was true for the guests, ministry and musical teams, and staff. Bruce and I were not ignored, in spite of the fact that our family times were limited.

Our closely knit circle included not only Mum and Dad, but our precious grandparents, Grandpa and Grandma Holliday and Len and Ness Aylett (Nana and Poppa to us). They were our mainstay throughout our growing up years. I considered my dear Nana to be my best friend. It was her counsel that I sought when troubled about decisions, or when I just wanted to chat. They too, along with many of our relatives were involved in conference ministry. Poppa's energy and work ethic meant that he was always up with the larks. He was happily whistling away at work, accomplishing more than staffers half his age. Nana, was faced with multiple health issues and considerable pain, but was never happier than when she was working in the bookroom. She used her many talents and abilities until the Lord called her home.

It was from my parents and grandparents that we learned how to work **with** people. Their example of patience and forbearance was key to helping those who came without any background of experience whatsoever. For many younger staff, it was their first summer job. They would learn as they went along. Some were homesick and probably felt like emotional refugees. Through love and support, of the staff team, these individuals gradually recovered and blossomed in their walk with the Lord. Down the road, some of the camp romances led to marriage or new job opportunities. It was also a challenge when some came as "special projects" . . . sent by anxious parents who were "at their wits end". The Lord did touch many lives, and continues to do so, even many years later.

Mum kept track of guest registration details. She and Alice Wadge fielded many aspects relating to the main conference office each day. They were usually the ones on call for late arrivals. My Dad had his office in the back. Somehow he managed to hear every conversation that took place in and around the office area. Nothing seemed to get past him. We often kidded him about having radar hearing.

Multiple chapters could be written about medical emergencies: heart and respiratory problems; an all-night search for a missing child at Widjiitiwin that involved the police and other agencies; falls; broken bones; ruptured spleens; sprains; bee stings; cuts; scrapes; anaphylactic reactions to various agents; dermatological issues; lightning strikes; etc., etc. I never could figure why most things seemed to require attention whenever it got dark. Ted and Corrine Hiltz regularly rendered assistance. From them I learned how to remain calm and focused in medical crises, human or animal. Indeed, it was to their home that I fled cradling a badly injured chicken from MacDonald's farm. They did not think it at all strange to operate on my bleeding friend and sew her back together on their dining room table.

Maintenance emergencies were a constant challenge. We all became fairly adept at creative problem-solving. Power outages, water crises, floods, leaks, road erosion, fallen trees, broken pipes; I truly think that we saw it all. Sewage systems always required priority care. My brother and I thought that our idea of issuing golden clothes pegs to all sewage system donors was inspired. There was the need to keep MBC grounds secure. We needed to be alert for on-site and outside people who were intent on being disruptive. Security patrols usually fell to my Dad. He would circle the grounds many a late night checking on the safety of people and equipment. I liked joining him for late night patrols. We both were so familiar with the grounds that we could quite literally walk anywhere without the aid of flashlights or other illumination. As time went on Elmer Potz became our Security Guard on night patrol. This seemed an unlikely task for such a gracious, kindly gentleman. He did it well !

Personal care and attention was accorded to everyone who visited the conference. As a family we were privileged to host the musicians and speakers in our home each week. We were introduced to a variety of music that included every conceivable instrument and spanned a wide range of styles. The best in speakers came from around the globe as part of regular conference programming. We became aware of the extraordinary uniqueness of each one, along with their special needs. We learned how God's grace and enablement were sufficient for these great men of faith, even in the face of health and personal trials. I do feel incredibly blessed to have personally met and visited with spiritual giants such as Dr. and Mrs. Howard Sugden, Dr. and Mrs. Warren Wiersbe, Dr. and Mrs. Charles Wagner, Dr. & Mrs. Joseph Stowell,(Sr & Jr), Dr. & Mrs. Paul Dixon, Dr. Jerry Falwell, Dr. and Mrs. James MacDonald, Dr. and Mrs. James T. Jeremiah, Dr. and Mrs. David Jeremiah, Dr. and Mrs. Marvin Rosenthal, Dr. and Mrs. Stephen Olford, Dr. and Mrs. Paige Patterson, Mr. Philip Yancy, Dr. and Mrs. Don Jennings, Dr. and Mrs. Paul Brand, Dr. John White, the HCJB Missions Team with the Joe and Betty Springer, Gene and Ruth Jordan, Lars and Elizabeth (Elliot) Gren, Abe and Marj (Saint) Vanderpuy and many more.

We enjoyed the blessing of laugher in their company and discovered that as Christians we can enjoy humour together. Some of the funniest stories I have ever heard have been told by pastors recounting funeral mishaps or other events. Coming to know these men of God in our home, helped us to value, even more deeply the burden which He had laid on their hearts to share.

My Dad was a bargain hunter and tried to find ways to economize. His efforts were not always applauded by those of us who had to carry out his ideas. There was "the turkey episode". A meat wholesaler called to ask if Dad wanted 70 turkeys. The wholesaler explained that his freezer was broken down, so he could bring the turkeys right to the conference for MBC kitchen use. Dad thought that the delivery truck was bringing frozen turkeys. When the transporter arrived it was loaded with cages, each containing thirty pound, LIVE turkeys. The urgent call went out to many of us. The whole process of butchering 70 very assertive turkeys, the plucking, the cleaning and placement in the freezer . . . what an experience! What a great group! My uncles, cousins, Ron Hartwick, Howard Wadge, Gord Stephenson and other summer staff . . . these claimed they were traumatized by this ordeal for months. Some stories need many years of distance before they become amusing. AND AGAIN … *"Fresh strawberries for the Dominion Day BBQ, What could be better"*, said Dad. Who knew how much work it would be to clean and husk all those flats of strawberries for 1500 people! AND AGAIN Dad's "Rock Festival" was a monumental project to build and fill the metal gabion wall baskets, to reclaim and preserve the beachfront and marina peninsula. The dozens of cottage and trailer park workers called it the "MBC Rock Festival".

Thankfully maple syrup operations were taken over by the very competent **Mr. Howard Wadge**. We all learned from him the critical timing of knowing when the sap was ready for pouring. Nearby he kept a pig's tail, suspended from a string. He would watch as the evaporator become a mound of foam. At the right time, Mr. Wadge would dip the pig's tail into the foam. If it was boiled to just the right temperature, the foam would immediately disappear from the surface of the syrup. It was then ready for pouring. It took 1000 gallons of sap to make 50 gallons of pure maple syrup.   DELICIOUS ! Every year we sold every drop.

Over the years we chased escapee horses (and other farm critters) down Hood Road, and around the grounds.   We wormed horses, and learned how to treat other equine and animal ailments. We discovered how to work with a twitch when trimming the hooves of a nervous horse. I recall one very exciting horse ride with my Dad. Chum (our pinto) liked to get the bit in his teeth and charge for home. Unfortunately we were approaching the main road with potential traffic. On my faithful friend, Topsy, I overtook Chum and cut my Dad off. I was hugely surprised (and delighted) when Chum jumped sideways into the ditch, and a deep stream at the side of the road. I will never forget the sight of my Dad's face. He was still going full pelt when he suddenly found himself 5 feet lower than the main road . . . in the water! My hilarity was not matched by his own!

Both my brother and I continued our involvement at MBC, even as we moved into university and other employment. We devoted most of our time off by partnering with our parents. It was satisfying to ease their load as much as we could. For me, this included driving north on a Friday from Cedarville, Ohio or my places of employment in London or Toronto. These would be for selected weekends to help out. I would return in time for classes or work on the Monday. Summers we worked in tandem to address the many challenges of staff schedules and other tasks. Having graduated as a nurse from Cedarville University I later decided to move to Edinburgh, Scotland to complete a Masters degree in nursing education. While there I arranged for a member of my church group and her friend to be employed at MBC during the summer. I requested that my brother Bruce keep an eye on the two girls. Events surpassed even my expectations. The rest is family history. Melanie, who was from Wales, eventually became my sister-in-law. They now have two sons, Joshua and Scott. Scotland was also a special place for me. That is where I found my husband David. Our family is comprised of two sons (David and Nicholas) and two daughters (Marilyn and Vanessa). David's first visit to Canada was to my home at MBC, where he came to know my parents and my extended family.

Bruce and I grew up at MBC. It was our home. Over the years, we lived in a variety of accommodations and then built our own house on the Port Sydney Road. We knew every inch of every building, roadway and trail. We never contemplated not being there. 'God knows the plans He has for us.' How poignant is Hebrews 13:14 "for here have we no continuing city, but we seek one to come."

Muskoka Baptist Conference has undoubtedly had an impact on many thousands of lives. The legacy of what so many have invested in time, energy, abilities and contributions is beyond calculation. God keeps the books. All that remains is for us to be faithful stewards of what He has entrusted to us.

Dr. Kimberly J. Sharp, RN, PhD,
Dean, School of Nursing & Allied Health
Professor of Nursing, Louisiana College, LA

Treasured Memories at MBC ~ **by Bruce Holliday**

My reflections of growing up at MBC, include many treasured memories. I began my MBC experience in my very first year, 1967. My father was Pastor of Emmanuel Church in Barrie. He was also on the Planning Committee for Muskoka Baptist Conference. My two sets of grandparents and other family members had been involved at MBC for years. When my Dad accepted the position as the first full-time Director, I was only 3 years old.

Early years on the conference grounds were exciting and interesting. I rode my first pony for a family photo-op. I enjoyed McDonald's Farm and still have a picture with other children, patting the animals. Not having a work schedule, I was able to be involved in the daily VBS programs, including Bible Story times with my Grandpa Holliday. How could I ever forget "Fu and Skalin" which was my cup is full and running over in Scottish, and "Your shack, my shack and a bungalow" rendition of Shadrach, Meshach and Abednego.

I did face one hazard! My grandparents had just returned from service in Zambia, Africa. We had met together in Barrie and were going on to MBC on Thursday. While waiting I was playing across the road with my friend, Peter. Two cars were leaving. My parents were anxious to get back to MBC. Dad left first, <u>knowing</u> that I would be taken north by my Mum. Mum left later, <u>knowing</u> that Dad had taken me with them. I watched and waved as each car left. Arriving at MBC, a phone call from Peter's mother alerted that I was still in Barrie. Mum was in the dining room getting ready for the smorgasbord. She was shocked to find out I was still in Barrie. Our neighbor friend thought it was hilarious and I joined them up north the next morning. Worrying thing was that when we called, I'm not sure they had missed me yet !!!

In younger years I participated in the children's choir led by Sandi Kernohan. There were friendships with other staff families. . . the Lawson boys, Lynnie and Lori Kernohan, Bruce and Kerri Lively and Ian Ross. As the years moved along, I fitted into staff duties. There were the many extra adventures made possible by the conference and its location. Horse riding from a toddler age to my first water skiing behind Peter Gibson's "200hp merc" at age 8. Midnight madness, fright nights at Dyer Memorial and roller skating are just a few memories. When my classmates in school played on their bikes in the summer, I was driving tractors, rock climbing, scuba diving, skiing, and being a "worker with". This was from a very young age. Summer's and any free time were never dull.

At MBC, so many lessons from the Lord have shaped, defined and guided my life. What better way to start the day than with staff devotions. We could all see those devotional lessons demonstrated. They prepared us for the challenges of each day.

Where else could you be cutting the grass one minute and suddenly be called to carry an injured horse rider a mile out of the bush? What a sensation to meet a wolf, while on horseback. How do you solve the problem of a trail ride of teenagers coming between a black bear and her cubs. It is amazing how 8 teenagers can be silenced in an instant!

Some important life skills to note... (1) always check which way a tree is going to fall before you cut, just in case it goes through the roof of a trailer. (2) Thin ice will never hold the weight of a tractor no matter how much you hold your breath ...not mentioning any names ... Dad. (3) In hindsight, driving a bus back from Widjiitiwin, with no brakes, is tricky on the hills and probably not advisable. (4) A can of beans will explode in a campfire. (5) Ground hogs may tend to get aggressive when locked in the horse feed bin. (6) Taking a running snow blower through the basement and up the stairs through the house is never a good idea, no matter how deep the snow may be outdoors. (7) Catching some air on your motorbike, too close the tennis court fence, this can be painful. (8) A 12volt alarm will set the carpet on fire when wired into the 110volt wall socket!

Working closely with my Poppa, Len Aylett, has made a lasting impression on me. We were busy in the shop one day. Dave Stevenson was driving the John Deere tractor into the shop . . . at the very moment that Poppa was welding. A spark ignited the leaking fuel tank under the tractor and set it on fire. Everyone shouted and darted in different directions. Poppa calmly turned off the torch. He opened the door and pushed the now blazing tractor out into the snow. The flames were quickly extinguished. My heart was still pounding as the smoke cleared. As I looked back, Poppa just said, "Ok, Ok". He had already returned to his work. No "fan fair" or "hype" . . . just back to work. It was such a labor of love, quietly serving the Lord. He never had an air of it being "MY work", but always a sense that it was the "LORD'S work". There are literally more adventures, experiences and answers to prayer than I am able to count. The work of God is not just produced by people or by sensational event planning. The real Muskoka Miracles which we have seen are by daily answers to prayer, and work done as unto the Lord.

It was at MBC and in our home that I came to know and admire so many speakers and spiritual leaders. Dr. Sugden made such a great impression on me. After one of his sermons I gave my life to the Lord. Speakers such as Dr. Joe Stowell and Dr. Charles Wagner also moved me. They had an influence concerning the choice about where to go to college. They not only challenged me spiritually, but also on the tennis courts as well!

After graduation from Huntsville High School and studies at Trinity Western University, I completed my degree and qualifications for flight and aircraft mechanics at Grand Rapids Baptist College and Seminary. During the summer of '89, Melanie Roberts, and a friend, came to MBC for summer employment and service on the ranch. She was a Welsh girl, studying in Edinburgh. She came to know my sister while attending Charlotte Chapel.

We met on the conference grounds, usually at meal times. Our first 'date', by chance, was on horseback. We had initially set out as a group of friends going for a trek. One by one, they pulled out for various reasons. It ended as just the two of us. So began a long distance relationship. Many cynics predicted that it would never last. So much for the 6 inch rule! The following summer Melanie returned to work at the conference. This time she returned to her home with a promise ring. We were engaged in April of '91, and married the following year. The rest, as they say, is history.

MBC has been such a big part of my family, life and spiritual development. In the course of my flight training I had the privilege of flying a plane home from Michigan to Muskoka. It provided a new perspective of the landscape, lakes and the wonder of God's handiwork in nature. We are blessed by such beautiful surroundings.

As I reflect upon the hand of the Lord through my years at MBC, I have a fresh appreciation of His guidance and blessing. I do pray that the conference, staff and speakers will continue to minister, challenge and move many more hearts over the days and years to come.

J. Bruce Holliday
Client Relationship Manager
Santander Bank, Swansea, Wales, UK

A FOOTNOTE BY THE AUTHOR . . .

It was at Muskoka Baptist Camp that I met Marilyn Aylett. She continues to this day as the joy and encourager of my life. We are of like godly parentage. Marilyn has served beside me in every endeavor. As observed by a beloved speaker, Lehman Strauss, *"God does not forget your work and labour of love which you have shown toward His name in that you have ministered to the saints, and continue ministering"*. Hebrews 6:10.

Chapter 22

There are many families with a three, four, or even five generation span of involvement in the ministry of Muskoka Baptist Conference. The forebears of the Ross family were a part of Fairbank Baptist Church when their Pastor, John F. Holliday, led in the first summer at Fisher's Glen, and then in Muskoka. Jim and Lil Ross Sr. were a part of those early years and their son's family, Jim and Elaine Ross, to this 80th year milestone. The family members, with Jim and Elaine have been diligent and faithful . Jim has been a Board Member for a number of years, six of them as President. They are examples of the Saviour's determined course, *"my meat is to do the will of Him who sent me, and to finish His work"* John 4:34.

The Lakeview Manor and other large projects were crucial for financial stability in the 1980's and beyond. The family now influences another generation by demonstrating commitment to the will of God and being *"finishers"* for God. We are grateful for the precious bonds of association as families.   RDH

＿＿＿＿＿＿＿＿＿＿＿＿＿＿＿＿＿＿＿＿＿

ANOTHER MUSKOKA MIRACLE ~ Jim Ross

M   The summer of 2007 was not a good one for M.B.C. Over the previous several years it had become apparent that our beloved conference centre was going down-hill. Operating deficits were increasing each year and now the outstanding debt had grown to 3 million dollars. Supporters and friends began to realize that there was a distinct possibility that M.B.C. could be lost to the Christian community, just as was Canadian Keswick 35 years earlier.

Many began to pray fervently for this ministry which had such a positive impact on hundreds and even thousands of lives since its founding in 1930.

Over the last several months of 2007 and early 2008, Elaine and I shared together regarding the conference centre. We even discussed the possibility of making a substantial investment in M.B.C. from our small family foundation.

However the obstacles to initiate any kind of action seemed impossible. One of the critical factors was the necessity of a capable leader to emerge. Who could or would ever want to take on this daunting task?

We, as well as a great number of others, continued to pray regarding the conference. In March Elaine and I went to Florida for our spring vacation. As usual our children and their families each came and spent a week with us. In the middle of the month it was time for Ian, Laura and their 5 children to join us. One afternoon the wind was blowing briskly over the gulf and so Ian, his daughter Brooklyn and I decided to rent a hobby cat and sail together. After a somewhat challenging start off we were soon enjoying the rolling waves and moved along at a considerable clip. After setting our sails Ian became a bit quiet and then said, "Dad, I was out running this morning and I just couldn't get M.B.C. off my mind." We talked about the present situation and the many challenges. I then shared with Ian some of the thoughts that Elaine and I had about possibly being willing to make a fairly large investment from our family controlled Ross-Shire Foundation. After some more discussion we returned to shore.

Ian immediately disappeared into his condo. A short time later he emerged and presented Elaine and I and his wife Laura with a document entitled "A Turn Around Plan for M.B.C.".

The plan was logical, daring and very challenging. One thing certain was that it would need to have complete support from the present board and also the M.B.C. constituency.

By the time Elaine and I returned home at the end of March an appointment was made for us to meet with the M.B.C. Board Chairman, Mike Nichol. He liked our plan. We then met and presented the plan to several other board members. They also liked the plan, and then it was presented to the whole board. At this meeting we got very strong support to move ahead. It was proposed to send a letter to the constituency to inform them. At the annual meeting on Saturday, May the 16th, our proposal would be presented to the voting members. The board recognized that there would probably be some opposition to the proposal, but that we would pray and trust the Lord for the outcome.

The basis of the plan was that the Ross-Shire Foundation would invest 2 million dollars into M.B.C. About 1.8 million dollars of it was to be earmarked for renovations and $200,000 to be used for debt reduction. These monies would be provided as a forgivable bond to the Ross-Shire Foundation. A viable financial plan was to be developed and followed with the goal that M.B.C. would prosper spiritually and financially. As part of the proposal, the Ross-Shire Foundation would have the right to nominate up to 3 members to the board of directors until the forgivable bonds were fully forgiven.

After sharing the story of how the plan had come about and the details of the plan, a motion for acceptance of the proposal was presented to the constituency. There was an overwhelming acceptance and a standing ovation. This will always be a memorable meeting for all those present.

Renovations began 4 or 5 days later. It was planned that the exteriors of all the main buildings would be completed by the 2008 summer conference opening, just 6 weeks later on June 26.

Bruce Fitter with his South Mary Lake Construction Company submitted estimates for the immediate renovations. His company was already fully committed for the summer but because of his whole hearted interest in the ministry of M.B.C. he threw himself and his people into the project.

One day Bruce and I met with the owner of a large painting firm from Barrie to get a price on painting the exteriors of all the main buildings. "Well," he said, "I will be happy to provide a quote for the job but there is no way we could get at this project until the fall. We are booked solid for the summer. In fact you'll never get any painter to do this job this summer. They are all booked completely".

During the next 5 weeks the work that was accomplished was unbelievable, in spite of a good rain shower nearly every day.

The Fellowship Centre building was repaired. Raccoons were driven out of the place and their holes covered over and siding repaired.

The worn roofing was replaced and the whole building completely painted.

Next the Hub and Chapel were tackled. It seemed that years had passed with minimal building maintenance or equipment care. New board and baton siding was installed where needed. The rotting deck on the roof and sagging timbers were replaced on the outer edges around the perimeter of the roof. The roof was brought into line again. New decorative timber frame members were also added to enhance the building and completely transformed the appearance. Along with a fresh coat of paint it was made into the elegant building it is today.

As this work was going on, Blyne Hutchin with his company "Attainable Landscaping" removed the formidable hill behind the Chapel. Over 200 large truck loads of soil were hauled away and then a new large interlocking stone patio installed. This was further enhanced with landscaping utilizing Muskoka granite for steps and walls.

Next were the dining room and lodge buildings. Again new board and baton siding was applied to the front exterior wall. Using his exceptional gifting in design, Bruce Fitter erected stunning timber frame trusses over the front entrance along with decorative stone pillars and other structural highlights. Again the building was further enhanced and accented with a new crisp paint job.

Repairs were made to the exterior of the motel and villa. New board and baton siding was applied the exterior walls of the manor as well as a new roof. All these buildings were also completely repainted.

It was our goal that all the exterior work described, would be completed by the opening day of the summer conference season, June 26, 2008. To accomplish this, a tight schedule had to be followed. The layout for a new set of sidewalks was planned, staked out, excavated and refilled with crushed stone to form a good base for the concrete.

On Tuesday, June 22, the cribbing was to be set up. A couple of workers from the cement contractor company arrived and erected about 30 feet of cribbing. They informed us, that was as far as they could go that week, and the pouring of the cement would not take place until at least the following week.

The next morning our dilemma was discussed with Bruce Fitter, who thought about it for a minute. Then he said, "I've got men who can do that job, and will". The cribs were installed the next day and the cement trucks were scheduled to start pouring cement at 7:00 a.m. Friday morning. By noon that day 150 cubic meters of cement had been poured. Immediately upon the departure of the cement trucks, a bulldozer moved in to level soil around the sidewalks. Sod was sitting, waiting to be laid. Soon a small army of volunteers were rolling out the sod on the freshly graded lawn area. By 8:00 that evening the sodding was complete along with the planting of some shrubs and trees.

Saturday we saw some flowers planted and cribs removed from the sidewalks. A general cleanup took place. We were now ready for our opening celebrations and barbeque! On Saturday afternoon June 26, the arriving guests stood in stunned silence as they viewed what had taken place since the annual meeting on May 16, only 6 weeks previous. Truly what had been accomplished over the last 6 weeks was indeed a miracle. The Lord had truly done a wonderful new thing. Somehow in spite of numerous hold ups, much rain and a number of surprises, the work was finished. It was very evident to all that the Lord had provided to enable this first step of many to be completed.

Earlier in this story I shared how the painter from Barrie had told us, "You will never get a painting crew up here in Muskoka at this time in the year, perhaps in the fall". On this last week before our opening one day I counted 17 painters on the job!

We serve a great God!

In addition to the repairing and refurbishing of the exteriors of the buildings, as well as the landscaping . . . other changes were occurring. The need for a Conference Director was met with the offer of our Conference Board Chairman Mike Nichol to take a leave of absence from his business to fulfill this position.

After the great opening celebrations, work was commenced on refurbishing the lodgings, all washrooms were upgraded, and each room had air-conditioning installed. The job of designing and choosing fabrics, paint colours, carpets and furnishings was carried out by Betty Davies along with Elaine Ross. Betty was on the job for more than 6 months. Bruce Fitter continued to fulfill the construction and servicing needs of each of the buildings.

As rooms were completed, they were immediately occupied by guests who came for the summer Ministry Program. By October most of the lodging renovations were complete. Over the summer the Hub also received a real upgrade with a new tile floor, pine ceiling, and designer lighting. New tables and chairs and leather couches made it more comfortable and commodious. The kitchen and serving area were also redesigned and new equipment installed.

As we approached the fall, the dining room was next to be tackled. Again a new beautiful tile floor was installed and the walls and beams painted. The windows were dressed up with new pull down shades and highlighted with beautiful draperies. Lastly, new lighting was installed as well as heating and air-conditioning for the comfort of our guests.

After a brief rest over Christmas of 2008, the front entrance, offices and lounge area were gutted and rebuilt to provide a very professional warm, cozy atmosphere for arriving guests. The offices on the lower floor were also completely renovated. To save on heating expenses, a new outdoor wood furnace was installed to supply most of the heat for the large gymnasium (Fellowship Centre), the Hub and Chapel as well as the dining room and offices.

The operations of the conference were carried on throughout that whole year of 2008. Mike Nichol continued to provide "on sight" oversight during the fall and winter and he made a remarkable contribution in leadership. However, the need for a new C.E.O. was a big concern for the board. After prayerful and careful consideration the firm of Robinson Fraser of Bracebridge was engaged to conduct a search for God's man for this very important position.

By February 2009 several good men were interviewed but one stood out from the rest as the one we believed had the background, expertise, people skills and, most importantly, the spiritual qualifications to fill the needs for this demanding position. This man was John Friesen, who had been managing very successfully the Fairhaven's Bible Conference Centre at Beaverton for the last 8 years. It was with great joy and thankfulness to God that John joined M.B.C. as it's Chief Executive Officer April 1, 2009.

M.B.C. has an amazing story from its early beginnings 80 years ago. Its story is best told by the great spiritual impact the ministry of the Word of God, at this special place, in so many people's lives. Truly it is a story of miracles in people's lives. It is also a miracle of God's <u>provisions</u> for its many needs, including facilities, directors and staff over these many years.

It's been a great pleasure, joy and honour for all of us who have had a part in the miracle which has taken place over the last 1 ½ years. The many friends and supporters who had a love for M.B.C., who believed in it, who cried to God that it would be revived . . . we thank you for your faithful prayers and commitment. We believe that what has been accomplished is for the glory of God. It would not have happened without the gracious goodness of our great God, the Father, Jesus Christ, His Son, and the work of the Holy Spirit.

Praise Him!

We would like to share with you the words of these scriptures from 2 Corinthians 9: 6-15 (New King James version). They have directed and brought much blessing to our lives. We pray that they will also bring much blessing and encouragement to each of you. . . . .

This is I say: He who sows sparingly will also reap sparingly, and he who sows bountifully will also reap bountifully. So let each one give as he purposes in his heart, not grudgingly or of necessity; for God loves a cheerful giver. And God is able to make all grace abound toward you, that you, always having all sufficiency in all things, may have an abundance for every good work.

As it is written: 'He has dispersed abroad, He has given to the poor; His righteousness endures forever'.

Now may He who supplies seed to the sower, and bread for food, supply and multiply the seed you have sown and increase the fruits of your righteousness, while you are enriched in every thing for all liberality, which causes thanksgiving through us to God.

For the administration of this service not only supplies the needs of the saints, but also is abounding through many thanksgivings to God, while, through the proof of this ministry, they glorify God for the obedience of your confession to the gospel of Christ, and for your liberal sharing with them and all men, and by their prayer for you, who long for you because of the exceeding grace of God in you.

Thanks be to God for His indescribable gift.!

Jim and Elaine Ross

all members of our Ross Family

and the Ross-Shire Foundation

Ross-shire Foundation improvements 2008-2010 MBC Lodge

Walkway to Chapel from Lodge

Entrance to the Hub for meals and meetings, and to the Book Room-Gift Shop

Access to Chapel patio and entrances

Fellowship and refreshments in the Hub

Chapel patio and overflow area

Memorial Chapel

Grove sitting area with Gazebo

Welcoming entrance sign to Muskoka Baptist Conference Centre

Acknowledgements and Appreciations

By Rev. Dr. Richard D. Holliday

*The lines are fallen unto me in pleasant places; yea,
I have a goodly heritage ~ Psalm 16:6*

To quote the author of the 40 year and 45 year anniversary editions of Muskoka Miracles, ***"This preparation has been very pleasant, but not an easy task."***. We are sincerely grateful to all who assisted us in this publication. More than just an 80th Anniversary edition, we have sought to provide a clear history of God's leadership through times of both testing and blessing.

The co-founders left copious files and detailed information which was expanded in more recent decades. We have incorporated two chapters from the writings of **Mr. Sydney L. White**. For many years he was the treasurer, president, and member of the conference board. He was well able to furnish significant material about Conference finances and corporate policy. He was a tower of strength by counsel, encouragement and a deep understanding of the past and prospects of MBC.

The other Founder, **Rev. Dr. John F. Holliday** was a faithful prophet of the Lord, with keen organization and promotional ability. He observed that -

> *"Sometimes in the hour of spectacular success, such as we are now enjoying, the contemporary contributors to the achievement are tempted to think that no one did anything before them. Worse still, the temptation to forget the standards and objectives of the institution which God has established."*

These men sought no personal honours, but gave testimony to *"what God hath wrought"*. *"There are thousands in the MBC family who are happy to recall our Conference heritage. We gladly pay tribute to the spiritual giants who shared in its administration and ministry"*.

The "goodly heritage" most certainly prompts a depth of gratitude, beyond repayment, for the personal impact of MBC leaders of the formative years. Not only the two couples who led, but others who served with them have affected the home of this writer and his siblings. His wife, Marilyn, had a common background by parents who were present from the first year. Her hands have typed this script. We are grateful for our Kimberly and Bruce who loved the place and its ministry.

A great history treasure has been prepared by brother-in-law, **Bruce Aylett.** It is a careful compilation of 600 pictures from 1930 to 2010. What an exercise of patience and diligence to visually express God's blessing upon MBC. It is now a **DVD** with pictures and background music titled . . . *"A Visual Journey ~ Celebrating 80 Years Of God's Blessings".* We are grateful for the finishing work by **Lloyd Knight** and his *Roundtable Associates* of Stouffville, ON.

THE TESTIMONIALS of friends and family are appreciated and will bless all who read.

- *Mary (White) Donald* . . . sharing reasons for her love for the conference and appreciation concerning her parents. We know that this was like "a second home"

- *Dorothy (Roblin) Mitchell* for her patience and love from the 1950's to the present

- *Betty (Garner) Munson* for cheerful service when there were very few helpers

- *Allison Fish (nee Milligan)* for recounting MBC's important role as a spiritual haven in times of need.

- *Sandra (Fitkin)Kernohan* for describing her parents, Arthur and Nancy Fitkin and sharing the blessings of MBC to Jim, Lori, Lynnie and family

- *Evelyn Thompson (and Ross)* for fellowship in Emmanuel, and the encouragement and leadership of yourself and Ross . . . 18 years Ladies' Conference, and Ross almost two decades on the Board.

- *JoAnn (Gillott) Kerr* . . . grateful thanks for your helpfulness, and patience, in typing the 1975 edition of Muskoka Miracles

- *Bruce Aylett* – for your years of interest and support of family . . .your love for MBC and the countless hours you spent in producing its visual history record.

- *Kimberly (Holliday) Sharp and Bruce Holliday* – our dear daughter and son. So much of our joy through years at MBC was the tremendous satisfaction and team work of serving together. All your efforts seemed with godly motivation and unusual maturity.

We are grateful for the tireless efforts and sanctified enthusiasm of **Dr. Roy W. Lawson**. Through his years of involvement in pastorates, the ministries of FBYPA and our Fellowship of Evangelical Baptist Churches in Canada, he has been a faithful helper at Muskoka Baptist Conference. His Chapter 8 first appeared in the early editions of Muskoka Miracles.

Our appreciation to **Rev. Robert W. Irvin** for "The Foreword". His early years included a strong involvement in Youth Retreats which were programmed by his home church, High Park Baptist in Toronto. For five years he served as co-Director with Roy Lawson at MBC Teen and Youth Weeks, identified as "Chief" and "Skip". In sixteen years, he pastored four Ontario churches of the Fellowship of Evangelical Baptists in Canada. Sixteen years he served in Christian Education as Dean of Students and Counselor at Moody Bible Institute, Chicago. For eight years he was the Canadian Director of the Slavic Gospel Association.

This 80th Anniversary Edition includes the basic text of 1975. As in that day, we are vividly aware of the changes that have taken place. Health, place of service, marriage, bereavement, achievements, retirement, promotion, calls to higher service. . . it has not been possible to make the many alterations necessary for an update.

It is interesting to trace the steps of progress in the growth of Muskoka Baptist Conference. The pioneer beginnings were primarily as a youth ministry, soon including families and then mission work in Muskoka. The camp period was limited to 10 days, then 2 weeks, and later, the whole summer. Committee leadership developed during the 1950's and 1960's. Three major considerations were addressed beginning in the later 1960's..

- The transfer of the Conference assets by the Fellowship of Evangelical Baptist Churches in Canada to the conference organization.

- The incorporation of the Conference under the laws of the Province of Ontario, established a fifteen member Board of Directors, directly accountable to an Annual Convention for reporting and the conduct of business.

- The decision to appoint a full-time M.B.C. Managing Director. In the minutes of 1949 there is record of a proposal to appoint a director for the "whole summer". More than twenty years passed before the appointment was made of a "full year Director".

Through the record of the years from 1965 you will notice threads of concern from our Board of Directors. There was the repeated counsel to plan for increased year round accommodation which would supply our full operating expenses. The new Chapel was desired, but wisely delayed until we could pay the full cost. It was recognized that a winterized activity building was important for use in all seasons. These considerations eventually led to the appointment of the Planning and Development Committee.

From the late 1960's the Directors faithfully coped with two kinds of persistent expense: (1) Extensive legal fees for representation against exorbitant proposed taxation. (2) Enormous costs for engineering and the mechanical facilities needed for Conference expansion. These did not limit the blessing of God through our greatest period of ministry growth. Behind it all was Jehovah Jireh. Graciously, abundantly, miraculously, He met the needs, demonstrating to us once again, that He is the God of miracles.

It is our prayer that these pages may bring glory to God, and help to further enlarge the ministry of Muskoka Baptist Conference.